Three Black Generations at the Crossroads

Three Black Generations at the Crossroads

Community, Culture, and Consciousness

Second Edition

Lois Benjamin

ROWMAN & LITTLEFIELD PUBLISHERS, INC.
Lanham • Boulder • New York • Toronto • Plymouth, UK

ROWMAN & LITTLEFIELD PUBLISHERS, INC.

Published in the United States of America
by Rowman & Littlefield Publishers, Inc.
A wholly owned subsidiary of The Rowman & Littlefield Publishing Group, Inc.
4501 Forbes Boulevard, Suite 200, Lanham, Maryland 20706
www.rowmanlittlefield.com

Estover Road
Plymouth PL6 7PY
United Kingdom

British Library Cataloguing in Publication Information Available

Library of Congress Cataloging-in-Publication Data

Benjamin, Lois, 1944–
    Three Black generations at the crossroads : community, culture, and consciousness /
Lois Benjamin. — [2nd ed.].
        p. cm.
    Includes bibliographical references and index.
    ISBN-13: 978-0-7425-6000-0 (cloth : alk. paper)
    ISBN-10: 0-7425-6000-7 (cloth : alk. paper)
    ISBN-13: 978-0-7425-6001-7 (pbk. : alk. paper)
    ISBN-10: 0-7425-6001-5 (pbk. : alk. paper)
    1. African Americans—Social conditions—20th century. 2. African Americans—
Economic conditions—20th century. 3. Intergenerational relations—United States. 4.
Community life—United States. 5. Social values—United States. 6. African American
professional employees—Interviews. I. Title.
    E185.86.B3793 2008
    305.896'073—dc22   2007016583

Printed in the United States of America

♾™ The paper used in this publication meets the minimum requirements of American
National Standard for Information Sciences—Permanence of Paper for Printed Library
Materials, ANSI/NISO Z39.48-1992.

To Bernice Fortson, my sister,
who is the wind beneath my wings

Contents

Preface ix

Introduction 1

1 The Way We Were 15

2 Educating for Living and Uplifting 39

3 Black Clergy: Salvation and Liberation 75

4 Black Physicians: The Community Healers 101

5 Black Entrepreneurs: Mixing Mission with Making Money 131

6 Black Politicians: The Bellwethers of the Post-Civil Rights Era 155

7 Black Artists: The Soul of Black Communities 199

8 Chaos or Community: Facing the Twenty-First Century 235

Notes 241

Index 251

About the Author 265

Preface

The past four decades of the twentieth century witnessed structural, socio-economic, cultural, and technological changes in the African American community, as well as in the larger society, which impacted the collective ethos and value system of blacks. The civil rights movement, which gave African Americans greater social and economic opportunities to participate in mainstream America, was integral to this transformation of values. Desegregation gave African Americans the chance to interact with whites on a more equal footing, thereby increasing the likelihood of members of the community adopting the more individualistic value system of the dominant group, and consequently altering a people's consciousness from a "We" ethos to an "I" ethos, especially for those who were born or who came of age after the civil rights era.

In the first edition, I use life histories of individuals in the traditional professional occupations of African Americans in the pre-civil rights era to illustrate the value shift. In linking the personal biographies of individuals in three generations to larger social forces that impinge upon them, I show how personal and social factors shape their value system and worldview according to their time period. Clearly, these structural and cultural shifts have affected African Americans' community, culture, and consciousness. To assess whether these patterns continue to manifest themselves in the diverse professional occupations in the post-civil rights era, in this new edition, I have added two new chapters on politicians and visual artists and included new literature.

I would like to thank Alan McClare of Rowman & Littlefield for encouraging me to revise this edition. I am also obliged to Michael McGandy of

Rowman & Littlefield for his editorial suggestions and timely feedback. I would like to thank the following individuals for their support, friendship, and encouragement: Janet Adeyiga, Bernice Fortson, Jeffrey Fortson, Reginald Fortson, Lawrence Jones, Brooke Obie, JoAnn Obie, Valerie Sweeney Prince, Yasmin Shiraz, Sheila Stevens, and Claudia Widdiss. In addition, I thank the following students for their support and assistance: Kendrick Henley, Christelle Larose, Stacy Robinson, Jasmine Davis, Tameka DePriest, and Kimberly Liburd. I am especially indebted to Frances Hawkins for her editorial and typing assistance and for her invaluable friendship.

Introduction

Frances Hawkins: In the decades of the 1920s, 1930s, and 1940s, when I was growing up, nearly every black family in the community shared a similar economic status, and people were truly sympathetic to the needs of their neighbors. In the midst of baking a cake, my mom might find that she was a little short on sugar. "Go over to Mrs. Scott's and borrow a cup of sugar," she would tell me, careful to provide the cup. "Tell her that I will send it back to her on Friday" (payday). Without hesitation, Mrs. Scott would dip a cup of sugar from her bin and hand it to me to take home. On Friday, after the four of us kids would go downtown and get the groceries, before putting them away, my mom would pour that cup of sugar in the same cup and send one of us to return it to Mrs. Scott. You see, it was almost an unspoken code. If you borrow something, be sure to return it. Economics placed as much importance on returning that cup of sugar as paying the rent. Everything had to be accounted for if a sufficient amount of supplies was to last from one pay period to the next. Thus, it was imperative that neighbors display a high degree of honesty to assure that the entire neighborhood survived. To break the code was to be as unwelcome as a pariah.

Maria Hatcher: When I grew up in the late 1940s, 1950s, and 1960s in a Southern city, I remember people borrowed from their neighbors, particularly those they felt close to. But it was important for neighbors not to borrow too much, because one should have one's own. We were better off economically than my parents, who grew up during the Depression. After I graduated from college, I moved away from my old working-class neighborhood. When I return, I don't see the amount of borrowing in the 1990s that I saw in my childhood, nor do I see that sense of community, except among some older neighbors. In my predominantly white middle-class community, borrowing seems rare, and I sure would be hesitant to ask for anything, let alone a cup of sugar. However, if I felt close to a black neighbor, I might ask her.

1

Sandra Jackson: My formative years were in a large Southern city in the mid-1960s, 1970s, and 1980s. I have no recollection of my mother borrowing from a neighbor and would not expect to borrow myself. We were not that close to neighbors. If someone did borrow a cup of sugar, I would not expect it to be returned. In fact, I expect those in my generation to keep not only the sugar but also the cup.

These vignettes about the economics and reciprocity of a cup of sugar illustrate the changing cultural tradition of sharing and caring in the black community. Yet, they capture, at a microcosmic layer, the zeitgeist that overlays the macrocosmic shifts in the black community, as summed up by three generations of black women. On the one hand, Frances Hawkins, the seventy-three-year-old retired college administrator, born and reared in a closely knit, small-town community in the Midwest and influenced by the World War I generation, recounts the collective ethos of community, culture, and consciousness that prevailed despite one's socioeconomic status. Maria Hatcher, the fifty-three-year-old university professor, seizes the spirit of the World War II generation, while Sandra Jackson, the thirty-three-year-old college professor, catches the cultural winds of the civil rights generation. What momentous cultural and structural alterations in the black community have contributed to these frayed connections among generations? Have they struck a blow at blacks' shared history of community, culture, and consciousness? If so, how has the historic sense of collective consciousness and collective action been transposed by these broken bonds? What larger cultural and structural forces overlaid such transpositions in the past century?

The twentieth century witnessed more dramatic events and changes in cultural phases, economic shifts, and technological transformations than at anytime in the entire span of human existence, and these alterations affected nearly every nook and cranny of planet Earth. Margaret Mead, anthropologist, identified three distinct cultural phases—the postfigurative, the cofigurative, and the prefigurative—all existing simultaneously in the twentieth century,[1] which coincided with significant economic evolutions and technological transmutations. In Mead's postfigurative culture, which represents the past, change is slow. Children learn from their elders, who transmit to them a sense of tradition and unchanging continuity. A break from the postfigurative culture may occur in the following ways: through war or a catastrophe; through the "development of new forms of technology" in which the elders are not adept; through "migration to a new land" where the senior members of a community are invariably regarded as outsiders; through conquest in which defeated populations are compelled to learn the language and customs of the conqueror; through "religious conversion, when adult converts try to bring children to embody new ideals they themselves never experienced" in their formative years; and by "a purposeful step in a revolution that establishes itself through the introduction of new and different lifestyles for the young."[2] In this resulting cofigurative culture, which represents the present, the experiences of the young are radically different from those of the elders in the family and community, so the children find it necessary to learn from their peers. While the principal paragon for members of society is the actions of their contemporaries, elders remain dominant in the sense that they set the style and the limits within which cofigurative behaviors are manifested in the young. For Mead, the prefigurative culture, which represents the future, has a totally new conception of living and alternative lifestyles that are emerging in the postmodern era. Here, in contrast to the postfigurative culture, elders learn from their children, and the young learn, even more than their cofigurative predecessors, from the electronic media and their peers.

While Mead's theory of cultural continuities and change is a heuristic framework for grasping some sweeping intergenerational alterations among blacks and for understanding some of the shifting dynamics within black communities during the twentieth century, I am mindful of the limitations of this paradigm. One major drawback of Mead's matrix is her deemphasis on the role of racial politics and power struggles and its relationship to the three cultural phases. It is arguable that specific historical events, such as the civil rights movement, have had a greater impact on intergenerational changes within black communities than any distinctive cultural phase.

Charles F. Simmons, historian and former dean of social sciences at Norfolk State University, suggested that World War I, World War II, and the civil rights movement were defining milestones in the twentieth century that impacted changes in black communities and altered black/white relations.[3] These events, in juxtaposition with major cultural, economic, and technological changes, have helped to shape a different sense of community, culture, and consciousness among three generations of blacks who were born, reared, and educated in these historical contexts. I shall refer to these three generational epochs as the World War I generation (1900–1924), the World War II generation (1925–1949), and the civil rights generation (1950–1975). Hereafter, in this work, the postfigurative culture is identified with the World War I generation, the cofigurative culture with the World War II generation, and the prefigurative culture with the civil rights generation. The collective contours of black life have been cast not only by these larger social forces and by the character of race relations in a specific era, but also individually by significant life events related to family, religion, education, economy, polity, personality, class, and geography. In highlighting the lived experiences of blacks from three cultural and generational epochs, my angle of vision slants toward the most privileged of the race, since they are more likely to assimilate the values and behaviors of the dominant culture. And more important, they have historically been in the forays of the color line as cultural and political leaders, championing the ideology of racial uplift, reform, and liberation.[4]

In the World War I generation, elders were the most important agents of socialization. The church and family took precedence in the primarily agriculturally oriented economy of the South, where most blacks resided. In this Southern culture, the color line, as well as the gender line, was rigidly embodied in the folkways, mores, and laws. The racial insularity fostered more homogeneous black communities and at the same time seemingly conserved the Africanity manifested in the more communalistic culture of blacks. Consequently, blacks were more culturally and structurally integrated into their familial, friendship, and institutional networks. Mentors and support networks were more likely derived from within the community, with the institutions of family, education, and religion working in tandem to reinforce the saliency of core values that stress the importance of family, educational achievement, a strong work ethic, and a strong religious orientation.[5] In the extended familial structure, where group honor took precedence, parenting was by a mother/father unit, with the support and involvement of community elders. In 1890 and 1940, for example, about 80 percent and 77 percent, respectively, of black families were two-parent families; in 1990, only 39 percent comprised two-parent families.[6] The percentage declined to 36 percent in 1996,[7] and in 2004, according to the National Center for Health Statistics, single women accounted for 69.3 percent of non-Hispanic black births.

In the World War I generation, blacks were primarily educated by other blacks in a dual educational system. In this era of less specialization, education was viewed as a means of living, not of making a living, and as a means toward social reform, uplift, and liberation. For the few blacks who were able to pursue professional occupations, segregation limited their mobility and occupational options to preacher, teacher, doctor, and entrepreneur. Since the black economy was more occupationally and professionally uniform than that of whites, blacks used their communitarian collaborative accomplishments as a means to uplift the community.[8] The church, the soul of the black community, sustained blacks' hope that they could, through stewardship, which was grounded in their spiritual faith, lift themselves from the depths of racial oppression and look for a more just world to come. Religion was also regarded as sacred and communal; the Judeo-Christian ethics, virtues, and rituals, to which most World War I generation blacks subscribed, were incorporated into their way of life. Respectability, family background, refinement, education, occupation, property ownership, and skin color were portentous and served as important criteria for stratification within black communities. Ontologically more spiritually oriented and group-centered, blacks' sacred/communal value orientation emphasized people before things—sharing, caring, service, hope, and probity—which contributed to more psychic continuity with the group and greater racial consciousness. Even black leadership, so often dominated by the clergy, was service oriented, with common goals.

The advent of World War II marked a split with the culture of the World War I generation. Individuals in Hawkins's age cohort, whose early developmental years were influenced by the black culture of World War I, found their adolescence through adulthood transformed by the emergence of a changing culture and economy. In the World War II generation, new technology appeared. The economy shifted to a more centralized, urban-based, manufacturing-oriented one, "where the primacy of land was replaced by the primacy of wage labor."[9] Although the window of opportunity for blacks opened somewhat in this sector of the economy after the 1924 National Origins Quota Act, which restricted Eastern and Southern European immigrants, it opened wider during World War II. Blacks migrated to the urban North and South to take advantage of jobs—in stockyards and steel mills; in aircraft, electronics, automotive, and chemical industries; in the railroad industry as Pullman porters; in retail trade as salespersons, clerks, bookkeepers, and buyers; and in government as clerks, secretaries, and postal employees—creating the basis for an emerging black middle class. The obdurate color line was challenged during the war and new control mechanisms emerged based on the urban economy. The gender line was also contested as more women went to work in war industries. After the war, passage of the GI Bill helped a generation of young blacks to obtain education or training, the primary pathway of collective and personal mobility for them.

Although the cultural values of the World War I generation existed concurrently with those of the World War II generation, the rise of urbanization and the influence of the media led to the decline in elders' authority; the loosening of established familial, religious, and communal ties; the emergence and acculturation of new styles of behaviors and values, such as material and individual success; and the emergence of class distinctions based more on education, occupation, wealth, and family status. The values of the World War I generation in which Hawkins was socialized during childhood, along with the World War II values that shaped her generation's adolescence and young adulthood, would remain the guiding ethos for that age cohort. However, the winds of the World War II culture were blowing in a different direction for the transitional cohort of this generation, those born between 1940 and 1949, like Maria Hatcher. These changing winds produced new styles and behaviors among this restless legion, who came of age in the 1960s and demanded alterations in the status quo along the color line.

The 1960s marked a distinctive value shift in community, culture, and consciousness between the culture of the World War II generation and the emerging culture of the civil rights generation. It was an era of rapid social and cultural change, and a renewed season of activism among blacks. The modern civil rights movement, which had its inception in the Montgomery boycott, crested in an all-out campaign to end legally enforced segregation in public accommodations, education, jobs, housing, and voting. The black power movement was an outgrowth of this. In fact, Aldon Morris, in *The Origins of the Civil Rights Movement*, argued that the movement "promoted the democratization process" nationally and internationally and provided inspiration and a model for oppressed groups in the 1960s—Native Americans, Chicanos, Asians, women, students, gays and lesbians, farm workers, environmentalists, and the physically challenged.[10] The turbulent 1960s also witnessed the assassinations of John F. Kennedy, Robert Kennedy, Martin Luther King, Jr., and Malcolm X; the rise of urban rebellions and Vietnam protests; the emergence of countercultures and youth movements; and the shift of societal values and norms.

The post-World War II norms of the 1950s, particularly among the white middle class, underwent radical change. *Making Sense of the Sixties*, a 1991 PBS documentary, noted that the norm to obey authority shifted to confront authority; "fit in with the group" changed to "do your own thing"; "don't even think about having sex before marriage" shifted to "if it feels good, do it"; "control your emotions" changed to "hang loose." Once-touted values, such as those that championed the centrality of the work ethic and identified progress as always good, were questioned.

The 1960s also brought changes to higher education. As students challenged the traditional authority of collegiate life that was dominant in the generations of World Wars I and II, protest movements erupted on both black campuses and white campuses across the country. Todd Gitlin, sociologist, concluded that "the genies that the 1960s loosed are still abroad in the land, inspiring and unsettling and offending, making trouble. For the civil rights and antiwar and countercultural and women's and the rest of that decade's movements forced upon us central issues for Western civilization—fundamental questions of value, fundamental divides of culture, fundamental debates about the good life."[11]

All these movements took place in the burgeoning economy of the post-World War II years. Here we began to see the emergence of an information-based economy in the service-oriented sector, where Benjamin Bowser noted that a shift from "wage labor to lifestyle–self-concept maintenance" began.[12] We enter into Mead's prefigurative culture, or the culture of the future. Some social critics argued that in this phase the young absorbed new values and norms. Along with the customary "utilitarian individualism" intrinsic to Euro-American culture, which values material acquisition and personal achievement, a fresh strain of "expressive individualism" surfaced,[13] particularly among young middle-class whites. This new ethic underscored the primacy of personal happiness, self-satisfaction, consumptive materialism, and a sense of entitlement. The old "ethic of self-denial," says Daniel Yankelovich, began to give way to the "ethic of self-fulfillment,"[14] embodied in the spirit of the "Me" generation of the 1970s. Christopher Lasch labeled this value shift the "culture of narcissism,"[15] as revealed in a survey of entering first-year college students in 1990. Seventy-four percent were committed to being "very well off financially," while only 39 percent held this commitment in 1970.[16] Some cultural critics, like Daniel Bell, Robert Bellah, and Amitai Etzioni, believe such an ethos undermines the basic institutions and commitment to the community.[17] This ethos promotes winning and achieving at any cost and has reified itself at the national government level in the Watergate scandal in the 1970s, at the corporate level in the savings and loan scandal in the 1980s, and the acceptance of widespread cheating among college students in the 1990s. For example, in a 1991 survey of 6,000 students from thirty-one elite universities, 67 percent said they had cheated. Similarly, in a survey of 1,800 state university students in 1993, nine out of ten said they cheated.[18] In another survey of "Who's Who among High School Students," 76 percent of the 3,351 students surveyed admitted cheating on their homework, and 39 percent said they had cheated on a test. It is riveting to know these same students felt that the "decline of moral and social values" is the greatest crisis confronting the nation and the top problem facing teens. Increasing apathy, narcissism, and pessimism may be outcomes of this value system. Certainly, narcissism bespeaks to the corporate dishonorableness of Enron and MCI in the twenty-first century.

This new ethic of "expressive individualism," along with the unabating core of "utilitarian individualism," is dominant in a context of structural changes, where the decline of industrial jobs, corporate downsizing, and educational cutbacks have created a downturn in the economy and a shrinking middle class since the 1980s. For Paul Rogat Loeb, in *Generation at the Crossroads*, "economic fears, materialist dreams, ethical timidity, and a relentless push to adapt—all flourish in America's current uncertain landscape."[19]

The eroding economic climate in the early 1990s contrasts with the over three decades of prosperity and growth in the post–World War II economy from 1945 to 1973, when a burgeoning stable middle class developed. Then, in the 1970s, technological and economic shifts from manufacturing to a service-oriented sector produced job dislocation.[20] In the 1990s, job dislocation happened through downsizing among the white-collar workforce. These cultural and economic transformations, buttressed by a conservative political climate, continued to make the American dream of upward mobility even more elusive for blacks, who made significant strides in the late 1960s. One study noted that since 1980, blacks have been "only half as likely" as whites to move up from low-income to middle-class status, and from there to the ranks of the rich. Moreover, middle-class blacks were more likely than whites to slip down to join the poor.[21]

Despite coming of age in a more precarious economic climate than the later-born cohort of the World War II generation, the civil rights generation, those born during the 1960s or who came into young adulthood after the 1960s, operated in an economic market that was broader than ever before. These new post-1960s privileged blacks, with increasing options, emerged and supplanted the old pre-1960s ones. Martin Kilson, in "The Black Bourgeoisie Revisited," summed up the distinctions between the new and old privileged blacks.

> For both the old and the new black bourgeoisie, racism hinders the quest for parity with the white bourgeoisie. This hindrance generates much frustration, for both the old and new black bourgeoisie, [and] distorts the character of bourgeois existence, especially the quality of its leadership role. . . . But here the similarities between old and new black bourgeoisie end, for there are more fundamental differences. The old black bourgeoisie's political economy was essentially ghetto-bound, while the new black bourgeoisie's political economy is essentially national. Now both the training milieu and job markets are mainly free of ghettoization. . . . [T]his deghettoization of the black bourgeoisie's education and job markets spawns a behavioral and structural metamorphosis that symbolically disentangles the new black bourgeoisie from the old.
>
> Above all, the occupational and professional milieus of the new black bourgeoisie intersect (though not necessarily directly) those of the white bourgeoisie. . . . Whereas the old black bourgeoisie's associations defended ghetto markets, the new black bourgeoisie's race bound associations function integratively. . . . The difference is fundamental: the old black bourgeoisie faced a fierce ceiling on its professional and social mobility; the new black bourgeoisie, while still confronting residual racism, takes over much of the professionalization and mobility of the white bourgeoisie.[22]

Within the context of a changing black political economy, a flexible postindustrial economy, a precarious economic climate of the early 1990s, and a changing value system incorporating greater expressive and utilitarian individualism, how do cultural and structural shifts within the larger society and within black communities mutually impact one another? Also from the liberal

1960s to the conservative 1990s, how have these significant transformations affected the community, culture, and consciousness of the most privileged blacks of the post-1960s civil rights generation? How do they differ from the pre-1960s generations of World War I and World War II, who helped to shape the social milieu of the 1960s that brought civil rights and the public policy priority of equal opportunity for blacks?

Here I return briefly to Hawkins's sugar bin for granules of wisdom to make the linkage between the reciprocal exchange of a cup of sugar from a neighbor and larger generational value shifts. Frances Hawkins, whose childhood was influenced by the values of the World War I culture, whose adolescence and adulthood were formed by those of the World War II culture, and whose middle and senior years are grazed by the civil rights culture, has seen differences since the 1960s among generations in the way they feel, think, and behave about borrowing and returning a cup of sugar. When this question was posed to individuals in the three generations, one twenty-four-year-old expressed, "I grew up during the Reagan years and its me, me generation. We would not borrow and may not loan." A thirty-two-year-old claimed, "Not only would my generation keep the cup and sugar, but would say, 'When you get a chance bring it over.'" A forty-year-old indicated, "I would borrow but would not feel obligated to pay back. I would take my own cup so I wouldn't have to return it or the sugar. I would not expect them to return the sugar if they borrowed." One fifty-year-old claimed, "I would borrow if needed, and return the cup. I may buy the neighbor a two-pound bag instead of sending back a cup of sugar." Since the sugar anecdote is a metaphor for the caring community, Hawkins attributes the generational value shifts—"the lack of civility and self-centeredness"—to its loss. Others in the post-civil rights generation may see these differences as a matter of class, that is, they possess greater material resources. Hence, they do not need to return the cup of sugar. Bemoaning the loss of black communalism and decrying the emerging ethic of individualism are unifying themes each generation is expressing, despite their attitudes toward borrowing or repaying a cup of sugar.

Many individuals, like Hawkins, perceive these value shifts as most discernable in the culture of the civil rights generation, which is characterized by a more heterogeneous community, with individuated lifestyles and greater stratification by socioeconomic status. In contrast to the World War I and World War II generations, the familial structure of the 1990s was more variant; parenting was more likely to be performed by a singular unit without community involvement and support. In 1996, about 64 percent of homes with children were headed by black single parents.[23] Along with increased urbanization, such structural factors as high unemployment among black males impact familial formation and its spiral disruption.[24] In a weakened black family structure, group honor is diminished and is supplanted by individual narcissism.

In the culture of the civil rights generation, the educational institution also changed. Education becomes more specialized, and it is seen as a way to make a living. Self before service is the dominant motif. Education is also more racially integrated, and black students are now more likely to be taught by white educators. Desegregation has increased professional mobility and occupational options in the black political economy to include corporate executives, legislators, scientists, and engineers. More than previous generations, the civil rights generation is more culturally and structurally integrated into the dominant white community, and correspondingly more isolated from black familial, friendship, and institutional networks. They are more likely to use their individual competitive accomplishments for self-fulfillment.

The pillar of the moral community, the black church of the past era, no longer holds sway over the competing individualistic system. Absolute ethics and faith are replaced by relative ethics and skepticism in an amoral community. Even black leadership, dominated more by politicians than clergy, reflects individual goals. Acculturation of the dominant group's more materialistic and individualistic, capitalistic value orientation and worldview, which emphasizes things before people—material success and self-fulfillment—has also contributed to more psychic discontinuity and less race consciousness in a society that is more covertly racist and sexist.

In Margaret Mead's words, the elders in the postfigurative culture and to some extent in the cofigurative culture say to the young with certainty: "You know, I have been young and you have never been old." Now, in the prefigurative culture, the youth can reply: "You have never been young in the world I am young in, and you can never be."[25]

CONCEPTUALIZING COMMUNITY, CULTURE, AND CONSCIOUSNESS

As previously mentioned, the 1960s stood symbolically as the transitional backdrop not only for the changing characteristics of the black elite, but also for major social, structural, cultural, economic, and psychological alterations between black communities and white communities and within black communities. These changes profoundly impacted black culture and consciousness. Here I define how community, culture, and consciousness are employed in this work. When I refer to community, the concept is not necessarily confined by geography. Rather, as Robert A. Nisbet noted, it "encompasses all forms of relationships which are characterized by a high degree of personal intimacy, emotional depth, moral commitment, social cohesion, and continuity in time. . . . Community is a fusion of feeling and thought, of tradition and commitment, of membership and volition,"[26] which finds its symbolic expressions in locality, race, religion, ethnicity, occupation, or nationality. Andrew Billingsley reminds us that blacks comprise a community in four respects.

> First, geographically, most black families live in neighborhoods where most of their neighbors are also black. . . . A second sense of the community among African Americans . . . is a shared set of values, which helps to define them. . . . Thirdly, most black people, wherever they live, continue to identify with their heritage to some considerable degree. . . . Finally, it is appropriate to speak of an African-American community in terms of a set of institutions and organizations which grow out of the African-American heritage, identify with it, and serve primarily African-American people and families.[27]

Culture is the social heritage of a people, the shared compass that guides their thinking, feeling, and acting and their philosophical assumptions and worldview. It includes a people's expressions of traditions, institutions, artifacts, and styles of life. It is also a dynamic process involving the complex interplay between the past and present. For example, several scholars have argued that an African worldview—for instance, the emphasis on collectivity, spirituality, and harmony with the cosmos—survived the New World experiences of blacks.[28] These retentions, such as communalism, were functional for blacks' survival in a hostile and oppressive society. Communalism also survived among other people of color in the United States, particularly among Native Americans.

Consciousness is a social process that is collectively constructed. It is a person's sense of identification—ideologically, behaviorally, emotionally, and spiritually—to the group or status of origin—race, class, sex, or ethnicity. Here, I am specifically referring to racial/ethnic consciousness. I postulate that community moves on culture and changes it: culture stirs consciousness. Consciousness is both collectively and individually cyclical. Pitts agrees, too, that it "emerges, changes, and declines."[29] Specifically, group racial consciousness varies according to historical time periods; the cultural, structural, and economic trends and transformations within the larger society; and in response to mobilization from within black communities.[30] Racial consciousness also changes in tandem with manifestations of mutable racism. Racism was more overt in the pre-1960s and more covert in the post-1960s.[31] In the 1990s, a resurgence of overt racism occurred, such as, the arson attacks on black churches in the South and the increasingly vociferousness of white hate groups, particularly via the Internet.

This nexus between mutable forms of racism and racial consciousness assumes that racism is a central feature of American social structure that continues to color the life chances of nondominant racial groups, although differentially. African Americans, the darkest hue, are still the "faces at the bottom of the well."[32] Their group mobility and quality of life, like other nondominant populations, are inextricably tied to and tempered by economic cycles, by structural and cultural changes in the larger society, and by political mobilization within the black community. These mutable forms of racism, as practiced by the dominant group toward nondominant groups, follow a cyclical rather than linear pattern. This theoretical position differs from those of scholars, such as William J. Wilson, who argue that the significance of race and racism is declining in a postindustrial society.[33]

In applying the concepts of community, culture, and consciousness to generational changes among blacks, I propose that the more blacks are structurally, culturally, and psychologically integrated into black communities, the more likely they are to postulate the permanence of racism and the more likely they are to manifest stronger group and personal racial identity clarity, racial consciousness, and a sense of communal ethic. The black elite of the pre-1960s, therefore, would be more integrated into black communities and black culture, and thus share a greater sense of group racial identity clarity, racial consciousness, and racial collectivity than the post-1960s black elite.[34] A typology of changing black community, culture, and collective consciousness in the pre-1960s and post-1960s is represented in Table 1.

These structural, cultural, and psychological shifts of which I speak represent a continuum rather than discrete changes, although they are more predominant in a particular epoch. For instance, in the traditional culture of the pre-1960s, the collective ethos of black leadership was service before self; but, as in any given time period, individuals manifest a discrepancy between ideal culture and real culture. Surely, the seven deadly sins know no historical boundaries or times.

In exploring the overarching theme of generational changes in community, culture, and consciousness, I focus on the dominant professions of blacks in the pre-1960s—teacher, preacher, physician, and entrepreneur. Black leaders, embodying the ideology of service and collective uplift, reform, and liberation of the group, emerged from these traditional occupations. These professions embraced the Ujima spirit, the collective work and responsibility, of the pre-1960s black community—its mind, soul, body, and socioeconomic heartbeat. Chapter 1, "The Way We Were," captures the essence of that collective specter in the lives of two World War I individuals. Chapter 2, "Educating for Living and Uplifting," looks at three generations of educators, the community's ministers to the mind, and depicts how the communitarian zest has eroded with each succeeding generation. Chapter 3, "Black Clergy: Salvation

Table 1. A Typology of Changing Community, Culture, and Consciousness

A. Community

Social, Structural, Cultural, and Psychological Forces	Homogeneous Mode (Pre-1960s)	Heterogeneous Male (Post-1960s)
Family	*Extended*	*Variant*
	Parenting by mother/father unit with extended family support and community involvement	Parenting by singular unit with minimal community involvement and support
	Group honor	Individual narcissism
Education	*Segregation*	*Desegration*
	Generalized credentials	Specialized credentials
	Education for living and group uplift	Education for making a living and self-fulfillment
Religion	*Sacred/Communal*	*Secular/Associational*
	Faith	Skepticism
	Moral community	Amoral community
Economy	Occupation and professional uniformity	Occupation and professional diversity
	Communitarian collaborative accomplishments	Individual competitive accomplishments
Polity	Race-linked	Class-linked
Race, Gender, and Class Structure		
	Overt separatism: more rigid color line and gender line	Covert separatism; less rigid color line and gender line
	Stratification based on both subjective and objective criteria within the black community: respectability, family background, education, occupation, property ownership and skin color*	Stratification on objective socioeconomic criteria within the black community and the larger society: occupation, income, and education

B. Culture

Social, Structural, Cultural, and Psychological Forces	Homogeneous Mode (Pre-1960s)	Heterogeneous Mode (Post-1960s)
Dominant Ethos	Service oriented	Self-fulfillment oriented
	Common goals	Individual goals
Ontology	People before things	Things before people

C. Consciousness

Social, Structural, Cultural, and Psychological Forces	Homogeneous Mode (Pre-1960s)	Heterogeneous Male (Post-1960s)
Individual and Group Identity	Race-linked	Race, ethnicity, class and/or gender linked
Individual and Group Identity Clarity	Collectivized	Individuated
Double Consciousness	Psychic continuity	Psychic discontinuity

*For a discussion of pre-1960s class criteria, see Norval D. Glenn, "Negro Prestige Criteria: A Case Study in the Bases of Prestige," *American Journal of Sociology* 68 (May 1963): 645–57.

and Liberation," focuses on preachers, the community's ministers to the soul, and records the generational changes from a candle of collective consciousness to a more individualistic one. Chapter 4, "Black Physicians: The Community Healers," spotlights the physicians, the community's ministers to the physical body, and illustrates the generational change from an ethic of service to an individualistic and profit-centered one. Chapter 5, "Black Entrepreneurs: Mixing Mission with Making Money," highlights the entrepreneurs, the community's socioeconomic heartbeat, and points out generational changes in community, culture, and consciousness. Chapter 6, "Black Politicians: The Bellwethers of the Post-Civil Rights Era" and chapter 7, "Black Artists: The Soul of Black Communities," introduce the new pieces in the second edition of this work, which focus on professional occupations that have opened up to African Americans since the civil rights movement. To assess whether generational changes continue to occur in these new professions, politicians and artists have been chosen to represent the myriad of professional opportunities that are now available to blacks. Chapter 8, "Chaos or Community: Facing the Twenty-First Century," concludes with a treatise on the political, social, and economic implications of a declining collective ethos in the twenty-first century.

The life histories in this work, culled from in-depth interviews, are part of an ongoing research project of black professionals in the United States that began in the mid-1980s and culminated in 2006. When necessary, follow-up, in-depth interviews were conducted. While some real names are used throughout this book, pseudonyms are employed to protect the identities of others.

1

The Way We Were

When the luminous and spirited Louise Thompson Patterson, educator, cultural critic, labor organizer, and social reformer, was born in Chicago, Illinois, in 1901, the dawn of the twentieth century, and the witty William Holmes Borders, minister, educator, and social activist, was born in 1905 in Macon, Georgia, it was a time of hope in America—an era of expansion and industrialization. And despite Du Bois' dictum that "the problem of the twentieth century is the problem of the color line," blacks, 89.7 percent of whom lived in the South,[1] were also hopeful that the new epoch would signal the demise of what Rayford Logan, black historian, called "the nadir."[2] This dismal period in African American history, beginning with the Compromise of 1877 and ending in the early twentieth century, sounded the death knell for civil and political rights and privileges gained during Reconstruction. During the nadir period, Black Codes were reenacted, and in 1883 the Supreme Court repealed the Civil Rights Act of 1875, making it again acceptable to deny blacks equal access to accommodations. The Court ruled also, in *Plessy v. Ferguson* in 1896, that separate facilities for blacks and whites were not a violation of the Thirteenth and Fourteenth Amendments. This "separate but equal doctrine" set the stage for race relations in the United States for the next six decades.

In this chapter, I tell the story of the unsung heroes and heroines of the World War I generation, epitomized by the voices of Louise Patterson and William Holmes Borders, who helped pave the stony path for the activism of the World War II generation in the 1960s. The changing racial landscape in the 1960s, dubbed as the age of rebellion and the most tumultuous of the twentieth century, ushered in a period of conflict and confrontation, a wave of activism and a proliferation of social movements, an era of breaking boundaries, and Kennedy's New Frontier. Full of vim and vigor, like the fresh faces of the social movements, the young President John F. Kennedy sounded a clarion call for a "grand and global alliance" against tyranny, poverty, disease, and war and broke boundaries in the technological race to space. The younger cohort of the World War II generation, who came of age at his inauguration in January 1961, carries a collective memory of the glaring sun that blinded the sight of the venerable Robert Frost and the wintry wind wafting at the notes of the old and frail poet, who painstakingly struggled to read his poem. Thirty-two years later, at Bill Clinton's inauguration, the white male was supplanted by a statuesque black woman, Maya Angelou, as the poet on whom the eyes and ears of a civil rights generation focused in its remembrance. The symbolic "passing of the torch" from a white male to a black female did not occur without the painful struggles of the World War II generation, who were on the frontline frays of the civil rights movement of the 1960s, and the Pattersons and Borders who trod the stony road and fought the fight before them.

The lives of Patterson and Borders capture the spirit of the World War I generation, one which embraced a collective ethos of racial uplift and service to others. Though both were exemplary actors in the racial frays to improve the socioeconomic status of the masses, significant personal and social life events created contrasting worldviews and values that shaped their collective consciousness and actions. In their formative years, Patterson and Borders were influenced by the racial uplift and service ideology of W. E. B. Du Bois and Booker T. Washington, two towering black leaders who responded differently to the nadir period. While the clay of Patterson's social consciousness was molded by the ideology of Du Bois, who demanded equality, economic and educational opportunities, and an end to segregation, Borders's social consciousness was shaped by Washington's urging of blacks to accept social and political inequality in exchange for economic and educational support, as outlined in his Atlanta Exposition speech of 1895.

SIGNIFICANT LIFE EVENTS:
COMING OF AGE IN THE WORLD WAR I ERA

Fueled by the intimidation and violence of the post-Reconstruction, as well as by the sluggish economy in the South, blacks began migrating to the expanding commercial and industrial northern and border cities such as Boston, Chicago, Cincinnati, Evansville, Indianapolis, Greater New York, Pittsburgh, and St. Louis. Between 1890 and 1915, for example, the black population increased in Chicago from less than fifteen thousand to fifty thousand. The majority of these migrants—43 percent—came from the upper South and Border States, with the largest number coming from Kentucky.[3] Louise Patterson's mulatto family was among this stream of migrants leaving Kentucky in the late nineteenth century and eventually flowing into Chicago. Passing through Ohio, the family split. Patterson's mother and her sisters remained within the race, but her brothers stayed in Ohio and passed for white. E. Franklin Frazier noted that the anonymity of the city allowed many blacks to pass for whites, often as Southern Europeans or South Americans, to enter occupations closed to blacks.[4]

After leaving Ohio, Patterson's mother moved to Chicago. Here she met and married her husband and gave birth to her only child, Louise Thompson Patterson. When Patterson was four, her mother divorced her father and, with her young daughter, settled on the West Coast, which was inhabited by less than 1 percent blacks in 1905. They moved first to Seattle, Washington, where they lived with the daughter of the first black to serve in the United States Senate during Reconstruction. Her mother soon married a restless chef, who moved his family to various small towns throughout the western states of Idaho, Oregon, Utah, Washington, and even Nevada during the famous silver and gold mine strikes.

Being constantly uprooted, Patterson experienced the pain of loneliness and social isolation. She attended over twenty elementary schools and "never knew what it was like to complete a semester." As the only black child in these white communities and schools, she longed for a supportive network of family, friends, church, or other black institutions. She described her existence as hell.[5] Being barred from attending Sunday school at a white church was one of many poignant racial episodes she encountered. Her devoted mother, a fair-complexioned woman, could have easily passed for white to seek better job opportunities. She chose, however, to work as a domestic so she could remain with her daughter and protect her from racial storms.

Growing up in white communities, Patterson learned only negative conceptions of black people. She lacked positive black role models; Booker T. Washington was the only successful black she heard of in school. At age eleven, her mother took her to hear him speak in a small town in Washington. She was sorely disappointed with his accommodative approach to race relations. Her knowledge of black people, their culture and issues remained practically nil until she was fifteen, when she moved to a black community. Here she became versed in black cultural lifestyles and traditions. She reminisced humorously about the ritual of straightening hair and the impact of white beauty standards upon her self-esteem. "When we moved to the black community, my mother's friends said to her, 'You know that child of yours would not look so bad if you did something to her hair.' Since my mother never heard of straightening hair, she asked, 'What do you do?' They suggested she should get my hair straightened."

Patterson felt ashamed and demeaned that her hair was not naturally straight. At school, she would avoid swimming classes because her hair was so long and thick that it would not dry in time for her next class. Since color and hair texture were important status distinctions and such high valuation was placed on them in this era, the young Patterson announced to her mother, "I don't care that you married a dark man, but why didn't you marry one with straight hair?" "Straight hair became the thing you longed to have, so you could swim, comb your hair easily, and do many things in life," said Patterson.

Despite Patterson's conflictive feelings about her blackness, she experienced a sense of community in northern California for the first time. She formed close friendships and learned to socialize with others. She stayed long enough in this community not only to complete a semester of school but also to finish high school. After graduating from high school, Patterson wanted to get a job, like all her friends; her mother insisted, however, that she attend college. She entered the University of California at Berkeley, at the end of the "Red Summer" of 1919, when lynching and race riots occurred.

The context of Patterson's college experience and young adulthood also took place during a period of international crisis and domestic social change in the United States. On the international front, World War I was coming to a close. Nationally, increased industrialization and urbanization, as well as the war, had set off the Great Migration, the large exodus of blacks from the South to the North. The migration and the 1924 National Origins Quota Act, restricting the numbers of eastern and southern European immigrants, increased the influx of unskilled and semiskilled blacks that were needed to work in northern industries. Bart Landry noted in *The New Black Middle Class* that the large pool of black workers contributed to the growth of the black middle class. "The burgeoning black urban communities provided an opportunity for the emergence of a black middle class of teachers, doctors, dentists, undertakers, realtors, insurance agents, ministers, newspaper editors, and small businessmen who attempted to meet the needs of a black community that whites were often unwilling to serve."[6] This class was distinctly different from the post-Emancipation, mostly mulatto black elite, primarily a status group who worked as domestics, servants, caterers, barbers, tailors, and small businessmen serving white communities.

But unlike the emerging professionals who resided in regions with larger black populations, Patterson lived in the West, where there were less than 1 percent blacks when she graduated from college in the 1920s. Although there was a greater concentration of blacks in Los Angeles and the San Francisco Bay area, Patterson, a cum laude graduate who had majored in business and minored in Spanish, was unable to find a position as a teacher. She lamented the gender line and color line: "Los Angeles had a larger and more established black community, so a black female could teach. We didn't have a black teacher in the Bay area, so the best thing for middle-class black girls was to make a successful marriage. Blacks worked in menial positions; even well-educated black men were caterers, post office workers, janitors, or redcaps. A woman could work in a department store if she wanted to be a maid or elevator operator. There were no salesgirls. You couldn't even get a job in the civil service."

Patterson was unprepared for the responsibility and restraints of marriage. Yet she could not find work, so she used her Spanish minor to pass for Hispanic and was hired in a civil service position. She had seen many blacks who migrated to San Francisco from New Orleans, Louisiana, and Dallas, Texas, pass for white or Hispanic. Often, the family would split up, like her own extended family, and some members would disappear into the white population.

Leading a double life was a poignant experience. On weekends, she would socialize with her black friends. When Mondays arrived, she led an existence apart from those friends, who worked in the financial district of San Francisco as runners and stock clerks. "My friends and I would take the same ferry across the bay. Here we've been having all this fun on Sunday, and [on Monday] they would walk past like they had never seen you." Sometimes Patterson's white boss would drop by her house on weekends, and the black friends would hide in her closet. At work, she constantly heard white colleagues say about blacks, "We'll get this nigger to do this and that." For Patterson, the double-consciousness created psychic conflict that was overwhelming. "I can't live like this to earn a living. You got to deny who you are. I can't take it," Patterson agonized before quitting her job and ending her double life.[7]

Patterson and her mother traveled to Chicago, where they reestablished contacts with relatives. There she worked in a small accounting firm, while her mother worked as a cook. In Chicago, Patterson began to read and learn more about black history and the "New Negro Movement." This movement sparked the Harlem Renaissance, and the adventurous Patterson wanted to be a part of it. When she met W. E. B. Du Bois again in 1924, and he invited her to New York, she wanted to go. Du Bois had inspired her racial awakening and racial pride when she was in college. She described her encounter with him "like meeting Jesus Christ." It was the first time she had seen a black person who exuded confidence and race pride. His demeanor contrasted sharply with Booker T. Washington's accommodative approach to race relations that she had observed a few years earlier. After Du Bois' invitation, two teaching experiences intervened before she went to New York to become, eventually, an important figure in the Harlem Renaissance.

Du Bois and Washington would blaze the different paths that the generation of Louise Patterson and William Holmes Borders would tread. Patterson, whose developmental years were shaped by her experiences in small white communities in the West, was influenced by Du Bois' protest leadership in race relations. In contrast, Borders, the Southerner, was more inspired by Washington's accommodative philosophy to race issues and the importance he placed on the dignity of labor. Yet he could also appreciate the contributions of Du Bois, who emphasized the dignity of the mind. Still, for Borders, a black boy coming of age in the segregated South during World War I, it was more feasible, in such a cultural milieu, to adopt Washington's conciliatory strategy toward whites as a survival mechanism.

Borders and Patterson were brought up in different ways, and this was the critical influence in their choice of their life paths. Patterson was constantly uprooted and lacked a stable network of kin and friends, while Borders, the seventh of ten children, grew up in a tightly knit extended family in Macon, Georgia, and remained in his community until he left for college. His father was a prominent Georgia minister, and his mother, a housewife, was an alumna of Spelman Seminary. They reinforced the racial pride, hope, and dignity of mind of Du Bois' *Souls of Black Folk* and the dignity of labor, self-help, and hard work of Washington's *Up from Slavery*.

Borders learned early the importance of determination, hard work, and thriftiness as necessary qualities to surmount racial roadblocks. At eight years old, he arose at four o'clock in the morning to deliver the *Macon Telegraph*. Making only four dollars a week, he gave his mother two dollars, saved one dollar, and spent the other. It was also paramount for Borders to develop his mind, for "being educated, no white man could take it away from you." Anxious to continue schooling, Borders picked peaches, carried mail, worked on a tobacco farm, washed windows, scrubbed floors, and raked leaves. Like Booker T. Washington, Borders, over six feet tall, wanted to be judged not by his height, but by the depths from which he came. He was the descendant of a mulatto slave grandfather, a blacksmith, who purchased his freedom at a cost of two thousand dollars and had almost paid for his wife's freedom when the Emancipation Proclamation was issued. Borders was inspired by his grandfather's character and wanted to be judged by his standards in his desire to improve the lot of others. The grandfather, also a minister, had symbolically passed on his personage when he handed down to young Borders his blacksmith hammer from slavery as a "symbol of burning desire and everlasting ambition for personal liberty and an opportunity to preach a social gospel."

After graduating from high school in the early 1920s, Borders was accepted at Morehouse College in Atlanta, Georgia, where he had a chance to be judged by his character. He did extremely well in his studies. But this honor student was asked by President John Hope of Morehouse to leave in his senior year, because he was unable to pay his debt to the college. The dean of the college wanted to see young Borders receive his degree, so the morning of graduation he called a conference with President Hope and Borders. After listening carefully Hope asked Borders, "If we allow you to graduate, will you promise to clear your debt?" Borders quipped, "If you handle a man for four years, and he won't pay his debt, then there is something wrong with the school." Hope retorted, "You are a fool. You are trying to graduate, not More- house. If we arrange to have you work on a tobacco farm in Hartford, Con- necticut, will you agree to pay back what you owe to the college?" Borders responded, "Yes! However, I should be sent as a boss, not as an ordinary worker." After much discussion, an agreement was reached; Borders would work in Connecticut. During the 1920s and beyond, Borders noted, many philanthropic organizations assisted black college students in obtaining sum- mer employment in the North.

Making a weekly salary of only fourteen dollars, Borders kept his promise to President Hope, sending seven dollars weekly to Morehouse and seven dol- lars to Macon, Georgia, to save his father's property. Many blacks were los- ing their livelihood and property several years prior to the onset of the Great Depression. The reckoning of debts was important to Borders, but it left him without money for room and board. To take care of other expenses, the en- terprising young man washed clothes for the boys who worked on the farm. In 1929, with his debt repaid and his degree from Morehouse College in hand, Borders entered Garrett Theological Seminary in Evanston, Illinois. He mar- ried Julia Pate, the inspiration of his life, in 1931. He worked his way through seminary, earning a bachelor of divinity degree in 1932. Eventually, the young couple had two children. While pastoring a church and providing for his young family during the Depression era, Borders received a master's de- gree from Northwestern in 1936 and continued his work toward a doctorate. He studied later at Union Theological Seminary and Columbia University in the 1940s.

EMBODYING THE TRADITION OF UPLIFT
AND SERVICE: TEACHING, PREACHING, AND REFORMING

In the 1920s and early 1930s, teaching and preaching were dominant occu- pations of the black elite. While men like William Holmes Borders could preach and teach, college-educated women of Louise Patterson's era could only teach.

After leaving Chicago in the mid-1920s, Patterson accepted a teaching appointment in Pine Bluff, Arkansas. She spent only a year at Pine Bluff, teaching shorthand to students who, she said, "couldn't write and business to those who couldn't add." She was disheartened not only by the quality of her students, but also by the quality of life for blacks in Arkansas. It was her first encounter with the most virulent forms of racism in the South. Patterson painfully recalled that, in 1925, the year the Dyer Anti-Lynching Bill was introduced into the Senate, the body of a black man who had been lynched was returned to his community and burned. This incident left an indelible mark on the young teacher. As she reflected over sixty-five years later, "I was in a rage at Pine Bluff. I remember going around hating everything white. I even hated white chickens."

The overt racism in Arkansas was too emotionally wrenching, so in 1927 Patterson accepted a position at Hampton Institute (now Hampton University) and soon found herself embroiled in a student protest. The ghost of Booker T. Washington, its most illustrious graduate, still haunted Hampton's hallowed halls, embodying the paternalistic spirit imparted by General Samuel Chapman Armstrong, his white headmaster. Like many black institutions, Hampton was dominated by whites who comprised the majority of faculty, trustees, and presidents in the 1920s. In *Long Memory*, Berry and Blassingame wrote:

> By the early years of the twentieth century, many of those whites had lost the missionary zeal characteristic of their predecessors in the Reconstruction Period. Instead, they were often domineering and paternalistic. The Northern financiers who controlled the board of trustees of many of the black colleges were often dictatorial and sometimes withheld money from institutions dedicated to protests.[8]

Such paternalistic attitudes precipitated many blacks to gain control of black educational institutions. Kelly Miller, of Howard University, argued that blacks would be well served if all philanthropies were stopped and blacks maintained their own institutions. Said Miller, "The white race has furnished leaders for us. No man of one group can ever furnish leaders to people of another group, unless he is willing to become naturalized into the group he seeks to lead."[9]

In the 1920s, the protest reached its zenith. As Berry and Blassingame wrote,

> Precipitated by the wholesale dismissal of radical students and professors, the demeaning remarks made by white presidents, James E. Gregg, J. Stanley Durkee and Fayette McKenzie, and the segregation policies practiced by these presidents, student riots and strikes occurred on the campus of Hampton Institute and Howard and Fisk Universities between 1925 and 1927.[10]

A turbulent social milieu marked the arrival of Patterson at Hampton Institute in 1927, both on campus and in the community. The Virginia legislature had passed the Massenburg Bill the previous year, which required segregation in public halls, theaters, motion picture houses, and all places of public entertainment and assemblage. The immediate target of the 1926 law was Hampton Institute, because the races were not segregated when they attended events in the campus auditorium. The publisher of Newport News *Daily Press*, who was in favor of the bill, warned that

> powerful influences were at work in the United States with the ultimate aim of racial amalgamation and that these influences were represented locally by Hampton Institute "which teaches and practices social equality between the white and negro races." . . . Amalgamation would mean the destruction of the Anglo-Saxon race in America. Rather than that should be [sic] we would prefer that every white child in the United States were sterilized and the Anglo-Saxon race left to perish in its purity.[11]

Against this historical backdrop, Patterson recounted her experiences at Hampton: "In contrast to the primitive school at Pine Bluff, Arkansas, Hampton was a beautiful campus and the racism more genteel. The head was white [President James Gregg, 1918–1929], and all the departments were headed by whites. All the matrons were white. We had only been at Hampton three days when the principal, a Congregationalist minister from the North, called a meeting of new teachers. We were the first blacks in each department. He said, when he called us together, that we should not walk along the campus front. A boil started inside of me and the strike came."

When the strike occurred, Patterson had been at Hampton for only three weeks. She and another black woman teacher were the only faculty who supported the students. She was perturbed about the paternalistic attitudes and behaviors of faculty and staff toward students. Patterson recounted that "Hampton had separate entrances to dining rooms and classrooms for faculty and students. I used to go galloping to my class and some little white clerk would say, 'Why are you coming out of this entry? You are not supposed to do that!' I didn't get angry for myself; I got angry that they were treating students like that." So Patterson, the rebel, had found a cause. She recalled the precipitating incident that led to Hampton's strike: "The strike started over the paternalistic attitude of the dean of women, a white woman who had never been to college. She required that couples be chaperoned when they viewed movies on Saturday nights. For every two couples, a teacher sat in the front and back of the auditorium. The dean said she didn't know what students did when the lights were out. She and other matrons had such evil minds, and most were old maids. When the dean turned the lights on in the movie, the

kids got up and walked out. The strike was on. It was a Gandhi strike of passive resistance."

The following day, General Jan Smuts from South Africa spoke on campus.
He once said, "Every man in South Africa, except those that are mad, quite
mad, believes in the suppression of the Negro."[12] Patterson said of Smuts'
visit: "The matrons were trying to round up students [and coach them] on
what they should say, and how they should act. At lunch, the students passively resisted his visit by refusing to sing the blessing. When students went
to chapel, which had a separate section for blacks and whites, an Uncle Tom
sang a spiritual, but the students refused to sing. I was so excited to see them
do this. When I expressed my joy in the presence of other black teachers at
the behavior of the students, I was called on the carpet."

Someone reported Patterson to the president, and he warned her not "to get
off on the wrong foot." She was not fired, but admonished "to understand the
Hampton spirit." Patterson wryly lamented, "The turmoil at Hampton really
set me on a course of rebellion." Patterson went to New York to get support
for the strike from W. E. B. Du Bois, while her friend visited the poet Alain
Locke, in Washington, D.C., to implore him to persuade Du Bois "to write ed-
itorially about what the strike was all about at Hampton." She followed up
with a long letter to Du Bois. The strike ended after two weeks, the students
who had participated in the strike were expelled, and classes resumed.

While crossing campus one day, a black colleague said to Patterson, "Look
what I got." She held up a copy of the *Crisis* in which Patterson's letter had
been reprinted, but her name had been withheld. The letter stated:

Very much depends on public opinion in this affair. The authorities are crediting
this strike as the work of disobedient boys and girls who were led to do what
they did. On the other hand, each student I have talked with has impressed me
with the serious attitude he has taken in the matter—with each one of them it became a holy cause. . . . It has been a terrible ordeal to witness the struggle some
of them have gone through, feeling they cannot stay, yet cannot go. . . . There
are others who will never return, and they are the best of the school. Dr. [James]
Gregg acknowledged that the leaders in the strike were the foremost men on the
campus and those who had been some years in the institution. The wholesale
slaughter that has come about of the school's best is too great for good to come
of it, and the Negro world should be made to see the justice in the students'
stand. . . . [Since] the iniquitous Massenburg Bill which required the separation
of the races in public halls of Virginia, including Hampton School, . . . the Principal of the school has been less social with the students than ever before; . . .
he has placed in some of the trades departments of the school white men from
the Ku Klux sections of the Peninsula, one of whom died and was buried with
honors from the Kluxers; . . . members of the faculty from the North have referred to the students as "heathen," without, of course, designating any particu-

lar misdemeanant, and . . . it has been assumed that the students were of such low character that they would undertake sexual contact during a play unless the lights were on, even to the extent of destroying the effect of the moving pictures or play. . . . The whole atmosphere at Hampton has changed since the Editor of the *Daily Press* sought and succeeded in having a law passed separating the races in public halls.[13]

"All over campus, faculty and staff were asking who was the snake in the grass," said Patterson. "I wanted to get up and say I wrote that letter." Her friend asked her not to admit to doing it. At first, the administration accused her friend; then they concluded it was a "composite letter of disloyal people on the campus." Although Patterson feared she and her friend would be fired, they wrote letters indicating they would return. The head of the department called her in for a talk: "We got your letter, and I want to know if you are coming back to Hampton?" "You got my letter and what did it say?" replied Patterson. "That you are coming back," he responded. "Why are you calling me in to talk with me?" asked Patterson. The department head remarked, "We thought you might be happy someplace else. If you are coming back, we are delighted."

Patterson finally received a letter asking her to return. She said, "It was that kind of hypocrisy that was worse than overt racism. My two years at Hampton were too much. I had become embittered. Everybody was picturing Hampton as a paradise for students, but I didn't see it that way."

Patterson was especially disheartened by the condescending attitude of whites during the strike: "After all those things we've done for them, how can they be disloyal? How ungrateful they are!" It was the swan song to her season of discontent. "I had enough of philanthropy. I had to get out of that atmosphere and out of the South. Hampton had set me on a course of rebellion."

About the time Patterson arrived in New York in the late 1920s, after her brief stint at Hampton, and William Holmes Borders accepted the pastorate in Evanston, Illinois, in the early 1930s, disillusionment about the promise of the North set in for the masses of blacks. With a faltering economy and a hostile racial climate, blacks saw little hope for improving their life chances and for participating fully in American democracy. A cadre of dynamic and diverse black leaders of protest movements emerged during this period to respond to these social and economic conditions. Marcus Garvey's Back-to-Africa Movement, which appealed to the masses, and the new Negro movement, the cultural renaissance that appealed to the middle class, were examples of protest movements. Through poetry, prose, and song, numerous black writers and intellectuals in the Harlem Renaissance railed against social and economic injustices. They protested against segregation and lynching; demanded higher wages, shorter hours, and better working conditions; and fought for full equality and against second-class citizenship. While many black intellectuals, political activists, and labor leaders formed the core of the National Association for the Advancement of Colored People (NAACP), others were involved as key players in the Communist and Socialist movements. While William Holmes Borders, a Republican, took the former path, working within the system, Patterson, a Communist, chose the latter.

Before joining the Communist Party in the 1930s and becoming involved in the Harlem Renaissance, Patterson received a scholarship to study at the New School for Social Work in New York, but she failed to complete her graduate degree. It was not her destiny. "After interning in a charitable organization, I knew I did not want to become a social worker. I was sent to see a psychiatrist because I refused to spy on a client." The psychiatrist concluded that Patterson was the "sanest person that she had seen in a long time."

By the time she left school, Patterson had become good friends with Langston Hughes, Alain Locke, and Aaron Douglas, who introduced her to other intellectuals in Harlem, like Ralph Ellison, Arna Bontemps, Horace Cayton, and Rudolph Fisher. Here she met and married Wallace Thurman, a writer and leading spokesperson for the movement. The marriage did not last long. And while she was feeling somewhat daunted about it, Alain Locke introduced her to Charlotte Louise Vandervere Quick Mason, the wealthy widow of Rufus Osgood Mason and one of many whites who supported the black cultural movement of the Harlem Renaissance. The wealthy widow offered Patterson a position as editorial secretary for Zora Neale Hurston and Langston Hughes for $150 a month, a good salary in the late 1920s. Since Patterson could work at home, she thought at first this was a "wonderful experience." However, the first indication of a problem between Patterson and Mason occurred when Hurston, "who was collecting book materials in the South," told Patterson in a letter: "Godmother [as Mason wanted her patrons to call her] is unhappy that you never sent her a thank-you note when you got your check." "I've been working all of my life and never had to send my boss a note thanking her for a check," remarked Patterson. She claimed that Mason wanted to control the lives of all black beneficiaries of her patronage, whom she treated condescendingly. "She wanted to tell you what time to get up, what to eat, and whom to see."

While Zora Neale Hurston obliged Mason's request for gratitude and submissiveness for material gains, Patterson could not wear the mask. Patterson's relationship with Mason gradually worsened, and Patterson was the first to end her affiliation with the philanthropist. The following year, Langston Hughes did the same. But Patterson did not know "what broke Zora." In 1930 she had worked closely with Zora Hurston in collaboration with Langston Hughes on *Mule Bones*, a play. The collaboration ultimately caused Zora and

Langston to part company—Hurston felt Hughes was making Patterson "too much a part of it."

For a brief juncture in the early 1930s, the racial politics of Louise Patterson and William Holmes Borders converged. They were both involved in interracial cooperation. After ending her patronage relationship with Mason, Patterson worked with the Congregational Education Society in its department of social relations, organizing race relations seminars from New York to the South. The interracial group included wealthy whites and prominent blacks, like educator Mary McLeod Bethune. Borders, who served as minister of the Second Baptist Church in Evanston, was also involved in "learning more about race relations"; he was a member of the Evanston Consumer Cooperative. While Borders was pleased with the success of his interracial ventures, Patterson, then editor of the Congregational Education Society's newsletter, was dissatisfied with the slow pace of change in race relations.

At this time in the early 1930s, Patterson came to the attention of James Ford, the first black vice president of the Communist Party. He had just received an invitation from the Meschrabpom Film Studio to make a movie in Moscow about black life in America. He encouraged Patterson, who was attending the workers school, to organize a committee of blacks to go to the Soviet Union. For most of the young intellectuals and artists in her entourage it was an adventure; but for Patterson and Langston Hughes, it was an opportunity to learn more about race relations. Though the movie project was a failure, they learned that being black in the Soviet Union entitled them to preferential treatment. Nevertheless, one aspect of their journey proved embarrassing:

> Meschrabpom Studio proposed that we all go to Odessa, take a cruise down the Black Sea and then come back to a location where the shooting of the picture would begin. However, after our relaxing journey to Batum and back we were met in Odessa by a Meschrabpom director with the information that Black and White had been cancelled. We also learned that our group had become "world news" because of stories sent out by American correspondents always on the alert for sensational ways to attack the USSR. We returned to Moscow to find excited cables from relatives and friends who read of our being stranded and destitute while we had been cruising deluxe on the scenic Black Sea coast, wining and dining in Odessa's beautiful Londres Hotel, and still receiving four hundred rubles a month from Meschrabpom.[14]

The trip to the Soviet Union was the defining event that crystallized her political perspective on race relations. When Patterson returned to the United States in the early thirties, the Scottsboro case, involving the alleged rape of two white women by black men, was one of the major political issues. She

felt compelled to do something about it. She returned to her job as editor of
the Congregational Education Society's newspaper and wrote an editorial
calling the incident a massacre. The editorial board reacted by asking that she
drop the word "massacre." Unable to "carry on the charade," Patterson began
to "see race relations as based on mutual interest, not do-gooder philanthropy." She was convinced that "if you want to change race relations, you
don't sit around and talk; you do something about it." Activism through socialism was the answer for Patterson.

Fighting racial injustice through the NAACP was not an option for Patterson. It was "too middle class" and too interested in soft-pedaling race relations. The Left movement offered her an option, so she joined the Communist
Party. Although a shift of black voters toward the Democratic Party began in
1928 and strengthened considerably in 1932, most blacks were overwhelmingly Republican when Franklin D. Roosevelt won the election in 1932. Of
the 25,536 who claimed membership in the Communist Party, only 2,500
were blacks.[15] The party's 1932 platform emphasized the disfranchisement,
discrimination, and economic exploitation of and violence against blacks.[16]

When Patterson joined the Communist Party, the NAACP and the International Labor Defense (ILD), an arm of the Communist Party, were in conflict
over the defense of the Scottsboro Boys. This incident took place on a train
traveling from Chattanooga to Memphis, March 25, 1931. It involved several
hitchhikers—black boys and white boys and two white girls. A fight ensued,
and the white boys were thrown off the train. The white boys told the towns-
people that nine black boys were riding the train with two white girls. The sta-
tionmaster telegraphed ahead, and when the train pulled into Paint Rock, Alabama, an angry posse was waiting. The boys fled, but were captured. Two
weeks later, eight of the boys were sentenced to the electric chair. The ILD
waged a virulent campaign against the NAACP, not so much as some believe
because of their interest in racial justice, but to criticize capitalism.[17] Eventually the ILD allowed other groups to share in the case. This new defense committee was successful in winning the acquittal of four of the boys and in laying the foundation for the release of the others.

Several black luminaries, like Du Bois, objected to Patterson's joining the
Communist Party. But she replied, "You have tried it your way, and I think some
of us young people want to do it another way." Du Bois had rejected communism in a 1931 *Crisis* article titled "The Negro and Communism." He did eventually become a member of the party when he was ninety-three years of age.[18]
Some leading black women of the day—Charlotte Hawkins Brown, Nannie
Burroughs, and Mary McLeod Bethune—for whom Patterson had deep respect,
opposed her political stance. Her friend Mary McLeod Bethune, "wondered
what had happened to her." Others thought she was crazy. Although Patterson

was still for reforms, she saw they were not going to solve the race and class issue. "Until you do away with exploitation, pitting one group against another, I see no way out—not only for the race question, but for peace and equality."

As a member of the Communist Party, Patterson never worked directly with the organization. She was affiliated for fifteen years, instead, with the International Workers Order (IWO), its powerful fraternal society. From 1933 to 1940, she lived in Chicago. As a national officer for the IWO, she traveled to Europe and across the United States as a labor, political, and social organizer. In the capacity of assistant secretary for the Scottsboro Boys Action Committee, she worked with Theodore Dreisden to organize the first demonstration on behalf of the "political prisoners." It drew more than three thousand demonstrators who demanded their release. She and James W. Ford were among the group of twenty-five whom President Franklin D. Roosevelt refused to meet with in the Scottsboro case.

As a labor organizer in Chicago in the 1930s, Patterson worked with packing-house and steel workers. She traveled to Pittsburgh and West Virginia to work with coal miners and to New Orleans and Birmingham to organize workers. On one of her trips to Birmingham, she was arrested and jailed.

"IWO was involved in a strike," said Patterson, "and I learned some facts that were helpful to the movement. I walked into a police raid in a white neighborhood where I was to meet some people. I was identified as one of the goddamn Yankee bitches." "Anything Communist" was arrested and jailed. She was told to give an assumed name and to say "Yes, Sir" and "No, Sir," because it would save her from hard knocks. The chief of police of Birmingham interviewed her. He asked if she had ever been to "Russha" (Russia). She replied, "No." He then warned, "Okay, you are in the South now, and when I ask you a question, you say, 'Yes, Sir.'"

"I was ready to die," said Patterson. "The next question he asked, I said 'No.' It was at the height of the Scottsboro trial, and the strike was on, so they didn't want any more trouble. I was transferred to the big modern jail—the same one as the Scottsboro Boys. I spent three days in jail. I didn't have fear, only anger at these white fascists. I was on one of the elevators with the chief of police when someone asked who I was. He answered, 'She's one of the goddamn Reds. We ought to put her in a corner and shoot her down like Mussolini does.' I don't know if they would have beaten me to a pulp if the IWO people had not found me at the jail. The jail official was bringing people to look at me like I was a strange animal. The only violence was when a black woman trustee struck me on the behind."

Patterson immediately left Birmingham. Upon arriving in Atlanta, she found that her picture was on the front page of the Atlanta *Constitution*. She was taken to the home of an IWO member. When the organization sent her a money order, she said, "I hit the road by myself and never breathed an easy breath until I got out of Georgia."

In 1940 Patterson married the executive secretary and attorney for the International Labor Defense and had one daughter. Eventually, she moved to Chicago and continued to work for the IWO until 1949, organizing immigrants who came to America to better relate to their new lives in a different country. This was one of the many projects she undertook in Chicago for the National Defense Committee, the intellectual arm of IWO until the late 1940s. Then the McCarthyism period had begun. The FBI was instrumental in destroying the IWO and other progressive organizations, such as the Council of African Affairs, where Patterson worked with W. E. B. Du Bois and Paul Robeson.

A new generation took up the banner in the post-World War II years. But throughout the decades of the 1950s, 1960s, and 1970s, Patterson remained active in a variety of organizations in the struggle for human liberation in the United States and Cuba. She was one of the founders of and a leading activist in the Civil Rights Congress (CRC) and a key player in forming the Sojourners for Truth and Justice, a black woman's auxiliary of the CRC. She assisted Herbert Aptheker with his Marxist studies and was involved in organizing the National Lawyers Association. When her husband died in 1980, she returned to California. In the late 1990s, she moved to New York where she remained true to her political ideals, until her death in 1999.

Reflecting on her life, Patterson said, "In all my radical activities, I was never afraid. I was free and could say what I wanted. I did pay a price. I don't have money, but I never wanted things too much. I've been able to travel through much of the world, and I've known people. I've lived a rich life. Socialism is still the way out, not only for the race question, but for peace, equality, and [erasing] poverty." For her contributions, she was honored with the Fannie Lou Hamer Award in the 1980s.

BORDERS'S SOCIAL GOSPEL

Although Patterson's and Borders's political philosophy and social activism converged at the same crossroad in the early 1930s, they quickly headed in strikingly different directions. Patterson, a Communist, chose to work outside the political system as a solution to the color and class line, while Borders, a Republican, viewed working within the capitalistic system as offering greater hope.

After leaving predominantly white Evanston in 1937, Borders returned to the black community as a teacher. President John Hope, remembering how Borders had faithfully paid his debt to Morehouse, invited him to return as professor of philosophy. Borders was also appointed pastor of the fledgling Wheat Street Baptist Church, which had been destroyed in the Atlanta fire of 1917. The young minister told his dispirited congregation, "Do not lose hope. We shall build here on Auburn Avenue in Atlanta, Georgia, a mighty fortress for our God." In building the "mighty fortress," he used it to preach the brand of social gospel taught by his grandfather. Blending the philosophy of Booker T. Washington and W. E. B. Du Bois, he encouraged economic development and civil liberties through his social gospel.

As the head of his flock, he acquired valuable land in the central city of Atlanta, where he built the Wheat Street complex, consisting of Wheat Street Church, the parsonage, the Christian Education Center, and a shopping center, as well as apartments for the elderly and low-income individuals. Until 1968 the church also operated a nursery school program. His work on the Board of the Consumer Cooperative in Evanston, Illinois, inspired him to establish the first church-sponsored federal credit union in the South. Under his leadership, Wheat Street, one of the largest black Baptist churches in the Southeast, developed the first housing project sponsored by a church in the United States.

To spread his social gospel, he evangelized from his pulpit, from his radio and television programs, and through his writings. Among his most noted works are *Follow Me*, *Men Must Live as Brothers*, *God Is Real*, *Big Rock Jail*, and *Seven Minutes at the Mike in the Deep South*, which contains the praise poem of African Americans, titled "I am Somebody."

Borders wanted to highlight the contributions of blacks to American culture, which contrasted sharply with the methods of Charles S. Johnson and E. Franklin Frazier, eminent sociologists, who negated African retentions among African Americans. In tandem with the noted scholars of his era, Du Bois and Melville J. Herskovits, Borders took an opposing view from the assimilationists. He noted African retentions in their family and community relations; in their music, folklore, and style of cooking; and in their spirituality. He claimed that "Southern hospitality crept through America's back door by way of slavery from Africa. Even masters who assumed themselves to be superior were taught better manners by contact with their slaves. Politeness was in the Negro's meek soul like corpuscles in his blood."[19]

Not only did Borders preach about the importance of black culture, but his church sponsored plays and distinguished artists, like Paul Robeson, Mattiwilda Dobbs, and Roland Hayes. It was his way of spiritually uplifting blacks by enhancing their sense of community, culture, and consciousness.

Borders also viewed his social gospel as a way of easing racial tension and pointing up the moral dilemmas in American democracy. This contradiction is reflected in one of his sermons during the early 1940s:

> Religion will work in race relations, in economic adjustment, in politics, in churches, in homes. We bark until the big dog of war, or dog of prejudice, or dog of hate trots over, then we fold up and flop. America, if you do not intend to let the Liberty Bell in front of Independence Hall ring out tolls of freedom for every race, color, and creed, quit bluffing. America, if you do not intend to give these boys in black a fair chance as they spill their blood and give their lives that this last fond hope shall not perish from the earth, quit bluffing. America, if you do not believe in the fatherhood of government and the brotherhood of man, quit bluffing. "If you ain't goin' bite, quit barking so much."[20]

Similarly, in a play titled *Beyond the Man*, Borders, portraying Jesus, viewed this medium as an opportunity to ameliorate racial tension. The play had an interracial and interdenominational cast of twenty-five hundred, but many white Atlantans in 1968 were, nevertheless, critical of the production for selecting a black man to play Christ. In addition, he was criticized because of his age and lack of experience.

Borders not only employed his social gospel to promote racial uplift and racial healing, he also used its message to speak out against economic and racial injustice. In one 1943 sermon, *Seven Minutes at the Mike in the Deep South*, he questioned, "Should the Negro Be Loyal to American Democracy?" He first described many of the injustices that blacks had to endure in a country that calls itself a democracy. He then pointed out that, although blacks have been loyal to the flag and helped to build this country through the sweat of their brows, they were denied voting privileges, economic rights and job opportunities, adequate education, and fair trials. "Because there is inherent evil and violations of democracy in these and many other instances, we know that we do not have democracy in America. . . ." He resolved the dilemma of being black in America by continuing the ideology of service and uplift to gain civil rights and justice.

> Speaking not of what ought to be but of what is—we are in war. We are faced with complete pacifism or continued struggle. We have chosen the latter. America is the Negro's home. He is no more an African than an American white man is a European. Justice under God will be his. The red stripes in our Flag were first dipped in the blood of Crispus Attucks, a Negro, on the hills of Boston in the American Revolution. "Old Glory" is the only flag we know. We stood by Theodore Roosevelt at San Juan Hill and supplied 38,000 soldiers from the immediate vicinity of Atlanta in the First World War. We must crush Hitler in Ger-

many and Hitlerism in Georgia. We must oppose forced labor as wrong in Czechoslovakia, and peonage farms in Georgia. We must rid Poland of evil ghettos and America of her slums. We must conquer Japan across the Pacific and Italy across the Atlantic—remembering, however, that democracy, like charity, begins at home and spreads abroad![21]

Matching his creed with his deed in the pursuit of social justice, Borders, in 1939, led one of the first voter registration drives in Atlanta. As a result of his efforts, the more "liberal" mayor hired the first black policemen in the city. In 1950 Borders, a lifelong NAACP member, was also active, through his church, in supporting workers' strikes and organizing laundry workers, who made only fifteen cents an hour. In 1957 Borders led the Triple "L" movement that was responsible for desegregation of buses in Atlanta. On January 8, 1957, he told an audience of twelve hundred Atlantans and one hundred ministers, "Tomorrow morning at ten o'clock, ministers will board buses and take seats heretofore reserved for whites only." The next day, armed with their Bibles, Borders and twenty others boarded a bus in downtown Atlanta, occupying seats in the front of the bus. The bus was declared "out of order," the passengers got off, and the bus was driven to its station. Though the Georgia National Guard was placed on stand-by alert, the following day, Borders and five other ministers again boarded the bus and sat in the "whites only" section. The bus returned to the station. While the ministers held a noon prayer meeting in the Wheat Street Church, a black detective entered with warrants for the arrest of Borders and five other ministers. For violating Jim Crow laws, they were jailed, then freed on a thousand dollar bond and indicted by the state government, which did not appear eager to bring them to trial. Later, a group of black ministers filed suit in the U.S. District Court requesting a federal injunction against segregation on public buses. On January 9, exactly two years after the attempted desegregation, federal judge Frank A. Hopper declared the bus segregation laws of the city and state unconstitutional.

In addition to leading the movement to integrate buses, Borders also participated in a student movement in the 1960s that integrated hotels, restaurants, and lunch counters in metropolitan Atlanta. Through the church, he worked with Thurgood Marshall, contributing money to the educational fund to fight segregated schools. He also participated in fund-raising activities for many civic, political, and social causes. For instance, in 1945 he led the black community in raising funds for Georgia's victims of lynching and offered rewards for the apprehension and conviction of the killers. Active in many organizations, Borders received numerous accolades for his contributions, including *Ebony* magazine's "Top Ten Preachers of Black America" in 1945 and Man of the Year and Atlanta Citizen of the Year in the 1960s.

The political leadership in the pre-1960s black community came primarily from ministers like Borders. The church was his vehicle for spreading his gospel for social change and to wield clout through the political process. Borders, a Republican, ran unsuccessfully for political office. He was, however, commissioned by the Nixon administration to make evangelical trips to Japan. As a strong supporter of Ronald Reagan, he remembered: "Reagan did what he could for me and my experiment with building for the elderly." Although Borders adopted a moderate political position, his association with the Republican Party and his political stance were sometimes controversial. In 1970, at the height of the black nationalist movement, when the governor of Georgia wanted Borders to give the prayer at the dedication ceremony of carvings of General Robert E. Lee, General Stonewall Jackson, and Jefferson Davis at Stone Mountain, Georgia, criticisms came from the black community accusing him of selling out, and declarations came from the white community that he was unwelcome. His prayer, a masterpiece of subtlety, follows:

Our Father—
  We thank thee for the United States, your nation, and our country.
  We thank thee that thou has helped us to make it the greatest on earth.
  We thank thee for our Constitution and your greatest political document.
  We thank thee for scientific technical intelligence, for economic and financial might, for our mastery of earth, sky, and sea.
  We thank thee for Robert E. Lee, Stonewall Jackson, Jefferson Davis, Abraham Lincoln, and Ulysses Grant.
  We thank thee for Herman Talmadge, your great senator; for Agnew, your great Vice-President; for Richard Nixon, your great, great President; for Governor Maddox, Congressmen Blackburn and Fletcher Thompson. Help us all to know that our President occupies the greatest and most powerful position in the world. Help us to know that his responsibilities at home and abroad stagger the most exaggerated imaginations.
  Help us to be critical of his leadership in love and equally critical of our fellowship in fear. Help us to know that mastery of the moon and clearing of slums are not mutually exclusive and that they are parts of the unitary totality.
  Help us to accept the challenge of polluted water, contaminated air, and corrupt morality. Help us to know that we are no higher than the lowest, no better than the worst, no more intelligent than the most ignorant, no richer than the poorest, no more advanced than the most delinquent, no wiser than the foolish, and no more Christian than the most pagan.
  Help us to be the quality nation, whom God can trust to give freedom to the world; the kind of nation, so loved and respected that we can conquer confusion among students by our sincere and sensible approach to their sincere protest, admitting mistakes in ourselves, and thereby asking them to admit their wrongs and cling to their rights; the kind of nation willing to spend money, brains, and

talent to train all children, jobs for all men and women, vote all eligibles, feed all stomachs; the kind of nation which can make those who gave their blood to give us survival value sleep more comfortable in their graves.

Help us to know "That except God build the house, they labor in vain that build."[22]

Participation in a ceremony honoring racist heroes is, without doubt, conflictive. The World War I generation of leaders, however, like Borders and Booker T. Washington, took such an occasion to engage in doublespeak or double-entendre as a tactic for subtle protest in the oppressive racial climate of the era. Borders was not unaware of the reality of racism: "You can find superior people in every race, but white people feel they have more folks in the driver's seat. They want to be in control, and they can't. Young people need to know the truth about race and fight like hell to change it. Some people think racism has disappeared, but that's the biggest [foolishness] in the world."

In his prayer at Stone Mountain, Borders used a more subtle approach to spread his racial gospel of equality, freedom, and justice to bring people together. His method of fighting against racism was by "striving to be better than Jesus." His liberation sermon—"Go Down Moses, Way Down in Egypt, and Tell Old Pharaoh, Let My People Go"—was his rallying cry for freedom.

While Borders reflected on his long life, I asked him about what things he would change and what meant most to him. He simply added, "I would rather have my wife. [Julia Pate Borders, his devoted wife, died in the 1960s.] She was something. She could challenge me and we stayed close." Surrounded by his two grown children, both physicians, his grandchildren, friends, and church members, he continued to teach, preach, and reach people for nearly thirty years after her death. With over fifty-five years as the minister of Wheat Street Baptist Church and in declining health, Borders continued to serve his flock. When unable to do so, his mere presence, "the patting of his feet and nodding of his head" was enough to inspire them. He died in 1994.

PASSING ON THE LEGACY

The lives of the late Louise Thompson Patterson and the late William Holmes Borders spanned three generations. They witnessed major events of the twentieth century, including the transition of three economic sectors: an agrarian economy, an urban-based manufacturing economy, and a service-oriented economy based on technology and communication. They saw firsthand how these changes impacted the color line, affected their lives, and transformed black communities. Patterson and Borders, whose formative years were in the World War I generation, were not only influenced by these major events and economic transitions that impacted the color line, but their social activism was instrumental in altering its contours.

In the generation of World War I, where race relations were more rigid and overt, Patterson and Borders had to fight in a larger economic, political, and social arena than succeeding generations. This is especially true of the civil rights generation, where hard-edged racial battles have been ameliorated and the color line is more flexible and subtle. Patterson's legacy to both the World War II and the civil rights generations is a model of sustaining commitment to obliterating the continuing oppressive skirmishes of racism, sexism, and classism. Borders's legacy is to use social gospel as a tool of racial and social liberation and empowerment. Together they leave a heritage of creative synthesis of disparate ideology and action that can be used in the human struggle for liberation and uplift.

Their lives and legacies embraced diametrically opposite philosophical positions and followed different political paths to fight for equality and social justice. Patterson's angle of collective consciousness was grounded, on the one hand, in the materialistic perspective of Marxism, which emphasizes conflict and collective responsibility and struggle of the have-nots against the haves as a means of securing political and social justice and liberation. On the other hand, Borders's angle of collective consciousness reflected Max Weber's and Hegel's realm of idealistic conditions of life. Thus Borders was guided by the spiritualism of Christianity, which stresses cooperation and individual responsibility, love, moral persuasion, and the belief in human redemption as a means to justice and liberation of the oppressed. While alike in their strong commitment to justice, their respective philosophic leanings took them on separate life courses. Patterson, a Communist, worked outside the system, taking a more radical stance on race relations and social injustices. Borders, a Christian, worked within the system, taking a more passive and moderate approach to the color line. His leadership base, mostly local, was derived from the black community, particularly the black church, while Patterson's leadership base, mostly national, was supported by whites, mostly left-wing Jewish intellectuals. For Patterson, race and class were intertwined, and through collective revolutionary struggle, the elimination of classism would lead to the demise of racism. While recognizing that race and class interfaced, Borders, in contrast, believed that race was a salient and permanent feature of our society. And, through nonviolent collective actions of blacks and "Christian-hearted whites," blacks could gain greater participation in the larger society.

Their respective responses to the color line were no doubt influenced by their personal biographies within the historical context of the time. As products of the Jim Crow era of World War I, Borders, the consensus leader, grew up in a Southern black community, with a strong kinship and friendship network. In contrast, Patterson, the protest leader, was constantly uprooted and lived in white communities, isolated from the network of black kin, friends, and institutions, which clearly affected her psyche. I should add, however, that while Patterson's formative years were not in black institutional settings, save for her immediate family and her momentary domicile in a black neighborhood, her communalistic values were imparted to her in that limited black context and through the ideological influence of black leaders like Du Bois, whom she admired. Notwithstanding the dissimilarity in the way Patterson and Borders responded to the color line, they shared, like their generation, traditional common ground—a service ethos and a strong sense of community, culture, and consciousness as expressed in the theme of racial uplift, reform, and liberation. Across time, however, succeeding generations would be impacted by the cultural and economic shifts and major events that challenge traditional common ground.

2

Educating for Living and Uplifting

James Weldon Johnson, composer of *Lift Every Voice and Sing*, recalled that in his education during the early part of the twentieth century at Atlanta University,

> the central idea embraced a term that is now almost a butt for laughter—"service." We were never allowed to entertain any thought of being educated as "go-getters": most of us knew that we were being educated for life work as underpaid teachers. The idea constantly held up to us was of education as a means of living, not of making a living.[1]

"Get an education and nobody can take it away from you," was the rallying cry for generations of blacks since Emancipation. Education, an avenue of opportunity that had been blocked during slavery, was regarded as a way to empower, uplift, and serve the black community and as a principal path to collective and personal upward mobility. Before the Supreme Court decision of 1954, the sign was pointed one way—separate and unequal. Since the 1960s, it has wavered in both directions. But one continuity from Emancipation to the present remains: The struggle for equality of educational opportunity persists as an uphill battle of progress and retreat. The foremost frontline warriors have been black educators, who fought to make education an instrument for collective liberation and uplift. Such leading luminaries as W. E. B. Du Bois and Booker T. Washington were exemplary fighters on the black educational frontiers, despite their philosophical differences. On the one hand, Du Bois advocated developing a cadre of educated leaders—the "Talented Tenth"—to uplift the masses, arguing that a liberal arts education would best prepare the black populace to empower themselves. On the other hand, Washington espoused the ideology that higher education was impractical for the black masses, so he championed an industrial education. In the changing economy of World War I, Du Bois' philosophy prevailed in most traditionally black private institutions.

Whether blacks received an industrial education at Hampton Institute or Tuskegee Institute or a classical training at Atlanta University or Morehouse College, these institutions produced teachers whose mission was to serve. Given the doleful status of black education in the World War I generation, it is clear why blacks widely regarded education as a serious mission. Black educators, the perennial touchstone of that calling, left their mark on their jewel charges as important mentors and role models. They encouraged the philosophy of education for living; reinforced the ethos of service and racial uplift; advocated a pedagogy of liberation; and stressed communal values of caring, sharing, self-reliance, hard work, and the hope for a better tomorrow. Behind the segregated walls, they taught respectability, race pride, strong spiritual and religious values, family pride and honor, strict discipline, and the need to excel, despite the racial restrictions of that era. In short, "service before self" embodied the dominant motif for achieving common goals. And for over half of the twentieth century, black educators were shaped by this value orientation, which emphasized collectivity over individuality.

Now the winds of education are sweeping in a new direction. Here, we reunite with Frances Hawkins and her generational successors to talk about the changing course in the following vignettes:

Frances Hawkins (born 1926): Black educators of my generation were more committed to their students. The attitude "I have mine and you have yours to get" was not the prevailing norm. If you had a job, whether in teaching or administration, you remained on it until retirement, unlike today's young people who are in constant search for better opportunities. At black colleges we trained students to teach, preach, and serve the community.

Lisa Allen (born 1946): When I entered white academia in 1977, I felt frustrated because I wanted to give more time to my students and my teaching, but if I did not conduct research or produce significant publications, I would not be tenured or promoted. Many academics in my generation who benefited from the resultant opportunities of the civil rights movement feel torn between our professional growth and giving back to the community that nurtured us.

Keith Walton (born 1966): Tenure and promotion are the coveted prizes at my university, and I published to get it. If I expect to become a recognized authority in my field of biology, I must compete for major research grants and continue to publish. Giving service to black students, the university, or the black community does not count toward my success nor does it help me to remain marketable for other career moves.

What binds these educators is the color line and their shared values of academic excellence and a high-achievement orientation, an early emphasis on reading, a strong work ethic a sense of self-efficacy and self-discipline, a supportive kin network and mentors, and for most a strong spiritual grounding. What separates them is their intergenerational response to education as a collective ethos of liberation and uplift versus education as an individual ethos of personal preservation and self-fulfillment. From the prism of African American educators—college presidents, senior level administrators, and faculty—these intergenerational value changes unfold through their lived experiences that interlocked with the historical time period of their birth and with the sociocultural influences of their formative years that helped to meld their sense of community, culture, and consciousness.

In unraveling the three generational perspectives of black educators toward service, this chapter first takes the reader into the educational milieu of traditionally black institutions. Next, it looks at black educators in traditionally white institutions since the 1960s. Finally, questions about the "loss of community" and the transfiguring stances toward service are raised in the context of broader changes occurring in higher education.

EDUCATING IN THE EBONY TOWER: A MISSION OF SERVICE

Yvonne Walker-Taylor: Teaching and Touching

For Yvonne Walker-Taylor, like other black women who came of age in the overtly racist, patriarchal culture of the World War I generation, how did this time period shape her consciousness as an educator? What significant life events helped to fuel her ideals? Walker-Taylor was born in 1916 in New Bedford, Massachusetts. Her father set the foundation for her personal accomplishments and her service-oriented ethos. She grew up in a well-educated and privileged household, where the importance of education was stressed by her father, a West Indian who had migrated to the United States at the turn of the century and who had earned a doctor of divinity degree from Boston University. Her mother, a housewife and a native New Englander, held a bachelor's degree in foreign languages from Wilberforce University. Through education, Walker-Taylor also found her place in the world. Her prominent father, D. Ormonde Walker, was a college president and bishop in the African Methodist Episcopal Church. Yvonne Walker-Taylor replicated her father's educational footsteps in 1984 when she became the first woman president of Wilberforce University, an African Methodist Episcopal church–supported institution in Ohio, from which she had earned a bachelor's degree in English and education in 1936. She earned a master's degree from

Boston University in 1937 and did further advanced study at the University of Kansas in 1964, earning an education specialist degree in education, administration, and instruction.

She began her work at Wilberforce University, one of the oldest black institutions in the nation, in 1955, advancing up the ladder from instructor to chair of the teacher education division; from assistant academic dean to academic dean; and from vice president to provost. Against all odds for women in her generation, she eventually assumed the presidency of an institution steeped in the patriarchal tradition. Despite shifting patterns within the last decade, most chief academic offices at historically black colleges and universities (HBCUs) are held by middle-aged black males. Although they have "similar career paths to the top office, female chief academic officers take longer to achieve the position and, once there, have different salaries and administrative responsibilities than men."[2] Though Walker-Taylor's path to the presidency had many roadblocks, she made successful detours by applying the lessons learned from her father, the sustaining moral and spiritual force and guiding influence in her life.

Walker-Taylor's father, an outspoken social activist who rose to prominence as an educator and minister from an impoverished background in the West Indies, instilled high self-esteem and aspirations in his daughter and inspired her to move beyond "a woman's place." He reinforced positive ideals of womanhood by telling her, "You've got brains, so you can do anything you want to do." He taught his daughter to believe in herself, but cautioned, "Never underestimate or overestimate yourself." She says her positive self-concept, her success, and her enthusiasm for life are undergirded by a strong religious and spiritual foundation, which she attributed to the teachings of her father. He also taught her the gentle art of persuasion and human management, as well as her political savoir faire. This political grounding, likewise gleaned from her close affiliation with the African Methodist Episcopal Church throughout her formative years, was the epoxy glue to her survival in her position as president of Wilberforce University.

Just as Walker-Taylor learned to negotiate the gender line from her father, a crusader for voting rights and black literacy, he also taught her how to walk the color line. Even though she was accepted in her white community in Chelsea, Massachusetts, where she spent most of her formative years, her father realized that sooner or later the color line would rear its ugly head. Walker-Taylor had to be prepared to deal with it. He urged her to "never take a back seat." And this she never did. Her self-assurance served her well in her life's work of service and uplift while battling and resisting racism and sexism.

Lifting as She Climbs

The apple did not fall too far from the tree. Walker-Taylor's commitment to the oppressed paralleled her father's. When he died in 1955, she picked up the banner, continuing the collective struggle for racial progress in the educational arena by teaching and touching young black men and women for over thirty-five years, without adequate monetary compensation. "At Wilberforce, we have worked for peanuts. But I feel a pride and joy at seeing black students develop and make something out of themselves," she exclaimed. She takes pride in the doctors, lawyers, teachers, scientists, engineers, social activists, and politicians who have graduated from Wilberforce. Like other HBCUs, Wilberforce has been a miracle worker for helping diamonds in the rough glow in the sun—taking the economically disadvantaged and academically unprepared and turning their lives into success stories. She remembered the young woman from Bronx, New York. "She came to us with the worst English I ever heard from a high school graduate. She had all A's in science, but she could not talk. She is in our engineering program with a 3.5 GPA. She can now get up at a banquet for the president and make a speech. I saw that girl had potential when she came here, and I love her to death."

Her voice rose as she pounded her fist on her desk, "Oh God, that is the joy of working here. Nobody can take that away. . . . I've seen girls who have come here and they've been told they are nothing all their lives. They didn't believe in themselves and acted like nothing—loud, boisterous, and cursed louder than any of the boys. Under the nurturance of a concerned faculty, they came to fruition as women of character. One girl in particular, a prostitute, was out in the streets at twelve. I bet someday that girl is going to be a judge. She came here dragging. She had been busted so many times, she had given up. We put into her a kind of confidence that she can do anything."

Walker-Taylor's own experience as an undergraduate at a predominantly black institution contributed to her understanding of how important a black undergraduate education is for black students. "They learn how to understand people. They learn confidence in their own abilities, because in a black school you can be president of the student body, serve on the board of trustees and standing committees, experience what it means to work with other people, and become comfortable with expressing yourself and not be inhibited by race, color, or creed." At a black college or university, students can also explore their racial identity and prepare themselves to cope in a racist society.

Deeming education to be a moral enterprise, Walker-Taylor believes preparing blacks to cope and resist in a racist society means setting high standards of excellence and encouraging them to work within the system for social change. Coping and resisting racism also means building a sense of community and encouraging economic self-sufficiency among students. Black educators, she says, become "the nucleus for our future to build on." Accordingly, they need to educate students "to trust one another and join ranks with one another and to combine interests and skills to complement each other. If I were in school now as an accounting major and I had a friend in design and another in merchandise sales, I would like to see those three individuals combine their thought processes and plan down the road to pool their resources to develop a firm."

Whether as teacher or administrator, Walker-Taylor was part of that "nucleus for our future to build on" as she ascended the academic ladder from instructor to the presidency. As the kernel for building and disseminating a knowledge base to uplift the black community, Walker-Taylor encountered much resistance along the way because of her gender. From the beginning, she reminds us, "I got slapped down each step of the way as I went up the ladder." Rather than react, she developed a proactive strategy to serve the university. As academic dean, Walker-Taylor utilized her knowledge and talents for personal and collective empowerment as women of the World War I generation were socialized to serve and nurture others. Although the president did not support her candidacy for that position, she still "fed him ideas," and he used her as a sounding board. "You have to, as a woman, feed ideas sometimes to a boss and not care who gets credit for it, as long as the idea gets over," said Walker-Taylor. When he asked her how to build up enrollment, she suggested a co-op. "The next time I heard this, the president was announcing that he thought of the idea of cooperative education. I didn't say a thing. I worked with him, and it was my job to sell it to the alumni, parents, and students." While being denied personal credit for the idea, Walker-Taylor worked diligently for the collective good in developing strategies to implement the program. "We worked day and night on it. Finally, in 1964, we made it mandatory, and we doubled the enrollment in one and one-half years. Co-op is the lifeblood of Wilberforce University now."

Walker-Taylor does have a tolerance limit for letting others accept credit for her ideas and hard work. She did not allow another president to take credit for the engineering program. If she fought for credit of all the ideas she developed and implemented at Wilberforce University, Walker-Taylor argued, "I would have alienated board members. I would have no longer been on the inside. You have to be on the inside to get anywhere. The way to stay on the inside is to not make waves that are too great. You make waves—you make them all the time—but make little ones. When you are agitating the boss man, be willing to back off." With male bosses, Walker-Taylor believes women sometimes need to wear the mask and "use the subtleties of their nature." She employed these subtle strategies with the bishop who chaired the board of trustees of the university and who subverted her presidency.

She fully understands that being a black woman is never to be good enough in the eyes of a racist and sexist society. "You have to be better than everybody. You have to stay way ahead." After the bishop forced her to step down, she wanted to make it easier for the next woman president, so she ran for the judicial council, the highest judiciary body of the AME church, and was the first woman elected. Not only could Walker-Taylor launch an attack on the gender line, she could contest church policies that negatively impact on AME-supported educational institutions like Wilberforce University. Walker-Taylor believes that women of her generation are more subtle in their approach than today's women, who will "stand toe-to-toe and nose-to-nose with the college president and male boss."

Gender discrimination thwarts the collective efforts of service and uplift that are so vital to strengthening the caring community. It also makes it trying for the transformational leadership style of women like Walker-Taylor to flourish. To battle both the gender and the color line, Walker-Taylor extracts courage and fortitude from black women ancestors—like the "strong slave mammies—who nursed, cooked, and cleaned Massa's house. We came from these loins, and they survived. We should not feel ashamed of them. We can draw from their strength. It is that strength that brought us through, a fervent belief in self." Moreover, her strong spiritual faith, belief in herself, and the lessons learned from her father help her to resist and to cope with the vicissitudes of life. When she is perturbed, she listens to the song, *He Is Only a Throne Away*, and it soothes her.

As educator, Walker-Taylor carries on the legacy of reaching back to uplift and educate not only black students but blacks in all walks of life. Yet she extends dignity and respect to all humanity, regardless of race, creed, color, or economic status. For her efforts, she was the recipient of the Southern Christian Leadership Conference's Drum Major for Justice Award. Clearly, the collective ethos of her service and uplift ideology is consistent with her praxis.

The first woman president of Wilberforce University, having enjoyed each stage of her life, is in a new phase. When she retired from the university in 1988, she was appointed distinguished professor at a neighboring university and an administrator at a seminary in the late 1990s. She is pursuing her long-standing research interests in history and literature, and she is writing her memoirs. The octogenarian feels she has something else to do before leaving this earth; her philosophy is "I'll wait on the Lord. I don't know exactly what is in store for me. I think because God has given me such energy and strong will, He has something in store. So whenever my time comes, sing no sad songs for me, because I will have lived and lived well."

William R. Harvey: The Enterprising Educator

William R. Harvey, president of Hampton University, was born during World War II and reached young adulthood during the civil rights movement. What definable patterns and ideals, besides gender, seemingly separate his generation's presidency from Walker-Taylor's? What attributes and paragons inextricably bind them? What cultural and structural changes might account for any value shifts? How have these changes impacted the collective ethos of educators' actions, attitudes, and values? Are the qualities of the World War II generation in synthesis or opposition to the collective ethos of service, uplift, and liberation?

We can begin to answer these questions by first discerning the shared intergenerational connection of Walker-Taylor and Harvey. They are linked by their leadership roles in private HBCUs; by their socialization to service and institutional affiliation and loyalty; by their deep commitment to excellence in education; by their desire to produce leaders to serve the black community and the world community; and by their aspiration to educate students to compete successfully in the global marketplace. Both Walker-Taylor and Harvey (who assumed the presidency in 1978 at age thirty-seven) see education as a moral enterprise. But Harvey differs from Walker-Taylor: he understands that education is also like a business enterprise. Accordingly, he must "run Hampton like a business for educational objectives." Both educators have retained the traditional HBCU mission of mining precious gems. However, Walker-Taylor, who came to the position of leadership in her late sixties, seemed to follow more closely the historic charge of refining and polishing diamonds in the rough—the less-prepared students in society. Is Harvey more interested in obtaining the cut, polished stones as an objective?

"I am not only interested in the cut, polished stones, I am also interested in the process to make them shine as brightly as they can. I think the process is very important because that helps to shape the outcome," says Harvey. This process involves "obtaining and retaining the best professors you can get." For Harvey, the team approach is also a part of that process. "It is important to provide opportunities for the best and brightest, along with giving some opportunities to those that may not be the best and brightest. Hampton does that inasmuch as we allow 10 percent of our current class to come to Hampton who may not have the prerequisites." These students "may have the scores but not the grades, or the grades but not the scores." "I don't think colleges ought to acquiesce because the student hasn't reached a certain level of development. Colleges and universities should not gear themselves to their clientele, but vice versa," he argues.[3] Hampton University recruits its student body from a more privileged background, while Wilberforce University enlists students from a more working-class background. As an entrepreneur and educator who was trained in the post-World War II consumer-driven and market-oriented economy, he sells Hampton—his product—to the corporate sector for fund-raising, but only as a means to the mission of the university. The college presidents of Walker-Taylor's World War I generation relied more on philanthropic do-gooders.

As Walker-Taylor's ideals were shaped by the cultural milieu of World War I, so Harvey's were shaped by the changing environs of World War II. Born in 1941 and reared in the small segregated town of Brewton, Alabama, Harvey's generation's life course was being catapulted by social forces already in motion in the 1940s. These forces had ushered in a new wave of black activism in the 1930s, which heightened in the 1940s and 1950s and crested in the 1960s. The NAACP, stepping up its attack on segregation in the 1930s, began systematic coordinated legal assaults on discrimination in education and won myriad judicial victories. As the old order of segregated education gave way, the Lanham Act, along with another transforming event, the GI Bill of Rights, democratized higher education for the first time in the history of America. Enrollment at black colleges in 1940 was 1.2 percent of the total U.S. enrollment, but by 1950, that enrollment had tripled.[4] The bill allowed an entire generation to go to college or to obtain some other form of higher education at both black and white institutions. The improved life chances of blacks in the prosperous market-driven and consumptive-oriented post-World War II economy and the expanded contact with the value system of the dominant group would eventually erode the collective ethic of service to and uplift of the black community. This erosion would become the emblematic Achilles' heel of that transitional age cohort at the tail end of the World War II generation.

These greater educational opportunities, heretofore unavailable, opened new doors to Harvey's generation. His contemporaries could now work in black or white institutions. But this educator and entrepreneur, who owns a Pepsi-Cola bottling plant, chose to serve in a leadership role at a historically black institution, after receiving offers at white universities. Because "strong, secure black leadership and direction are needed more in a black educational institution and community," he sensed his background would prepare him to serve and mold future black leaders, and his success would give him the "opportunity for leadership and service" in black education. He believes that black education has a place in "the twenty-first century, not only as a place for transfer of knowledge for a high quality education" but also as a place to train black leaders, instill character, "and learn about history and heritage."

What significant life events prepared Harvey for leadership and service? Moreover, how has he negotiated the conflict of his generation's corroding collective ethic of service and uplift and the emerging individual ethic of self-fulfillment? In the small community of Brewton where he grew up, his parents and extended supportive network of family, friends, neighbors, teachers, and ministers contributed to the development of his leadership qualities and his desire to serve. The community reinforced a strong, positive self-image, emphasized character building, and promoted the ethic of caring and sharing. His mother, a housewife and the first high school graduate in her family, was an exemplar of "decency, dignity, and fair play." She influenced him to incorporate these values into his own philosophy of life. The caring black community of Brewton approved adults sanctioning the behavior of its children and nurturing its youths in social, educational, and religious activities. These structured community activities reinforced the cultural values, norms, and behaviors of group honor taught by his parents, neighbors, and ministers and by the teachers of Southern Normal, a reputable private black boarding school in Brewton, where he attended elementary through high school. This school, established by the Dutch Reformed Church of America, stressed excellence and emphasized discipline. This Brewton school has an impressive history of producing physicians, lawyers, professors, and a former superintendent of the Chicago public school system.

Harvey's parents were also the inspiration for Harvey's keen business acumen and money management skills, his abilities to take risks, and his motivation for service and leadership. Harvey's mother taught him about the art of money management, "If you have a dollar, you can't spend one dollar and twenty-five cents." From his father, a successful businessman who dropped out of high school and a civil rights leader, he learned both the import of economic self-sufficiency and leadership qualities. In the 1940s and 1950s, when the supremacy ideology of Jim Crow reigned in every arena, economic independence was essential for racial progress and harmony. Since his father, the owner of a contracting business and the titular black leader of Brewton, was economically independent of whites, he assisted other blacks "when they got in trouble." His father was threatened many times by whites; however, the way his father stood up to racist practices and challenged the color line influenced Harvey to be fearless. "My father would say to me and my sister, 'If you are right, don't worry about the consequences.'" His father, who knew the prominent civil rights leaders of the 1960s, did not concern himself with the consequences of their home being designated as one of the "safe places" in "the county where civil rights leaders and workers could eat and stay overnight." In the early 1960s, blacks could not stay in motels or eat in restaurants in the South.

After graduating from high school, Harvey entered Talladega College, a historically black institution in Alabama. Coming of age at the height of the civil rights movement in the deep South, Harvey became a student leader in the movement at Talladega College. Like thousands of other black college students, he believed that the civil rights movement offered hope for a better tomorrow and more opportunities. When he graduated from college at age twenty, Harvey enlisted in the armed services and became a history writer for the Department of the Army in Europe. This experience reinforced the importance of discipline. After his duties in the army, he studied for his master's degree at Virginia State University, where he met the most important person in his life, his wife, Norma. He left Virginia State before completing his thesis and enrolled at Harvard University, where he earned a doctorate in education.

The Challenge to Serve and Uplift

Remembering the excellent education he acquired at Southern Normal in Brewton, Harvey wanted to return to the South to invest his talents and energies in a predominantly black setting. "I feel black role models are important and whites have a quantity of role models. I had something to offer—training and experience—that I could best use in a setting for blacks rather than whites." He was in the forefront of a dynamic new breed of black college presidents who emerged in the post-civil rights era and who operated in a larger social arena. For example, they serve on corporate boards. With more professional ties to the larger community, they are often expert fund-raisers, unlike black college presidents of the World War I generation who went "begging with their hats in hands" to philanthropists. The newer breed, like Harvey, is also interested in making black institutions more self-reliant. Harvey has employed his entrepreneurial expertise to construct a shopping mall and a commercial housing complex on campus to generate revenue. In 1978, when he took over the reins of then Hampton Institute from a traditional president, it was a struggling undergraduate college with a $29 million endowment and an operating budget in the red. Now Hampton University has one of the largest endowments of any of the historically black colleges and universities and attracts the most promising students from the best secondary schools.

Harvey instituted curricular changes and enhanced and expanded the physical facilities of the university, graduate programs, and the student enrollment from twenty-seven hundred to nearly six thousand. To maintain a competitive edge, he undertook a strategic planning process to ensure the survival of the black university in the twenty-first century. This plan called for an increased emphasis on science and technology, for faculty research opportunities, and for increasing the endowment. Hampton University now offers doctoral programs in nursing, physics, pharmacy, and physical therapy. Whether in the arts or athletics, Harvey "dares to be great."

Harvey's success at transforming the school from an institute to university status has been applauded nationally. For his myriad accomplishments, the twelfth president of Hampton University has received numerous awards, but his greatest reward is that people from all over the country send their children to study under his tutelage. Yet, there are critics who say black institutions like Hampton, Spelman, and Morehouse are becoming elitist and no longer interested in polishing diamonds in the rough. Dissenting with such critics, Harvey says, "I believe very strongly in giving people an opportunity and at the same time recognizing the best and the brightest that Hampton can attract. But even further, I believe that I am and must be a servant of Hampton University." Despite naysayers, his primary mission is to leave a legacy of black excellence in higher education and to educate students for life and for ethical leadership and service in the black community and in the global marketplace.

In his keynote address for Hampton University's 125th Anniversary Gala Celebration (1993), Harvey spoke of the importance of ethical leadership:

> Our world today cries out for men and women who are willing to exercise the courage of their own convictions, and promote what is *right* and what is *fair*. . . . It is not enough for educational institutions to produce successful physicians, accountants, or systems analysts if they are unwilling or unable to transfer those experiences and sound values to those who walk beside them and to those who will succeed them. (Hampton University Archives)

For Harvey, too many black leaders are not measuring up to the task. They "entertain people, rather than provide leadership." They should "empower the black community by owning businesses and keeping the money in the community." Though Harvey, also a Sunday school teacher, preaches the importance of economic self-sufficiency and development, he thinks the moral crisis is the more urgent problem facing the black community. Like many others of his generation, he bemoans the loss of community and civility since the 1960s. To restore it, Harvey feels we should look back to the moral values and economic self-sufficiency of the pre-1960s black communities like his Brewton.

IMPACT OF THE CHANGING ETHIC

Increasingly, since the 1960s, as upwardly mobile blacks have become more structurally integrated into the mainstream society, they have often adopted the dominant group's more individualistic orientation. This more narcissistic worldview negates a service orientation and stresses self-fulfillment. It is a direction that is particularly detrimental to the survival of HBCUs and their struggle for existence in the new millennium.

Bart Thompson [Pseudonym]: Service Leadership in Conflict

Bart Thompson, a former president of a financially beleaguered public HBCU, was forced to resign under a cloud of controversy. His story illustrates the changing ethic of "self before service." Charged with mismanagement by the board of regents of his state, his resignation was a condition for granting additional funds to the institution. Thompson assumed a position in a black corporation, far away from the ivory tower. But the university he left in ruins is struggling for its existence as faculty, staff, and programs are pared back in financial exigency. His dreams of serving as president of his alma mater for life were turned into nightmares. While some see the near collapse of the institution as the failure of the state to appropriate sufficient funding because of its discriminatory racial practices, others see it as the consequence of mismanagement brought on by an eroding collective ethic of its leader. No doubt the truth lies somewhere in between.

It is true that historically black public institutions have not received funding equal to that of white public institutions. Likewise, many public black colleges have been under fire for mismanagement, and legislators have employed white business managers to control them.[5] Moreover, they have been under siege from desegregation orders since the mid-1970s with plans to be closed, to be subsumed by an adjacent white university, or to be altered in their basic racial composition.

Thompson, who accepted the presidency in the mid-1980s at the age of forty-five, had an opportunity for leadership in white institutions, but chose, like Harvey, to remain at a black one. He believed in the viability of black institutions and was willing to fight for the preservation of his alma mater. To ensure its future survival, he intended to establish the financial solvency of the university and to improve the quality and quantity of its educational programs. Cognizant that the existence of HBCUs has been questioned since the Supreme Court decision of 1954, Thompson was keenly conscious that the forty-nine all-black public institutions, which enrolled about 71.4 percent of black college and university students, were under siege.[6]

Despite Thompson's well-meaning intentions to improve his institution's funding and the quality of instruction for the collective good, did his individual interest prevail in the self-indulgent milieu of the 1980s? What significant life events might have shaped his choices?

Bart Thompson, who was born in the late 1930s and grew up in a single-parent home in an urban Northeast city, was shaped by the tough streets of his neighborhood in the 1940s and 1950s. His impressionable years were spent navigating a precarious tightrope between the lure of crime in the street and aspiring to the life of the crème de la crème in the corporate suite. His mother, a divorced domestic with a twelfth-grade education, was the primary guiding influence. She kept him from misstepping by encouraging him and building up his self-esteem. She always taught him to "take no disrespect from anyone." His minister and his religious training reinforced his mother's influence, which was often in direct competition with his street peers. Perhaps the influence of sports, which added regimentation, determination, and discipline, along with his mother and minister, kept him on a straight course, in spite of impediments. Thompson recalled one such hindrance. A white teacher once told him, "You will never amount to anything." Though this teacher's admonition was devastating to him, it served as the motivating catalyst "to prove her wrong." To challenge the messenger of failure, he was determined to excel academically.

After graduating from high school, Thompson attended an all-black college, which was a significant turning point in his development. There he was influenced by the spirit of the civil rights movement and the belief in greater possibilities for himself and other blacks. Under the influence of his college president and several of his professors, particularly a male sociologist and a female historian, these possibilities were realized. They served as positive role models for Thompson and fostered an appreciation and understanding of black history, instilled in him the importance of academic excellence, encouraged a belief in self, and inculcated a sense of dignity and racial pride. As Thompson stated, "They made me want to maintain my allegiance with the black community." Under his teachers, he excelled academically and honed his street-smart leadership style and skills, knowing his ultimate goal was to someday become president of his alma mater.

After graduating from college, he continued his education at major white universities in the Midwest and East, earning his master's degree and doctorate in education. Thompson, who had mostly white teachers throughout his formative years, knew he wanted to become an advocator, an educator, and a motivator of black youths to counter the attitudes of teachers who felt they would "never amount to anything."

Creativity and Crisis in Serving

Though Thompson's ambition was to become president of his alma mater, he never cloaked his "cool pose" persona, the way "Black males use coolness as a coping mechanism."[7] His rhythmic style of speaking and walking remained an integral part of his being. Always tastefully and immaculately dressed, from school principal to college president, he presented himself to his inner-city black students as a role model. During the emergence of the black power movement, he gained much notoriety in his community as a social advocate for his work with high school students, instilling race pride and advocating for student rights. He was fired from his position and jailed for this offense and other civil rights activities.

After his controversial tenure in the public school system, he became director of a newly developed black cultural center on the campus of a predominantly white university. Later he was hired as vice president for academic affairs at his alma mater, and finally he became head of the university. Extremely dedicated to black youth, he stretched himself to the limits to aid them in getting an education. He was an exemplary motivational leader. In his weekly sermonettes, he exhorted students to study, to go to the library, and to do their best, knowing black students had to be twice as good as white students to achieve the same goals. Thompson brought to the campus prominent black role models to appear before the student body in weekly university convocations. He was also interested in improving the status of faculty. His efforts to bring the salaries of his faculty in line with those of other state institutions probably helped contribute to the dire financial problems of the university. However, he was firm in his resolve to enhance the financial status of the faculty and staff at any cost. In addition, Thompson cultivated extensive ties with African universities and governments.

Considering Bart Thompson's creative energies to serve and uplift, some will, no doubt, wonder if he sacrificed himself and his career for the salvation of the school that he so dearly loved and the inner-city black youths who comprised his student body at the four-year public university. Others might wonder if the savvy "opportunist" sacrificed the university for his personal interest. When he began his presidency, the headline in the local newspaper editorialized "Now It's Make-or-Break." He launched his presidential tenure on a stormy note when several members of the faculty sued him. Thompson had summarily dismissed them for writing a letter in an effort to prevent his being hired as president. The suit was settled in the midst of the trial, and damages were awarded the aggrieved faculty. Bart Thompson found himself wrapped in a similar controversy when he sought "creative measures" to remedy the underfunding of his university by the state. He was accused by the board of regents of padding the university's enrollment figures by listing members of the faculty and staff, some of whom were deceased, as being enrolled in classes. Several of his close associates were dismissed or retired as a result of this incident. Thompson defended his actions by accusing the state of underfunding and discriminating against the university.

With controversy swirling around him, eventually Thompson was forced to resign for financial mismanagement, leaving the school in ruins. Since his departure, many survivors of the World War I generation, who were socialized in the culture of service and who were affiliated with the university, came forth to volunteer their time and talents to save "their school." Among those was a seventy-eight-year-old woman, former chair of physical education, who returned, without pay, to head the department and to teach four courses, one of which was weight lifting. In contrast to the older generation, diverse younger faculty and administrators sought greener pastures in other venues.

Did this man in the forefront of advocating for students' rights forget the struggles? He would vehemently disagree, noting that for him success means developing not only his "maximum potential" but "giving something back to others and paving the way for future generations." He reminds us that, as president, he recruited mostly inner-city students whom teachers felt "would never amount to anything" and brought them to the university to get an education, and he increased the enrollment of his campus. Yet, for the academically unprepared students, the university became a revolving door, with most of each annual cohort leaving after one or two quarters. Critics accused Thompson of not following up on their attrition and not seeking the more academically prepared and motivated students. Whatever one thinks, his life energy, ebbing like the tides of the sea, has flowed between collective creativity, respectability, and responsibility and individual scandals, snafus, and slip-ups, always leaving controversy in its wake.

As the collective ethos of service waned in the 1960s, perhaps Thompson was inextricably caught up in the web of change. The traditional culture of service before self that characterized the black community in the pre-1960s, and which began to shift somewhat in the World War II generation, was often in conflict with the more narcissistic and individualistic culture of the civil rights generation. Bart Thompson's prevailing ethos reflects a clash of cultures—that of his youth, espousing service, and that of his young adult to middle years, emphasizing self.

In sum, while Taylor is more reflective of the culture of the World War I generation, Harvey is more typical of the World War II culture. Bart Thompson is also a cohort of this era, but his actions and ideals are juxtaposed with the individualistic culture of the civil rights generation. As black college leaders move forward in the twenty-first century, their model of leadership is becoming more complex and more accountable to conflicting constituents. Ernie Suggs, writing in *Black Issues in Higher Education*, claims, "Today's black college leaders are being asked to navigate their faculty, students, funding sources, alumni, and governments through an ever-changing sea of academic turmoil."[8] What impact then will these conflicting demands have upon the traditional ethic of service?

BLACK FACULTY: THE GENERATION GAP

Under the intrepid leadership of chief academic officers like William R. Harvey, a few HBCUs have achieved fiscal success and national visibility. Too many others, however, are struggling with a litany of traditional predicaments: underenrollment, overconcentration of underprepared students, serious fiscal problems, low endowments, poor management, a shortage of library resources, inadequate curricula, and a high faculty turnover. In addition, they now confront new challenges resulting from desegregation and diversity. One issue of desegregation is the brain drain of black scholars from black institutions since the 1960s, a pattern compounded by the shrinking supply of black Ph.D.s. Prior to the 1960s, most blacks taught at HBCUs; now, about 47.7 percent of black professors are employed at HBCUs.[9] They comprise slightly less than 60 percent of the faculty of the forty-one HBCUs in the United Negro College Fund, while nearly 40 percent of faculty are made up of nonblacks, most of whom are white.[10] Some individuals, like Kufra Akpan, professor of history, see this issue as a grave concern. They argue that only black institutions can truly instill self-confidence and pride in black youth and educate them for service, uplift, and liberation. He typifies black faculty who have remained at black colleges and universities, despite excessive teaching loads and committee work, lack of research time, and lack of study leave. Despite such disadvantages, intangible rewards at black institutions, such as the commitment to train future black leaders and the comfort factor of being in a black setting, can compete with the tangible benefits of white institutions.

Kufra Akpan chose to remain in a black institution because he felt a strong responsibility to blacks and because he understood the power and pedagogy of others educating black youth. He wanted to educate his own in a holistic way. What social factors fueled Akpan's collective consciousness?

Kufra Akpan [Pseudonym]: Teaching Blacks and Giving Back

Kufra Akpan was born in Pittsburgh, Pennsylvania, in 1930. No doubt this history professor's worldview was shaped by the harsh memories of the Depression during his youth and the misery, hunger, and death that hovered over coal-mining communities of West Virginia, Ohio, and Pennsylvania. His father, a drifter with a tenth-grade education, worked as a coal miner, steel mill worker, construction worker, custodian, and a bootlegger in the coal-mining mountain towns of West Virginia, Ohio, and Pennsylvania. Akpan's father was not influential in his life—Akpan did not live with him until he was ten years old. However, the small-town, close-knit communities of Ohio and West Virginia, which emphasized sharing and caring, deeply influenced him and shaped the foundation for a collective racial consciousness that is summed up in the biblical aphorism, "Bear ye one another's burden."

After Akpan's mother died when he was two, the community of relatives and friends bore the burden of caring for him. His prescient mother had asked one of her friends, whom Akpan referred to as "Aunt," to take care of him if something happened to her. This friend and her husband reared Akpan until he was ten. His fictional aunt, with a third-grade education, encouraged him to read early and taught him the value of hard work and perseverance, and the importance of an education. She also taught Akpan to always stand up for himself. The memory of not being able to defend himself at age nine against the racism that overlaid the mining towns of West Virginia like coal dust still haunts him. While waiting in line at a store, Akpan remembers one white man saying, "Push that little boy out the way. He ain't nothing but a nigger." This incident and others helped to shape his conviction about the color line and his warrior posture in confronting the color line wherever a racial arrow strikes.

Akpan also recalls the influence of another neighbor, James Patterson, an activist in a labor union, who frequently watched him "hustle pop bottles" and who would say to the young boy, "You are going to amount to something one day." When Patterson purchased books for his daughter, he encouraged Akpan to read them, and he inspired him to study the dictionary. Akpan was able to translate his aunt's and James Patterson's messages into stepping-stones for success.

Though he was shunted among different households of fictive kin and extended relatives, Akpan thinks of the joy of those days in his close-knit community, where he absorbed the collective ethos of honor, sharing, and caring. "Although people fought and sometimes killed each other, people shared fundamentally good relationships with one another. The elderly people were respected, and all were of equal importance to the community. Their sense of dignity and honor was never violated. A respect for humanity existed." He relates one example of this dignity. "If you were a teacher's child or coal miner's child in that one room school, you got equal treatment. The teachers assumed their pupils could learn, never mind how poor. There were no special educational classes. People moved along together through the educational process and got through high school with lots of pride."

Living with varied relatives and fictive kin who were impoverished and uneducated, Akpan often wondered what motivated him to go to college, since there was no family tradition of education. He attributed his escape to a "combination of luck, circumstances, and being in the right place at the right time." Moreover, he is clear that the decisive influence of James Patterson and his aunt, the influence of sports, which served as an outlet for his aggression, and the influence of his black teachers, who did not want their students to work in coal mines and get black lung disease, were instrumental.

After finishing high school in Pittsburgh, Akpan enlisted in the air force during the Korean conflict. He admitted that during this stage of his career, he was not so noble or politically conscious about the need for collectivity as a way to advance the group. One incident came to mind. When he enlisted in the air force, he admonished himself for selling out black troops. "I chose to serve with white troops rather than go out into the jungle with the black unit, I was selfish and accepted integration, so I could live in these nice stucco buildings with nice showers and wood floors as opposed to going out with the ammunition carriers. I was a Negro emerging into the white world." After spending several years in the air force, he studied full-time under the GI Bill at Ohio State University, completing his Ph.D. in history.

Paying the Price to Serve

Remembering his childhood as a coal miner's son, Akpan felt his responsibility was to return his talents to a black institution, in spite of the black brain drain to the white higher education academy that began in the 1960s. It was a place where he felt he could practice his training in history and his commitment to empowering black youths. "I think black people ought to assume the same posture as Jews who educate their own children. We should assume unqualified responsibility for their education and development, balancing psychological, academic, and physical development of our people." To assume responsibility, he waged battles inside and outside the university walls to educate academically underprepared, low-income black youths and to fight against misconceptions of their inferiority. During the 1960s, black youths were labeled as disadvantaged by whites, and an underlying assumption was that they could not learn. His own experience in segregated settings taught him differently, so he has spent much energy over the past thirty-five years negating the "blacks can't learn" syndrome. Instead, he has "promoted their usefulness, their sanity, their stability, their ability to cope and to enhance their self-esteem."

In addition to promoting his liberation pedagogy for black youths, Akpan has continued his scholarly activities and research to correct and expand perceptions of blacks' roles in history. Moreover, he has retained leadership roles in professional organizations to promote blacks' interests and to make the connection between the interlocking categories of class and race. As community leader, he rails against discriminatory social and economic practices in his locale. He is frequently labeled as a "black troublemaker," whether it is organizing black parents in his community to fight injustices in the school system or challenging an insulting racial remark. He often feels isolated and alone: "Even on a black campus, I am in the minority in terms of ideology, blackness, and Africanism." But he always reminds himself, "No matter what you do, you are going to get kicked in the teeth anyway, but go ahead and do it. The price you pay as a leader is not really ever being appreciated. But you don't need to be appreciated or need to be loved. Do what you got to do and hope it is good, right, proper, and just, even though individuals may be unjust, unforgiving, and ungrateful. Love them anyway."

Akpan wants to leave the legacy that through caring any students can be inspired and be receptive to learning no matter their class or color. He advises young people to "work hard at discovering what they like to do, but don't be motivated by income alone." He reminds us to "bear ye one another's burden. Those who succeed have a special obligation to empower those less powerful." He knows our predecessors have "created the opportunity for us to be successful, and we have an obligation to share our skills, knowledge, and wealth with more oppressed blacks." And he speculates about "a day of reckoning for successful black men and women who want to set themselves apart." For those who have benefited from the 1960s, he says, "we are just accidents. I am supposed to be in the coal mines somewhere looking at pictures of my black lungs. Many people brighter than I didn't get a chance and didn't have the 'accident' along the way; therefore, I have a responsibility."

Sandra Jackson [Pseudonym]:
A New Generation's Call to Bear the Burden

Prior to the 1960s, it was the zeitgeist of dedicated and committed black teachers, like Akpan, to exhort their students to a life of service. Teaching and serving were synonymous. Although a sprinkling of researchers were part of the black higher education academy, most teachers were disseminators of knowledge rather than producers of knowledge. This teaching tradition still prevails. However, in the post-1960s, as a result of the greater availability of federal and private funding sources, research and grant writing activities are assuming a new priority for tenure, promotion, and retention even in the black academy. For younger faculty members, such as Sandra Jackson, who are socialized in the publish-or-perish mode at predominantly white research universities, the black tradition of teaching, service, uplift, and liberation poses new challenges. Unlike Kufra Akpan, Sandra Jackson, assistant professor of psychology, did not feel blacks had a responsibility to educate other blacks prior to her appointment in a private HBCU. In fact, in the preencounter stage of her black identity development,[11] she held negative stereotypes about black universities, and part of her felt somewhat grateful that she was not educated in one. This notion was reinforced when she taught at a public HBCU, as an adjunct professor, while working on her dissertation. She was surprised and dismayed that her students could not adequately read or write a complete essay. "In my elitist attitude, I angrily asked: 'What type of people would let someone graduate with such poor skills?'" She felt alienated from her students, whom she viewed as hopeless and helpless and whose rough edges she felt no calling to polish. The encounter with black students in her present position in an elite HBCU has helped to change her attitude toward them and black institutions.

What generational alterations separate Sandra Jackson's preencounter individualistic ideology from Kufra Akpan's collectivistic ideology toward educating blacks? When Jackson was born in 1965, the civil rights movement was winding down, and a new social order was beginning. Her impressionable years were never seared with the collective memory of sitting at the back of the bus, of drinking from a separate water fountain, of using a colored-only bathroom, of viewing movies from the balcony of a theater, of eating in segregated dining facilities, of playing in segregated parks, of attending segregated schools, or of prohibiting interracial marriages. While she hears her mother and grandmother speak of the old order of segregation, it seems almost as distant as slavery.

Jackson grew up in a middle-class, devout Catholic family in a large city in the South. Her mother, a secretary with two years of college at an HBCU, and her father, a computer programmer with a BS degree from an HBCU, stressed the importance of the work ethic, honesty, independence, personal responsibility, and compassion. They wanted their two children to have the best education possible and the best quality of life this new order would bring. She was educated in private schools from the primary grades through graduate school. Until the eighth grade, she was in a black Catholic school in her black neighborhood before transferring to a white Catholic high school in the ninth grade. She remembers insensitive remarks from white teachers and white students, slights from teachers who did not recognize blacks' achievements, and negative stereotyping of blacks in school. Yet, she never encountered the virulent racism of the pre-civil rights era. These more covert encounters with racism fashioned her extremely competitive attitude toward white peers. She strove to be the best in her academic studies, and to that end she spent long hours studying. Her life was remarkably unfettered, save for the traumatic death of a sibling during graduate school.

After graduating from high school, she attended white universities for her B.A., M.A., and Ph.D. During her undergraduate and graduate studies, she limited her contacts with the few blacks on campus, preferring not to participate politically or socially in black groups. She viewed blacks' camaraderie on campus as unnecessary and activities like black Greek step shows (choreographed group dances) as frivolous and embarrassing. She felt blacks should have been in the library engaged in serious study. She was familiar with the stereotypes of blacks and wanted to distance herself from the negativity. Jackson was unversed in the rich heritage and history of blacks, and she had no overpowering desire to understand it. Her graduate mentors, white males except for one black female, were grounded in the quantitative Western scientific tradition, which has an ahistorical approach. With encouragement and support, they wanted Jackson to conduct research employing this paradigm and to teach at a major research university.

Jackson questioned her career path as professor and researcher only when she taught as an adjunct instructor at three universities, two white and one black, while completing her dissertation. On the one hand, she found herself at the white universities alienated from her white students, who were disruptive and who questioned her authority. She also speculated about collegiality and isolation in a white milieu. On the other hand, at the black college, she could not identify with her academically underprepared black students for whom the chair had asked her to "dumb down the class." Indeed, she was at a crossroad and felt less of a desire to teach. After several offers at major white research universities, she interviewed at a prestigious black institution. Although her major professor warned her against the appointment, she accepted it. When she presented her research during the interview, she said, "I was shocked how smart the students were and it changed my perception. I thought I could really have an effect on students and help them. It began to change my way of thinking. I said to myself, 'This is where you should be, making a difference.'"

She has been at the university for a few years "making a difference" and balancing her heavy teaching load with research and service. As she moves to the immersion-emersion stage of her black identity, where she negates her old negative perspective of blacks and fashions a new frame of reference,[12] she sees the HBCUs as having a critical role in the lives of blacks and as instilling self-confidence. She wants to help students fulfill their dreams and be their best. Where once her idea of service and personal compassion was confined to the Catholic Church, it has expanded to the black community. She has also embraced the notion that a group can progress only through collective efforts. In addition to her research on urban youth, she has become involved in community activities to assist poor black youths. Jackson describes her experience at the university as a "sense of coming home. I am comfortable with myself and proud of my heritage." While her legacy is somewhere blowing in the distant future winds, the ancestral spirits of the past cry out to the present and call her to dance with their rising winds.

EDUCATING IN THE IVORY TOWER

Prior to 1900 only three blacks had taught in white institutions. By 1985, over 50 percent of the black professoriate was employed in white institutions.[13] The time period of the late 1960s and early 1970s was a significant turning point in the educational venue of the black community. Racial restrictions were lifted. With the commencement of the 1964 Civil Rights Act and affirmative action policies, blacks crossed new thresholds in higher education. Colleges in the North, caught up in the spirit of the civil rights movement and in the protest movements of black students, began to woo black administrators and faculty away from black institutions.

Frank Hale, retired college administrator from The Ohio State University, exemplified the brain drain from black colleges and this demographic shift to white institutions. Thus, today not only are the majority of black professors in white institutions, but the bulk of black students are being educated there as well. For Cornel West, there is a cost. "The quantity and quality of black intellectual exchange is at its worst since the Civil War. . . . This tragedy is, in part, the price for integration—which has yielded mere marginal black groups within the professional disciplines of a fragmented academic community. But this tragedy also has to do with the refusal of black intellectuals to establish and sustain their own institutional mechanisms of criticism and self-criticism, organized in such a way that people of whatever color would be able to contribute to them."[14]

How then does the lack of "quantity and quality of black intellectual exchange" among black scholars affect their attitudes, values, and behaviors toward social change and collective racial liberation in the black community? Moreover, since the mission of traditional white universities has not been service, uplift, and liberation for racially nondominant groups or the economically poor, how has the scholar-activist tradition of black intellectuals been negotiated, resisted, muted, or even embraced in this milieu? The scholar-activist has been a long-standing tradition in the black community, particularly in the discipline of sociology. W. E. B. Du Bois, E. Franklin Frazier, and Charles Johnson are exemplary of this heritage. Is this legacy fading among contemporary black sociologists? Although Cedric Herring, a past president of the Association of Black Sociologists, believes black sociologists should be in the trenches as change agents in the black community, he notes, "Our association is made up of people who think and write for a living; we're not good at organizing. It's not realistic for us to consider mobilizing whole black communities. We are people who meet in hotels."[15] Frank W. Hale, Jr., an academic of the World War I generation, would disagree with his successors of the civil rights generation. He embraces his generation's heritage of education for social change and service.

Frank W. Hale, Jr.: Educating for Collective Empowerment

Hale, a distinguished scholar and political activist, was born in the 1920s in Kansas City, Missouri. He chose to enter white academia in the 1970s, after serving for two decades at several HBCUs as a teacher and as an administrator. He had greater opportunities for professional development, that is, to conduct research as a producer of knowledge in a major university rather than merely as a disseminator of knowledge in a small black college. But more important, Hale was grounded in a service orientation, reinforced by his strong familial, religious, and communal ties that were fostered during the era of segregation. He felt that he could make a difference for the increasing numbers of blacks who pioneered at white universities across the United States and who were increasingly isolated on campuses. Hale wanted to use his energies to achieve collective empowerment of blacks rather than solely for personal gain.

Having grown up in a segregated black community in Topeka, Kansas, Hale never wanted to escape his identification with that source of his strength and success, which he attributes to his strong religious background, his communal and familial ties, his strong academic preparation in elementary and high school, and his own sense of assertiveness. His father, a respected furniture and bookstore owner with an eleventh-grade education, and his mother in particular, a housewife with a high school education, played an important role in their only child's life. They always listened to him and very early instilled in him the value of an education and the importance of reading.

Hale's parents were quite race conscious. They held before him examples of "people who were good role models," and they showed him how to cope with race through modeling. They took him to see Marian Anderson, Roland Hayes, and Paul Robeson, and persuaded him to introduce himself to them. After he spent an unsuccessful year at a white school in Ohio, he returned to Kansas, where his fourth-grade teacher played a critical role in his academic success. This black teacher was so inspirational that, at the end of his school year, Hale skipped three grades. After the intervention of this teacher, Hale continued to excel academically.

At the age of sixteen, Hale graduated from a predominantly white high school with honors. One racial incident there tainted his achievements and indelibly imprinted the impact of racial injustice in his memory. With an A– average and in the top 10 percent of his class, he expected to obtain several offers of scholarships from top white schools. The expectation went unfulfilled. When the sixty names of students with a B– average and above were called, he had only one offer, and it was not even from his hometown. He was not deterred. Instead, he became "more sensitive and focused and wanted to address those kinds of concerns for black students." As a student leader and activist in high school, he fought against separate racial proms and separate athletic activities.

After attending Oakwood, a black college in Alabama, in the mid-1940s, Hale transferred to Union College, a small white school in Nebraska, where his racial consciousness was further heightened. This private white college maintained segregated seating in the 1940s, so he continued his activism with a student group to "break down the barriers." He left the college to complete his undergraduate studies at the University of Nebraska. There he obtained a master's in communications and political science. Then he went on to The Ohio State University for his Ph.D., also in communications.

An Agent of Change

Frank Hale, retired vice provost for minority affairs and professor of communications at The Ohio State University (OSU), was in higher education for thirty-five years in both predominantly black and white institutions as teacher, scholar, and administrator. He served as president of Oakwood College, as chair at two black institutions, and as associate dean of OSU. Though Hale indicated that he preferred to remain in a black educational milieu, the limited resources constrained his professional creativity and network. His venue changed but not his culture of service orientation.

"I spent twenty years in black education, and the only reason I came to [a white] campus is that I realized a large number of blacks were isolated in a sea of whiteness on campus. They have fewer points to touch base when they need academic help. I have felt gratified to work in this particular arena for the benefit of black students."

As a change agent and advocate for cultural diversity, he worked tirelessly within his institution to bring more black students, faculty, and staff to campus. He initiated one of the most successful recruitment programs for minorities in the country, and the university became one of the leading producers of black Ph.D.s. Hale advocated a mentoring system, which stressed the importance of black faculty reaching out to assist others. Often he chastised those blacks at white campuses who "made no effort to reach down and assist others in how to negotiate that system." Hale especially had ire for black faculty who said, "Don't send me anything minority." "There are plenty of them," he lamented. He reminded such colleagues, "You are here because students laid down their lives. We have a lot of proficient blacks, but proficiency didn't get you in here. It was bricks and Molotov cocktails. Now you are going to tell me you are coming in here and sit down and don't give a damn and insult me and black students by saying, 'Don't you send me anything minority.' And they made it possible for you to get in here. You may think I am crazy, but I think you are crazy, too."

Hale wore many different hats. From his campus, he was expected to serve on all kinds of university-wide committees. And at the same time, he was expected to serve his black constituents within and outside the university community. He handled those often contradictory expectations by organizing community leaders to do "what is necessary." Otherwise, "You cut off your nose to spite your face, and you won't be here to do what little you can do." In speaking out for what he believes, he earned the respect of both black and white colleagues and students. The OSU Black Cultural Center is named in honor of Hale.

Hale retired from his position with a tribute from educators and community leaders throughout the country. Married, with three grown children, he is active as an educational consultant in higher education and within the university, the black communities, and the larger society, serving on twenty-one different boards. In 1999 Hale was appointed to a new part-time position as distinguished university representative and consultant for student recruitment, fund-raising, and alumni relations at OSU. A liberal Democrat, Hale remains a fighter as he continues to reach back to the black community. However, he said, "I am not a full-time fighter. Nobody is a full-time fighter. I pick and choose my issues." The legacy he leaves is his commitment to educate and nurture black youth whenever he can. He advises young people against the philosophy, "Get all you can; can all you get; and sit on the can." Instead, he imparts the message, "We are in this world to help somebody else." This ethos of service has guided his collective consciousness.

It has also guided James B. Stewart. Although Stewart and Hale are separated in age by a generation, their philosophies converge in a shared collective ethic of service and uplift. Having held similar positions as supportive players at major white universities, their titles—vice provost for minority affairs (Hale) and vice provost for educational equity (Stewart)—also reflect the shift from the focus on blacks in the late 1960s to multiculturalism in the 1990s. Stewart, former director of the black studies program and professor of labor studies and industrial relations at Pennsylvania State University, exemplifies this transition. While the late 1960s and the decade of the 1970s saw black students and faculty protesting over black studies, the late 1980s and

1990s witnessed raging debates over multiculturalism in the liberal arts curriculum as more white women and more men and women of color entered higher education in the 1980s. Born on the tail end of the World War II generation, James B. Stewart was among the first generation of educators with the option of beginning their professional careers in an integrated milieu. As new entrants into the white higher education academy, they found the old guard was changing its standards for retention in the academy. Publishing in mainstream journals and standard publishing outlets became a priority for tenure and promotion. Not only were they required to publish more, they had to be effective teachers, to serve as token blacks on committees, and to act as mentors to black students. But they were still less likely than whites to be tenured or promoted. In essence, as Lisa Allen articulated in the earlier vignette, Stewart's generational cohort was more conflicted about balancing their research, publishing, and teaching with service to the community. Stewart found his safety net and a way to walk the academic tightrope.

James B. Stewart: Servant of the People

As vice provost of educational equity at Pennsylvania State University, James B. Stewart views himself as the servant of the people. "I have been given talents by whatever creator that be, and it is my responsibility to use those talents for the betterment of all people. I focus on my ability to analyze, interpret, guide, and strategize for the liberation of humankind. I try not to be distracted by concerns for material prosperity, individual stakes, and achievement. Although I have achieved a number of honors, those things have never been important to me. I'd rather see the fruits of my labor emerge in better living situations for oppressed people."

What forces fueled the energies of James B. Stewart, a man born in 1947, the post-World War II era? Perhaps his strong consciousness springs from his family origins in a working-class black community in Cleveland, Ohio, where he was born and grew up as an only child. His father and mother were newlywed sharecroppers from Mississippi when they came to Cleveland seeking a better life during the Great Migration in the 1940s. Stewart's father, who had a ninth-grade education, found work as a laborer in the brickyard, making bricks and kilns; he worked there most of his life. Stewart's mother, who had a seventh-grade education, was a housewife. She eventually did domestic work to pay for his college education. Stewart's parents instilled in him that education, hard work, and discipline were the keys to success.

Although he lived in a prosperous working-class neighborhood, where people took pride in their homes and in their aspirations for their children, Stewart still found a dearth of role models to emulate or to guide his hopes and expectations. Most of the men had low-paying work in factories as blue-collar laborers. His first role model was a minister, one of the most respected persons in the black community, so for a while, Stewart wanted to become a minister. The next most respected person was a doctor, so for a time he wanted to be a doctor, until he realized how much educational training he would need. The teachers in his community, where a close collaboration existed between parents and teachers, also played important mentoring roles.

Despite Stewart's limited supply of role models, his community recognized his special talents and had faith in his academic achievements. After Stewart left elementary school, his teachers had less impact, and peer influence became more important. He said his older male contemporaries acted as his big brothers and protectors. They would say, "You're going to college and we are not going anywhere," and would take it upon themselves to protect him. Of course, growing up in the 1950s, the brickmaker's son never expected or dreamed that he would earn a Ph.D. in economics.

Stewart attended a small, primarily white technical school in the Midwest, where he received a B.S. degree in mathematics and engineering in 1969. His college experience was a significant event in his life. There he had several racial incidents, which became the catalyst for awakening his black consciousness and his involvement in the black power movement. This collegiate seasoning also laid the foundation for his present professional activities in the area of black studies. After college, he married and began his career as the only professional black in a private corporation.

Then, with the economic support of his wife (and while rearing three children), he completed an M.A. and a Ph.D. in economics at the University of Notre Dame. While studying for his doctorate, he came under the influence of a Jamaican professor of economics and minister. From him, Stewart learned how to merge such diverse viewpoints as the politics of black nationalism and the skepticism of science that were influential in activating his consciousness. Moreover, this scholar taught him to "see patterns where other people see points, and to draw connections from different areas and show how they connect." He also augmented Stewart's evolving spiritual connection and taught him "how to link data, using what he had learned from Western science in a much more expansive way than whites knew how to use it."

Though a distinguished scholar, Stewart yearned to employ his prestige and his knowledge to empower others and to bring "something back that would benefit and serve blacks." In his position as vice provost of educational equity and in his previous position as the director of a black studies program, he has brought back something for blacks, despite the publish or perish mandate at his research university. Blessed with intuition, strong networks of colleagues, family, and friends, and the desire to be the best ambassador for the race, Stewart armed himself to cope in the role as "servant of the people." In fact, his long-standing commitment to serve influenced his decision to enter higher education. While working in an electrical utility company as an engineer, welfare rights organizations started lobbying for lower electric rates for the poor. Even though he believed in this concept, in his position he felt "forced to support company policy," since he had a family to maintain. This internal conflict between his political ideology and action created cognitive dissonance and served as the impetus for a career change.

As director of black studies and professor of economics and labor studies, Stewart became a recognized authority. In promoting the Afrocentric perspective, he made major contributions to the development of the field. Then, as now, he actively recruited black faculty and students, served on committees within the university and within professional organizations, worked with grassroots and national sociopolitical organizations in whatever way he could, and acted as a facilitator in encouraging others to give their best back to the black community.

Oftentimes, when he volunteers for committees on campus, he confronts issues directly. Other times he knows he will not have an immediate effect, but he wants to learn how these committees operate so that he can have a future impact, or use that information as a later reference point. He mentors young blacks, encouraging them to have an Afrocentric orientation, to have a positive attitude toward self, and to obtain knowledge for social change in society.

In his position as vice provost for educational equity, his campus role expanded from race-based politics to include the politics of ethnicity, gender, class, ableism, and sexual orientation. That transition was not a difficult one, because, in addition to his responsibilities in black studies, he chaired a committee that provided funding to programs designed to help transform his institution into a multicultural university. Stewart's multicultural penchant and his negotiatory skills have helped him to mediate the various confrontations and competing interests of African Americans, Asian Americans, Latinos, Native Americans, women, the lesbian, gay, and bisexual communities, and the differently abled. Possessed with the mental acumen to connect knowledge and to promote the importance of diverse views, he encourages group pride. Moreover, he uses the different ways of thinking and knowing of other cultures as an advantage—of "having one leg up"—in effectively dealing with whites. In working with various constituents on campus, Stewart does not feel that he has compromised his commitment to blacks. Even though Stewart still holds the same basic Afrocentric philosophy, his strategy has changed. He said, "I have become effective as an advocate for other groups that I am responsible for."

Some people question whether he can be an effective advocate for such diverse constituencies since he is an African American male with a background in black studies. Moreover, an underlying suspicion is that he will favor the African American agenda over others. To that concern he responded, "I have to be very careful and demonstrate that that is not the case. In fact, I think I have been able to advance women's issues, lesbian and bisexual issues, in particular, and also, I would say, Latino issues. Because I am not gay, when I speak professionally for gays, it has a different impact on the gay community."

This balancing act causes some blacks to raise concerns about the neglect of their agenda. He rebutted, saying, "I have had to put the African American agenda in context, because if you look at some of the contemporary popular approaches to Afrocentrism, many people see this as a sort of 'Aunt Jemima' in the same way as in the 1960s when the African American owned that agenda for all others." Some critics might ask whether black women ever owned the agenda in the 1960s. In a similar vein, some might ask, "Will the interests of black women, and also black men, be shoved in the background and overlooked in the multicultural spirit of the twenty-first century?" In balancing the interests of African Americans with other groups, he said, "I am not a sell-out. I have been a part of the institutional history and [black colleagues] know I've fought these issues from the ground up, whereas an outside person would not have the same credibility." For the young black students of the 1990s, he pointed to the "battle scars of the sixties" and said, "Don't tell me about being militant." He argued that "an international perspective is required to produce a better situation for African American people." Stewart sees conflict as emerging with groups, because each views its interests as paramount. "They must learn to see interests cooperatively," he said.

Though Stewart's major aim is to assist diverse groups to respect the interests of one another, personal life events—family illness, the death of his mother, and the death of a close friend who was important to the black struggle—have forced this "servant of the people" to refocus his priorities and ask, "What legacy do I want to leave to the next generation?" Stewart would like to bequeath a theory of social change in the tradition of great thinkers like W. E. B. Du Bois, Arnold Toynbee, and Pitrim Sorokin, and would also like to leave a systematic study of black issues. He desires to secure the field of Africana studies in terms of its intellectual foundation, focusing on science and the economy. When his time comes, he would like his tombstone to read, "I've struck a few solid blows for black liberation and the dignity of all humanity."

Keith Walton [Pseudonym]:
Servant of Self, the Credo of a New Generation

Keith Walton would probably want his tombstone to read, "I've struck many solid blows for my personal salvation and the dignity of myself." In life he would probably embrace the admonition of Frank Hale, "Get all you can; can all you get; and sit on the can." Walton is a product of the culture of the civil rights generation, where the collective ethos of self-fulfillment dominates. For the civil rights generation, in contrast to the World War II generation, the conflict of balancing professional concerns versus community concerns has lessened, and the civil rights generation is clearly distinct from the World War I generation. Walton's life is a microcosm for helping us to understand those generational shifts.

Keith Walton, born in 1966, grew up in an upper-middle-class household in a mostly white suburb in a northern California town. He feels the gap not only between generations but between the poor blacks of the inner city and the white-suburbia-dwelling black upper middle class. He was born, reared, and educated in a white milieu from kindergarten through his postdoctoral studies. He is employed at a major research university on the East Coast as the lone black professor in a biology department. Since he does not belong to any professional black organizations, his contact with other blacks is still as minimal as in his formative years. He stated, "I don't feel I should join a black organization. Blacks should not separate themselves. We are Americans and should strive to be accepted on our own merit and not hide behind race." Increasingly, many young African Americans who were born during or after the civil rights movement and who were reared and educated in predominantly Euro-American communities lack a feeling of identity with other blacks unless they are integrated into a network of blacks. Thus their personal ideology and behavior are more likely to be aligned with the dominant white value system of individualism and the ethos of personal survival over group survival than previous generations. William Cross, black psychologist, would characterize such individuals as being in the preencounter stage of black identity development, characterized by "low salience to race neutrality to anti-black."[16] Individuals born in the World War I and World War II eras, especially those born in the segregated South, were aware of racism since it was more blatant. Those born in the last phase of the civil rights movement, or after it, are more likely to be in denial about racism or to be unaware of its more subtle contemporary forms. While the time period of birth and formative years is important, other sociocultural influences shape consciousness and intervene to mitigate against assimilating the dominant group's value system or reinforcing it.

Walton's father, a physician, and his mother, a secondary school science teacher, grew up in California. Their parents had migrated from Texas to California during World War II. Walton's paternal grandfather worked in the war industry. Unable to find a job as a teacher because of racial discrimination, his maternal grandfather worked as a Pullman porter. His maternal and paternal grandmothers had been elementary teachers in Texas; they, too, were unable to find work in California, so they remained housewives. Both sets of grandparents had come to California not only to seek better economic opportunities, but also to obtain better educational opportunities for their children. After graduating from a medical school in California, Walton's father set up a successful practice in northern California. His mother, who earned a master's degree, taught biology in high school. They encouraged Walton to succeed, providing him with a stimulating intellectual environment in the home and in the private schools he attended. "My parents gave me the best of everything, materially and educationally. I was educated in the best private schools all the way from elementary to my graduate studies. I was in the same class as corporate leaders' sons and daughters. I had the best education money could buy. My family traveled to Europe each summer, and I learned to speak fluent French and German. I spent one year studying abroad in my sophomore year in college and another when I did post-doctoral studies in France," Walton added.

Religion was not a significant part of his formative years, although Walton's parents were members of a white Unitarian church. They taught him to respect all people and accept everyone on an individual basis rather than as a group or stereotype. When I asked him about his racial socialization and experiences, the fair-complected young professor hesitated before commenting. "I cannot recall any really negative experiences. People who are prejudiced are just ignorant, and I was taught to ignore them. I rarely saw other black people besides my parents and grandparents except on television, and my life was not like that, so I could not identify with them except for the *Bill Cosby Show*. I was accepted by friends, neighbors, and teachers as one of the guys. My race was not important, so I didn't think much about it nor did my parents stress race. Their friends were mostly white, too, and my father's practice was also mostly white, with some Asians and a few blacks. I really don't concentrate on race, and I am uncomfortable talking about it. Too many blacks use race as an excuse not to succeed or to pull themselves up."

Walton does not feel blacks who are successful have an obligation to assist other blacks in improving their life chances. "Each person is responsible for helping himself. Through hard work and a good education, [one] can go as high as [one] desire[s]." A seemingly quiet man of few words, he continues to move up the academic ladder, doing important research in biomedicine. He is very active in his professional societies, presenting his cutting-edge research. However, occasionally, when a colleague hints his success is the result of affirmative action, he eschews that notion. "I don't need affirmative action. I have worked hard and succeeded on my own merit. I don't like being stereotyped. I don't like affirmative action, because it stereotypes all blacks as being given something and being not up to the task. I want to be seen as an individual who has accomplished in my field, and I don't want to be seen as an affirmative action black or even as a role model for blacks."

With the declining number of blacks, particularly males, pursuing doctorates or careers in university teaching, his critics would argue that Walton, despite his protest, is a role model for the underrepresented young blacks in science and engineering, whether or not he chooses to accept that responsibility or share his success. The political independent, who is married to a white woman and has two children, would say that his "idea of success is to obtain material comforts and personal achievement" and recognition in his field, which "does not involve service to others." Walton believes color will not inhibit him from "making it in this society."

A warning for Walton and those of his generation who share his feelings comes from a distant voice of the World War II generation—Crystal Miller, a professor of black studies, that I interviewed. "Black people are facing their greatest challenge since slavery because of the sophistication of racism. The few blacks who make it are held up as examples of what you can do with hard work. It gives credence to the idea that all those people who don't make it— the poor, teenage mothers, black men in jail, young people on drugs—it is their fault. I am not sure any one [black] really makes it in society, because of racism. People who do 'make it' have to take a hard look at what is happening in this society and their own isolation that made it possible for them to be where they are."

In summary, striking distinctions exist among the three generations of professors and administrators, whether employed in the ebony or ivory tower. Educators like Yvonne Walker-Taylor and Frank Hale, who grew up in the traditional culture of the World War I generation, were collectively socialized to embrace education as not solely for the shaping of the mind and making a living, but also for the shaping and molding of character to serve humanity, for empowering people as change agents, for building caring communities, and for self-awareness. In the culture of the World War II generation, William R. Harvey, Bart Thompson, James B. Stewart, and to a lesser extent Kufra Akpan were collectively socialized into a dual ethic: one of service, uplift, and liberation in their youth and one of self-fulfillment in their young adulthood. How this dual ethic unveils itself depends on significant life events and the historical context and place of their formative years, such as the geographical region, an urban versus rural setting, or a predominantly white versus black milieu. It may also hinge on age cohorts within the World War II generation. Generally, the older the cohorts, the more likely they are to embrace the collective ethos. In the culture of the civil rights generation, Sandra Jackson and Keith Walton are symbols. They have been collectively socialized into an individualistic ethic: Their ideals are guided by self-fulfillment or the "Me-First" model. Of course, a shift to embrace a collective ethic may occur at critical junctures in one's life cycle. For example, Sandra Jackson's collective consciousness was raised in young adulthood when she accepted a professorship at an HBCU. Familial influences, matriculating at an HBCU or maintaining other racial affiliations, significant racial life events, as well as a general knowledge of black history, might mitigate the individualistic orientation. The likelihood is nil that the Keith Waltons of the civil rights generation, who were socialized in white milieus, would have a pivotal juncture in racial awakening or would adopt a collective ethos.

For many in the World War I and II generations, the likes of Keith Walton is an alarming phenomenon, especially because too many of his generation view education solely as an avenue of personal mobility rather than as a collective pathway. The previous generations ponder the fate of racial progress and ask: What are the implications for collective group consciousness and collective action in the twenty-first century? And how likely is it to occur, since the majority of blacks are educated at white colleges and universities, and the majority of black students, in the K-12 grades, are usually taught by white teachers? Moreover, since there is an increasing presence of white faculty and students at HBCUs, what will be the impact of changing demographics on the collective racial consciousness?[17] What will be the long-term outcome of social, political, and educational public policies, such as the cutbacks in financial assistance to low-income students and the growing legal and political attacks on affirmative action, on the supply of doctorates, on enrollment among black college students, especially males, and on the quality of education for blacks? How will these issues affect the collective racial consciousness?

How will the changing milieu of higher education impact on racial consciousness? Arthur Levine, president of Teachers College, Columbia University, identified five external forces that are changing the landscape of higher education and propelling the academy toward a big business model: the shrinking revenues and rising costs for campuses, new technologies, the changing conditions of faculty employment in higher education, the changing characteristics of college students, and the growth of private sector competitors.[18] How will such issues as accountability, the higher education academy's financial crisis in general, its governance, the attacks on the tenure system, the changing demographic shifts, and diversity in a postmodern society affect education and black educators? Can fiscally strapped HBCUs, which have been the purveyors of black leaders, the cultivators of polished and unpolished gems, and the culture bearers of the ideology of service, uplift, and liberation retain their mission in the twenty-first century as education shifts to a multicultural, market-driven, business-oriented model?

Unless we begin to address these questions, the traditional track of education as a conveyor for black collective progress is on a downhill course. For our survival in a global community, the discourse must begin now. The emerging ideal of education as a business enterprise represents a paradigmatic shift, yet this model is likely to be an integral entity of our times.[19] To rethink these issues in education and the role of black educators, we cannot return to the past. Yet we are haunted by George Santayana's claim, "Those who cannot remember the past are condemned to repeat it." It is imperative, therefore, as an instrument of collective survival and liberation that we look backward to the traditional ideal of education as a moral enterprise to counterbalance the model of education as a business enterprise. William R. Harvey's leadership model of blending the moral enterprise of timeless values with the business enterprise is a starting point.

3

Black Clergy: Salvation and Liberation

Preachers predominated more than teachers in the black professional class in 1900, which included 21,267 ministers and 15,528 educators.[1] Can the prevalence of preachers in the World War I generation be explained by a divine interpretation or a sociological fact? Though Jim Hall was not born until 1928, his sociological explanation for choosing the ministry sums up the popularity of this profession before the 1960s. "I don't know if the Lord called me to the ministry. But I did see the ministry as one way to escape the horrors of holding down a job as custodian, bellhop, or chauffeur. As a black man living in the United States, it was one of the few positions then that would give me a decent living and the opportunity to do some good." Perhaps like Hall, it offered others a source of independence, dignity, respect, prestige, and a window of opportunity "to do some good." Whether preachers heeded the "divine calling" or whether they chose the profession in order to be the Moses that frees Pharaoh's black people in America, their role was to mediate for both worldly and otherworldly deliverance. No doubt Wyatt Tee Walker was acutely aware of this role when he asserted, in *The Soul of Black Worship*, that the preacher is the cardinal figure in the black religious experience and historically "the most revered figure in the black community." Walker affirms that, from slavery to the present, the "black preacher fired the hopes and aspirations of the oppressed community and became, in turn, a symbolic 'medicine man' for all the ills that occur."[2] The conservatory for those hopes and aspirations was the nurturing community of the black church. Noted historians Mary Frances Berry and John W. Blassingame, in *Long Memory*, articulated, "What distinguished the black church from its white counterpart was its adherence to a nationalistic theology of liberation, reform and uplift."[3] Moreover, James Tyms, in *The Black Church as Nurturing Community*, insisted that the black preacher, the "chief communicator of the nurturing community" and the herald of a Supreme Being, stood "between the oppressed and oppressor" and affirmed and proclaimed a gospel of "liberation, human dignity, justice"[4] and ethics that sustained and inspired resistance. Thus preaching was the medium for conveying a nationalistic theology of liberation, reform, and uplift. And historically, Christian ministers, such as Henry M. Turner, Martin Luther King, and Samuel Proctor, and somewhat later the Nation of Islam's ministers like Malcolm X and Louis Farrakhan, became black communities' messengers, their conservators of black culture, and their conscience.[5]

In essence, leaders of the largely Christian black clergy, as well as the ones in the Nation of Islam, incorporate the dual elements of German sociologist Max Weber's distinction between priest and prophet. On the one hand, the priest, a conservator or saver, is involved with the specific tradition of the faith in which he or she is a trained and an ordained leader. On the other hand, the prophet, a charismatic mortal, is an agent for a new social order.[6]

Since the traditional function of the black clergy incorporated both priest and prophet, has this role changed in the post-1960s? If so, how? Are there generational differences among the "chief communicators" of the nurturing community? If so, what are the implications for the black church in its traditional role in the social struggle for equality and justice and in the social transformation of black people, the nation, and the world? What are the ramifications of these changes for the church as the ideal caring, moral community? To unlock answers to these questions, we turn to the following scenarios of ministers from different generations.

From the World War I generation, we hear the voice of winter's season, James Tyms, who was born in 1905 on a farm in rural Mississippi and retired from Howard University as professor and as a former dean of its seminary. "Older generations of ministers were 'called' to the ministry with not much emphasis placed on being educated for the profession, although these differences have depended on the congregation. By and large, older ministers are less selfish in their orientation and are more interested in ministering to the people, despite the younger ones' training in pastoral care—a recent development in black church/ministry," contended Tyms. "Younger ministers are less conservative and more open to women ministers." Additionally, Tyms declared that more black parishioners and preachers are involved in white churches.

From the World War II generation, we listen to a hint of fall's season in the articulation of John Peterson Sr. Born in 1934 in rural Virginia, this pastor of the Alfred Street Baptist Church in Alexandria, Virginia, like Tyms, has also observed notable differences in the black ministerial role. Peterson, although himself highly trained, notes that the ministry is now looked upon as a chosen profession, whereas in his generation it was a sacred calling and "a divine urge on your life." He posited that many young ministers observe the relatively comfortable lifestyle of established ministers and choose the profession "without giving it the kind of dedication my elders and to some degree those of my generation have given it." Speaking of his own commitment as a young minister, he claimed, "I was very happy when I received a letter to supply a pulpit in a rural area. After two years, I was happy to go to an area for only two Sundays a month for $15 per week. But young theologians want to go into a big house. Younger ministers also do not want to be an assistant [pastor]; they want to have their own church. They look at the ministry as a profession and, therefore, demand their charge."

When Peterson started pastoring in 1953, oftentimes ministers, particularly those in rural areas, were given live chickens or a "sister gave canned peaches in Mason jars because they were unable to pay. And pastors were grateful." Even though Peterson never received a chicken when he served as a minister at an urban church in 1964, he did not receive sufficient pay to take care of his bills, so he needed to teach as a second profession. Although he acknowledged that he gave more than he received, he felt compelled to do it then and now. After a heart attack, he chose full-time ministry. As Peterson's church grew, it became more specialized, and his salary more competitive. But he quickly reminded me that he was not above visiting the sick and infirm.

In his course on practical theology, the adjunct university professor reminds young ministers that pastoring is more than "standing up in front of people and looking good. It has every facet from mopping floors to preaching on Sunday morning." He cited this example of a young minister and graduate student who was hired to assist at a ministerial retreat. When a heavy downpour left water standing on the floor, Peterson requested the young seminarian's assistance. "That's not for me to do," was his rejoinder, as the other ministers pitched in to aid. Chiding him, Peterson uttered, "Son, when you received your master's degree, it was preparing your hands to hold a mop. You have to do what has to be done in order to serve God's people." He attributed the changing attitudes to more formal education.

Agreeing with Peterson, Al Sharpton, born in 1954 at the dawn of the civil rights generation, said that more education and greater options have influenced the value shift. The president of the New York–based National Action Network reiterated that younger ministers have "greater options than those born in the earlier part of the twentieth century. [They] had to adjust to a more limited ministry in terms of access to society, different pulpits, different schools, than we had to. It automatically changes your perspective. But I also think those born earlier had a stronger commitment to certain values because they had to survive against more obstacles. We have more educational and economic options and weaker values."

Many of Sharpton's colleagues support his premise that formal education is changing ministers' worldview. Others differentiate that it is more formal education in predominantly white milieus and greater participation in more integrated settings that have contributed to these value changes.

Jesse Battle, a Pentecostal pastor trained at a white seminary and the fifth-generation minister in his family, thinks education has created a generational gap, but he does not feel his generation's values are weaker, only different. Born in 1949 in St. Louis, Missouri, on the cusp of the civil rights generation, his attitude toward the ministry differs markedly from Peterson's, as well as that of his father's. Battle, registered parliamentarian for the Twelfth Episcopal District of the Pentecostal Assemblies of the World, theorized that ministers in his age cohort fall into two categories—the trained and the untrained. The latter ministers work primarily from the premise that they were called, while the former have chosen ministry as a profession. Although he adds, "those of us who have been trained were at some point in our lives called into the ministry of mission. But we see it in a more secular way as a profession. I would probably be more representative of the trained type, but I work in an environment of mostly untrained ministers in the Pentecostal denomination. The untrained type is characterized by excessive emotionalism, is void of substance, is not geared toward long-term identifiable goals, and operates with very little system. I am involved with trained ministers whose philosophy has to do with comparing last year's figures with this year's figures and who are involved with record keeping, outreach, and retention programs. That's the difference."

While studying at the ultraconservative Lutheran divinity school, Hammond Theological Seminary, he began seeing religion from a different perspective. "I learned to put more value on style, systems, reason, and development as it relates to training ministers. After all, [ministry] is a business, a dollar and cents kind of thing."

He pointed out that "ministers go through four years of undergraduate and three years of graduate school to receive their master's degrees, and then some go on to get a Doctor of Divinity or some other form of doctorate. We look at all that training and feel we ought to be compensated, based upon experience, background, and education." While younger ministers are more concerned "about dollars," Battle said, "those over fifty-five view their ministry as strictly a calling, unless they have already gotten involved with the economics of the ministry. Ministers [age] fifty-five or sixty in the Pentecostal denomination will go wherever the will of God calls them without regard to money. In other religious denominations, trained older ministers are more concerned about the dollar, but not to the same extent as the younger ones. If you serve on a search committee, you'll find for the older trained minister that will be their fifth question. For me, it will be my first question." This is where Battle parts company with his father, who "will go wherever the Lord leads him." But Battle asserted, "I don't care where I work as long as it meets my standards, i.e., how many people in the congregation, how much money is it going to pay, budget, flexibility. Once those issues are settled, whether the church is in New York or Florida is of very little concern to me. I feel that wherever I go, God has led me [laughed] because things worked out economically."

Regarding the attitudes of younger ministers, he stated, "Most older untrained ministers feel we are renegades, ungodly, carnal minded, worldly, devils, unsaved, anything bad, and we are the people to whom they should be preaching. My father thinks it's awful to think about ministry and money in the same sentence. It's disgusting to him for a minister to ask, 'How much are you paying?' His attitude is 'It should not matter what they are paying: you are working for God, not them.' My father and I [disagree] all the time about this issue. For instance, I will not come to your church without some understanding of monetary contribution. He would not dare think of money as it relates to preaching. I write books. If you can't pay for them, you can't have them. My father would not think of selling the Gospel, as he puts it. It is a sacred thing, a God thing. I am just as committed to the God factor; it is just as important to me, maybe because I understand it better. I have a responsibility of being a good steward, but I also have a responsibility to make sure I am as marketable as possible."

In reference to pastoral care, Battle said, "I do visitations, but I don't do many of them, and the reason I don't is because, as a trained minister, I can't do everything. So I train associate ministers of visitations. I do weddings and funerals occasionally, but I charge a fee that will discourage that, and they'll get an associate minister. I may charge a couple $200. They can have an assistant minister for $50. My father didn't charge anything." Battle concluded, "My commitment to God is no less. My commitment to ministry is no less. My calling is not less, but my attitude toward life is different."

Clarence E. Brown, born in 1968 and reared in Buffalo, New York, grew up in the culture of the post-civil rights years. The young minister agrees that Battle captures the spirit of the civil rights generation. "My generation was influenced by television, videos, and parents who were more lax. They too often lost the importance of their responsibility and were too concerned about the almighty dollar and getting more at any cost. The focus of what ministers do now is, therefore, for self-gratification and self-glorification. They get puffed up about big sermons, big churches, and they do not see themselves as a vehicle for carrying the message of Christ and the message of liberation. With my generation, we are caught up into getting a lot of things and talking about prosperity. Our parents fought in the civil rights movement, and they wanted their children to have more material goods than they did. There is a sense of entitlement. We were taught to give [ourselves], instead of giving. Christ taught us to serve, but the service component is gone. My generation feels that instead of serving the masses, they should serve you. We have always been served, been given everything, and always been receiving. We have never been shown how to give."

What unites each generation of ministers is their keen sense of self-efficacy derived from a cavernous religious and spiritual grounding and their struggle in resolving the seemingly dialectical tension between salvation and liberation. A careful examination of the above scenarios suggests, however, several value shifts among three generations of black ministers, particularly those born during or after the civil rights movement. These differences can be summarized as follows: Black clerics who were born or grew up in the pre-1960s have a persona and theological orientation that is more sacred and communal. The cohort of post-1960s ministers is more secular and associational. The former is more otherworldly and spiritual; the latter is more worldly and materialistic. The pre-1960's ministers operate more in the context of the moral community, characterized by faith, while the post-1960s ministers function more in the framework of the amoral community, depicted by skepticism. Furthermore, the pre-1960s clerics are more parochial and exclusive; the post-1960s clerics are more ecumenical and inclusive.

Some polarities, like worldly and otherworldly, appear to be in dialectical tension. But are they? William C. Turner, Jr., in Jon Michael Spencer's *Sacred Symphony: The Chanted Sermon of the Black Preacher*, argues that

> The content and musicality of black preaching moved hearers away from the history that had unleashed terror upon them. . . . Black Americans have had to look away from their historical circumstances to find a source of dignity and worth. Only through perpetuating their quarrel with history while simultaneously sidestepping its terror could they forge a new identity for themselves.[7]

While trying to sidestep history's terror, traditional black theologians could sustain their quarrel with it, because they perceived the world as ruled by the "providence of an almighty God."[8] It was the God of the Old Testament whose presence and power manifested itself in their daily lives. Michael Battle, the former chaplain of Hampton University and director of its Ministers' Conference, said this God "is actively involved in the vindication and secularization of people—vindication deals with the total liberation of the person—mind, body, soul, spirit."[9] Accordingly, black preachers could proclaim a message of hope to the downtrodden with broken spirits, employing Old Testament stories to illuminate the communicants' plight—their longing for a more peaceful existence in the hereafter and for a more hopeful tomorrow. Battle maintains that the black Christian church's theology was based historically on the Old Testament theology of liberation, but changed in the 1940s and 1950s to embrace a traditional New Testament salvation theology. With the advent of the civil rights movement, "we have a maturation of black ministers' theological supposition," where they recognize that the "dichotomy between the sacred and the secular is a Western theological approach and not an African philosophical approach," said Battle. Each generation of black clerics, and each minister within his or her generation, must grapple with this set of existential polarities, which reflects the sociological conditions, the times, the circumstances, and the choices.

THE MINISTRY OF THE SOUL

Joseph Lowery: Prophet, Priest, and Pastor

James D. Tyms, in *The Black Church as Nurturing Community*, declared that "'The Mystic Trumpeter'. . . has ceaselessly lifted high an affirmed vision of God and proclaimed that the will of God for black folks is that, 'I want to see a mighty flood of justice—a torrent of doing good.'"[10] No doubt Tyms would include Joseph Lowery, civil rights leader and one of the cofounders of the Southern Christian Leadership Conference with Martin Luther King, Jr., as a symbol of the "Mystic Trumpeter." He synthesizes, in the finest tradition of black religious experience, the dialectical tension between priest and prophet. While adhering to the moral imperatives of his faith, he incorporates Old Testament biblical characters who have a strong social consciousness as a guide for confronting social injustices of this world. He, therefore, equated his participation in the civil rights movement with his ministerial duty. For Lowery, it was a way to let the mighty flood of justice roll down the southern hills of Alabama, Georgia, Mississippi, and across the country. For him, "the real basis of civil rights is moral, religious, and theological. I don't think you can talk about the fatherhood of God and the oneness of the human family without talking about justice; without talking about an end to hunger, homelessness, and war. You have to talk about peace with justice. All of these relate to the moral imperative of the Christian faith."

From black ministers of his childhood, he learned about the moral imperative of the Christian faith. He was also deeply influenced by biblical characters in the Old Testament like Amos who had a great social consciousness and by Jesus who committed his life "to justice and brotherhood and to giving dignity." These influences sensitized Lowery toward social injustices in this world. Young Lowery had an incident that brought home inequity in "a dramatic and traumatic way."

One day, when Lowery was leaving his father's ice cream parlor, two white policemen jabbed him in the stomach with their nightsticks and said, "Get back nigger! Don't you see a white man coming?" His father complained about the boy's treatment to the chief of police, but his response was it's the "natural order of the day." This incident marked an important event in young Lowery's life: It planted the seeds for his strong social consciousness of racial injustices in America. For a while, he was embittered by this incident. But as he "experienced the Christian religion," his "bitterness faded into determination to change the system and to work with people's hearts and minds." He did not know this resolve would someday place him among the cadre of moral leaders that would steer the South, the nation, and indeed the world to a new social order. What were his formative influences?

Joseph Lowery, the clever pastor emeritus of Cascade United Methodist Church in Atlanta and past president and national chair of the Southern Christian Leadership Conference (SCLC), was born October 6, 1924, in Huntsville, Alabama. His "moral imperative" to serve is grounded in the deep faith of the black community in rural Alabama where he grew up in the twenties and thirties. That deep faith was born of hard times in a racially divided society, where school, church, and social activities were segregated. While whites held limited expectations and aspirations for blacks in his community of mostly small farmers and sharecroppers, Lowery's parents had higher ones for their children. His father, a small businessman, dropped out of elementary school; his mother, a housewife and former teacher, completed normal school. They encouraged their children to "study hard, work hard, be honest, and be persistent." By studying, working hard, and having faith, along with "a little luck," Lowery achieved the A.B., B.D., and L.L.D. degrees while matriculating at predominantly black Knoxville College and Paine College, and then Wayne State University, Payne Theological Seminary, and Chicago Ecumenical Institute. Lowery, the former school teacher, newspaper editor, and visiting instructor at Emory University's School of Theology, has been the recipient of several honorary degrees and numerous awards, including *Ebony* magazine's Black Achievement Award in two categories—advancement of the cause of equality and religion and the Alpha Phi Alpha Outstanding Leadership Award in the field of civil rights.

The Good Shepherd

"Being a Christian means to serve," said Lowery, who is married with three adult children. "In trying to be a responsible child of God and a Christian minister, I want to serve the community, God, and my family." Since his days as a young student of religion and philosophy in the 1940s, Lowery fought to be the good shepherd, "bearing the infirmities of the weak," by leading marches and speaking out against economic and racial injustices from South Carolina to South Africa. A decade before meeting Martin Luther King, Jr., he began his social activism in college, where he worked to change the inequities in facilities for blacks and whites during World War II. After graduating from divinity school, the young minister "never separated civil rights from the divine order."

In the 1950s, the youthful pastor was one of the leaders in the forefront of the civil rights movement, spearheading protests in Mobile, Alabama, while Fred Shuttlesworth led them in Birmingham and Martin Luther King, Jr. in Montgomery. He also worked with the NAACP, which was outlawed in Alabama because the organization refused to submit its membership lists to the state. There he organized various protest groups in the community and headed the ones in Mobile. His leadership activities in Mobile placed him in the forefront as one of the prominent leaders of the civil rights movement. When the desegregation of the Montgomery bus movement began, Lowery supported King and the boycott in Montgomery. The interaction between King and Lowery, as well as other ministers, led to the formation of the Southern Christian Leadership Conference, which spearheaded the desegregation of restaurants and hotels in the 1960s. While Martin Luther King, Jr. served as chair of SCLC, Lowery became one of its vice presidents, a position he held until 1967. He was then elected chair of the board. In 1977 he was elected the third president of SCLC, which marked his genesis as a national leader.

As leader of the SCLC, Lowery campaigned against the Ku Klux Klan and police brutality and fought for voting rights, better employment, and economic opportunities for blacks and other oppressed groups. He called for defense cuts and for a new policy that would reorder our priorities: one that works for "peace, full employment, tax reform, health care, and reducing homelessness." He was twice jailed for waging a campaign against dumping toxic waste in a black community in North Carolina. This led to a congressional investigation, which found an overutilization of toxic waste disposal sites in poor and black communities.

When Lowery speaks out against social concerns, so intertwined are his politics and religion that his rationale is biblically grounded. Take his example of affirmative action: "Affirmative action . . . ain't perfect, but it's old. Jesus talked about his shepherd who had one hundred sheep and ninety-nine were safety tucked away. When he tucked them in and said good night, he went out into the wilderness to look for the lost one. That is affirmative action. It is old. It is also preferential treatment, and nothing is wrong with preferential treatment."

In confronting these social and economic issues, we see an evolution of Lowery's beliefs about the complexity of social change in the larger society and within black communities. During the civil rights movement, Lowery felt "integration was the answer" and "the movement would lead to the demise of racism." But its leaders had not confronted the issue of "economic justice and the extent to which the system itself, even if integrated, was not designed to deal with massive liberation and equity" of blacks and the poor. Lowery learned that changing the system is a complex process. Altering it can be brought about only "through certain basic external economic, moral, and po- litical methods—through pressures, and those pressures are available in your body, in marches, in jamming up the streets, and in disrupting the system." He believes blacks have to pressure both the private and the public sectors to ef- fect change. Along with altering the system, Lowery insists "we have to work with the black psyche, because there are so many factors that make blacks re- gard themselves as inferior and as incapable of achieving." There are issues of black isolation in white milieus, and a litany of other issues facing the black community—stress, despair, drugs, health, familial breakdown, youth vio- lence, and teenage pregnancy. To free the negative psyche, Lowery has urged blacks since 1985 to develop a "Liberation Lifestyle." This spiritual orienta- tion incorporates a strong familial and religious value system; emphasizes good health, a strong racial consciousness, positive individual and group iden- tity, and compassion for the less fortunate; and espouses peace and justice. His social action model juxtaposes individual and societal responsibility.

Lowery views the waning faith, narcissism, and skepticism in the black community as related to integration. The white definition of integration has "dulled our sensitivities to those spiritual aspects of the black experience that have helped us to get over." Lowery draws upon the sentiment of an old spir- itual, *How I Got Over*: "I got over through the Lord, through faith, leaning on the everlasting arm."

Lowery is concerned about human rights and justice not only in this coun- try, but also in third world or peripheral nations. In the 1980s, Lowery ex- tended his leadership and SCLC's involvement in foreign policy and the peace movement, holding meetings with such world leaders as Yasser Arafat and Daniel Ortega. He was among the first to lead the fight for divestment of U.S. business from South Africa. He was also among the first five protesters ar- rested in November 1984 in the South African embassy in Washington, D.C.

As a change agent in the global arena, he sees a special role for blacks: "Black people have to help this country to learn that there is a new world per- spective and order. Three out of four people in the world are not white. Al- most two out of five in the United States are not white. The Third World coun- tries are taking their place and America has to learn to deal not only with

Japan, but also with an emerging world economy that requires an entirely different perspective on economics than this country has experienced."

He reminds us that this new global perspective involves working for a legitimate peace, that is, "peace with justice so that nations can develop freely and be respected. . . . The exploitation by the superpowers of natural resources has to be eliminated. We have to develop relationships that are not bellicose. We've got to see all the world's people as human beings. We've got to see no country is exempt from the ravages of war and disease. For our own salvation, we've got to help save the world and see people of the world as our equals, as our brothers and sisters, and not as our puppets."

Whether in the local, national, or global arena, Lowery feels it is important to have strong black institutions like the church and independent leaders like himself who are not controlled by the white establishment. By working with black establishment leaders, independent leaders make it easier for the black elected officials and for those blacks working within corporations. "We always need 'house niggers.' I use the term affectionately. We are trying to get them in the house. I just don't want them to forget the field nigger. In slavery time, the house nigger and the field nigger worked together. SCLC has always been the field nigger. The house niggers need to keep us strong and independent, so we can fight for them. If you close your independent forces, where will you return?" said Lowery. He is quite concerned that the "house niggers," or blacks in white settings, are becoming increasingly isolated. But he cautions blacks in white corporations and integrated milieus to maintain contact with the black church. Because of the diverse membership within black churches, he believes, this institution allows the best opportunity for maintaining contact and allows blacks to cope more effectively with racism.

Lowery retired as president of SCLC in 1997. He imparts the legacy of the good shepherd who watches over "the poor, hungry, helpless, hopeless, and the wronged," and continues his fight as the good shepherd who "bears the infirmities of the weak." His Liberation Lifestyle, he said, allows him to "do what I can do and what I can't do, I don't worry about. I leave it in God's hands. If I can't get to it, I hope the Lord will."

Jim Hall: Priest and Pastor

Born in 1928, Jim Hall, retired Episcopalian rector from St. Cyprian's, a black parish in Hampton, Virginia, has many commonalities with Lowery, but there are differences. Both Hall's and Lowery's religious activities were similarly situated in largely white denominations. The two men differ in their theological orientation and their styles of worship. On the one hand, Hall follows the Anglican Church's liturgy, which embraces a New Testament theology.

On the other hand, Lowery is steeped in the black religious tradition, which espouses a theology of liberation based on the Old Testament. Both Hall and Lowery see themselves as pastor, priest, and prophet. Hall performed more in the position of priest, while Lowery enacted the part of prophet. Yet they both share a strong commitment to the service tradition characteristic of their era. Lowery's model of servant leadership can be identified as more ecumenical, while Hall's is more parochial. Lowery, whose racial ideology evolved from integrationist to pluralist, worked outside the system as head of the SCLC to bring about change. Hall, an integrationist who headed both black and white parishes, worked within the Episcopal denomination for racial reform. In the 1960s, Hall, like Lowery, was a participant in the civil rights movement in Florida, active backstage rather than on center stage. Unlike Lowery, Hall could not oblige the movement's philosophy of nonviolence to achieve racial integration. "I was involved in two demonstrations. When I was attacked, I attacked back. I cannot kneel down, pray, and sing *We Shall Overcome* while somebody is beating the hell out of me. The first time I was in a demonstration, a guy took the sign out of my hand and kicked me in the thigh. I took the stick that he had torn off one sign and went up side his head and laid it open. The civil rights movement had to be nonviolent, it could not have succeeded otherwise."

Like countless other blacks of his generation, Hall believes that the movement was a defining moment in his young adult life. Blacks could now be actors in forming their destiny rather than being acted upon. "It meant the system could work for us, but it meant somebody had to die," avouched Hall. Consequently, he had more than an abiding collective interest in the movement succeeding; it was deeply personal as well. Growing up in the 1930s and 1940s in Miami, Florida, Hall recalls how blacks could be arrested for loitering in white neighborhoods. "One of the most frightening experiences was when I was thirteen or fourteen and my aunt got me a job painting in a white neighborhood in Miami. I was returning home and the police stopped me and asked what I was doing in the neighborhood. When I told them my reason, they said, 'Ain't nobody live in this neighborhood by that name. Are you looking for white girls? Well, don't let me catch your black ass around here any more. Head on to niggertown and we are going to follow you to make sure you get to niggertown.' I started walking rapidly toward home. They said, 'You are not walking fast enough.' I started running, thinking I would be stopped any minute. They only stopped when I got to a traffic light and I kept running through the traffic."

He had a similar confrontation some years later when he was chased out of a white community. Not only did these incidents make him sad and angry, he professed, "I carried the hatred around with me for years and had no love for policemen. Like many blacks growing up in the South, I had no particular love for white people. I thought they were all SOBs and whatever other foul names." He developed a "different outlook on whites" after graduating from a black college and leaving his segregated community. He entered a predominantly white seminary in Wisconsin in the early 1950s to study for the priesthood. Although his racial experiences were mild in Wisconsin, the conservative, politically independent cleric's encounters in Montana as the rector of a white church had a more profound impact on him. "I got a chance to live with whites, and it changed my attitude. I equated conservatism with racism. Yet I had conservative Republicans as parishioners, and I was their pastor. Seven or eight Southern-bred individuals were my biggest boosters. I had to stop putting a racial face on everything. I related to people as people."

For over forty-three years, whether in a black or a white congregation in Montana, Washington, Tennessee, or Virginia, pastoral care was an essential mission of his ministry. The faithful shepherd tended his flock—counseling and visiting the sick and infirm, the bereaved, the institutionalized. In addition, he challenged the church community to cherish the tenets of Christianity. But he was always mindful of his pastoral duties—of "binding up wounds" of parishioners. "The congregation will forgive you for stealing money, but not forgive you if you do not meet their personal needs. You have to grieve with them when they suffer." He pointed out that younger ministers are not as committed to pastoral care. "Some have the idea that if you can't do anything for me, I don't have any use for you, that is, if you do not give money or do the church some good. I was never interested in what somebody gave to the church." His pastoral mission and priesthood were influenced by the gemeinschaft, the intimate caring community of his youth.

The Caring Community

The caring community nurtured Hall after the death of his mother. Hall's mother, a domestic with one year of college, died when he was twelve years old. After his mother divorced his absent father, a chauffeur, when Hall was three years old, his mother's sister, a domestic with a ninth-grade education, reared him. While his mother laid the foundation for his strong sense of independence and his "desire to learn," he remembered his aunt as "an uneducated soul sister" who yearned for only the best for him. Although as a young man Hall was unappreciative of her efforts, he claimed, "She kept me out of a lot of trouble by laying down the law and putting the fear of God in me." She "worked her fingers to the bone" to put Hall through a historically black college. Though he started at Talladega College in Alabama, he later transferred to St. Augustine College in North Carolina, also a black school, where he graduated with a bachelor's degree in social sciences with a minor in music. His mother's brother, a high school biology teacher with a master's degree, became his surrogate father. Despite holding a chauvinistic, macho view of females, his uncle wanted Hall to be well educated and to grow up to be a "wholesome male." His uncle also encouraged Hall to participate in sports. No doubt Hall's love of learning, inspired by his mother, and his uncle's encouragement kindled in him the desire for an education. Ultimately, he obtained an advanced degree in anthropology at the University of Montana.

The community where Hall grew up was an extension of his family. "Everybody was concerned about one another." His family and community role models—maids and chauffeurs possessed with positive self-images—taught him that he was "as good as or better than anyone, and nobody was inherently superior to anyone. People in the community would say, 'You have to make something of yourself.'" He cited an example to illustrate their concern: "My buddies and I had sneaked a bottle of beer from someplace and were swaggering down the street drinking it from a brown paper bag and acting higher than we were. When a neighbor drove past and stopped his car, he called me over and asked, 'What do you have in your hand?' I pulled it out and gave the bottle to him. He held it up, shook his head and called, 'Clara [Hall's mother's name]. You know Clara is turning over in her grave; you ought to be ashamed of yourself.' He turned the bottle up and poured it out on the ground, and said, 'I am going to tell Lucille' [Hall's aunt]."

Bemoaning the loss of the caring community and the civility of his youth, he mused: "We don't want people to stick their noses into our business today. In the past they did, if they thought you were not acting properly. . . . I recall one day after school, I was planning to slip a little girl home and I was going to have some fun. We walked toward my house and we got within a hundred feet of the house, and an old woman who lived across the street came out and started sweeping her sidewalk in one spot. She could have seen from the inside, but she thought if I did not see her, I would have slipped the girl inside the house and gotten her pregnant. The old lady continued to sweep until she wore that broom down to a nub."

The ethos of the caring community was, "If you are going to make something out of yourself, you can't have a baby holding you back." Although Hall and the young woman "mumbled unkind things about the old woman across the street," he can appreciate her concern today. "Who knows what I was saved from—syphilis, gonorrhea, a pregnancy. My life could have been ruined. Today, nobody would care enough to intervene. If you say something today, you might wind up dead or sliced with a knife," said Hall.

Jim Hall and his wife, Pauline, moved to Nashville, Tennessee, when he retired. Hall sees the caring black community of his youth evolving into a more individualistic and materialistic one, "where a sense of entitlement has emerged in this generation." This attitude also infects younger clergy. He, like others, wonders how this me-first model will impact pastoral care. With the retirement of ministers of his generation, seemingly this prototype of pastoral care, so integral to the nurturing community of the black church, will indeed be weakened. Al Sharpton, civil rights activist whom we met earlier, agrees, attributing the loss of the caring and nurturing black community largely as a casualty of integration: "I think that those in the earlier twentieth century had to build stronger communities because they had no one but each other. People in my generation went beyond the community and never looked back, which weakened the infrastructure of our own political and economic quest."

THE MINISTRY OF THE SOUL AND SELF IN STRIFE

Jonathan Walden [Pseudonym]: Prophet of a Relevant Social Gospel

Born in 1947, Jonathan Walden, Baptist minister, is one who looks back to the bridge in the black community that helped him get across. And yet he also moves forward toward strengthening its political and economic infrastructure. He is a link between the elders and the youth. He is old enough to remember the struggles and hopes of the civil rights movement, yet young enough to identify with the narcissism and skepticism of some gangsta rappers. As an avid reader of current events and black literature in high school, Walden credits the civil rights movement with changing his life from one of passivity to one of activism and with inspiring his strong interest in politics. "I began to observe Dr. King in the early 1960s. I wanted to be like him in the sense that I had a better understanding of racism and wanted to cry out against an evil, so I participated in high school speeches and debates."

Along with the civil rights movement, the assassinations of King and the Kennedys, the black nationalist movement, and the Vietnam War, when many of his friends and acquaintances were killed, shaped Walden's politics and his "caring attitude and commitment to the black cause." The student/athlete was a leader on campus during the waning years of the civil rights movement and the beginning of the black nationalist movement. The National Guard was called to his predominantly black campus, then considered a bedrock for black nationalist activists, after an incident near the campus. Although Walden claimed there was no provocation by students, the guard unit invaded the campus looking for suspects. "In a matter of minutes, you saw them lined up, and the next thing you knew there was a riot. Folks' heads were beaten. When students scrambled to their dormitories and locked themselves in, they came with their riot guns, knocking out doors, air vents, and forced everybody out of the rooms. The media were there, and they claimed we started the riot," states Walden. This event moved Jonathan to fight racism "not physically, but through the mind." It was a real awakening and a turning point in his life, which fueled his activism in the black nationalist movement.

Walden's ministry of social action is rooted not only in the civil rights movement, but also in the "theology" of black liberation, an ideology influenced by the black nationalist movement. In the mid-1960s when the political winds shifted from the civil rights movement in the South to the black power movement in the urban North, a group of clergy affirmed the use of power in the struggle for justice.[11] Suitably, a new theology rose among the more educated black clergy that called for confronting racism and for becoming more involved in economic empowerment in the black community. As more whites and middle-class blacks left the central city in the 1960s, their flight eroded the tax base. They left behind poor blacks who were besieged by crime, violence, drugs, inadequate housing and health care, unemployment, and teenage pregnancy. Accordingly, the church and its clergy began responding to these needs by expanding its services to a larger community and by providing social outreach programs, like government-sponsored Head Start programs, child care, housing, and tutorial programs.

These post-1960s ministers embraced what Michael Battle says is essentially an African philosophy and religion, which does not see a distinction between the sacred and secular elements "because all life is sacred. And we must take a sacred kind of response to secular problems confronting us." Battle professes that black theology shifted to the "belief of a realized eschatology, the notion of an empowering God in the struggle toward liberation" as opposed to otherworldly eschatology, which emphasized "pie in the sky." For Michael Battle, it is the "relevant black church" that must confront these secular problems in a "holistic fashion," because "the black church is still the foundation of African American life, our soul, our political and economic survival, our cultural continuity, and our spiritual sense of empowerment."

Married with five children, Walden operates within the tradition of Battle's holistic approach. He believes the ministry is an "active calling to be involved in worldly problems of drugs, unemployment, youth alienation, teenage pregnancy, drugs, racism, and economic empowerment." But for numerous inner-city youths, Battle affirmed that the church is not the internal control support system for their "disconnected lives." The "enabling songs of spirituals," which offered hope in the pre-1960s, are supplanted "by crippling songs of some rap and hip-hop lyrics, which degrade women and emphasize violence." Although Walden agrees with Battle, he deems his ministry as a "calling from God and His will to be used as an instrument" to make a contribution to the spiritual success of young people. He wants to empower them and instill a sense of ethics, meaning black pride and dignity in their lives. "I don't separate the work of the ministry and the church from the development of young folks. They are the future. They are branches of the vine. If we don't nourish them, prune them, and keep them strong, they will lose their worthiness, value, and contributions they can make to society."

The collective racial ethos of Walden was fueled not only by the civil rights and black nationalist movements, but also by his family and community. Walden, the son of a minister/coal miner and a nurse, was born in a small segregated town in West Virginia. His father, a disciplinarian, always "spoke his piece and established his rules." He expected his son to adhere to them. His mother was the stabilizing and nurturing force in his life. "The caring and giving part I took from her and made it a part of my ministry." Both parents instilled in their three children the values of discipline, independence, and a strong work ethic; taught the importance of education; inspired academic excellence; and encouraged them to achieve their goals. One goal for Walden was to obtain a good education. He received a B.A. from a historically black university, with a major in elementary education; he earned a master's in educational administration from a major university in the West and a master of divinity from a predominantly white university. He attributes much of his educational achievement to an older sister, who reared him in the absence of his working parents and who inspired his aspirations. His closely knit community was also supportive of his ambitions—the church, school, and neighbors. His parents and grandmother also gave him a strong religious foundation, to which he gives primary credit for his success. Desiring to emulate his father, Walden always attended church services and church business meetings with him. He was also active in youth groups. In church, he developed the art of human relations skills and learned the politics of religion, which he later transferred with such deftness to his ministry and to the political arena.

After completing his undergraduate education, Walden taught elementary school in a predominantly black school in the Midwest. Remembering the racial injustices he had endured while in his integrated junior high, he felt it was important to instill self-pride and dignity in black children for their survival and success in a white world. Consequently, he wrote plays for students to perform in school, plays which taught them about their black heritage and about striving for excellence. Walden left teaching to continue his graduate studies before stepping into the corporate world. There the racial atmosphere was extremely challenging, and he battled the system unsuccessfully for two years before retreating. Leaving the corporate world, he fell into politics. He organized the first Young Black Republican Party in his state and ran several unsuccessful races for political office.

Walden claimed that he had to "back up" from politics to take up a religious calling. "The revelation came to me at around thirty-two years of age. God was more than just words, going to church on Sunday, and singing in the choir. He was a Being who was the dominant part of my life." He related the following story, which foretold his calling: "I was in Kansas City for an Operation Push convention, and a lady I'd not met before spoke to me one evening in a store and she raised the question to me. She said, 'Son, do you know who made you?' and I thought I didn't have to answer because I didn't know her. And so, initially, I didn't answer. So she asked me again. Rather than deal with the personal side of what I really thought, then, I said, 'My mother and father made me.' She said the Lord made me and 'you should never forget that as long as you live!' She said, 'The Lord has great work for you to do. He wants you to speak for Him. He wants you to use your mouth and your face. He will give you masses of people to speak to.' I was twenty-nine years old when it happened."

The recurrent dream of the old lady inspired him to go into the ministry. His social gospel sermons revolve around the "issue of black folks and how they need to deal in a racist society." Usually, the message is, "Be the best you can and have self-pride." He also addresses the ravages of drugs, violence, family dissolution, racism, and economic empowerment in the church and the secular world.

Although social activist ministers of Jonathan Walden's generation do work outside the system for change, they are more likely to confront these issues by working within the system as a change agent. They differ somewhat from Lowery's generation, which is more likely to choose the former. Walden, a politically active, moderate Republican, has run several times for political office, managed campaigns, organized the Young Black Republican Party, and served on numerous civic and political boards in his local community and in his state. He understands how decisions are made and plans to run for an elected office in the future. Though he recognizes his motivation is for selfish reasons, it is also because of a strong social consciousness: "I tend to think anybody who aspires for political office has a selfish motivation, but I don't think that's bad, because striving for political office is work. It is a person's career and like other careers, one also strives for self-gratification and personal success. But I believe that there are some who not only see success in it for themselves, but who also have a sincere commitment to others."

If Jonathan ever runs for office again, he thinks having an independent base is critical, which the church represents for him. But, he said, it doesn't make much difference what the setting is, "I will speak what I believe as I have done so throughout my life. If the issues need to be addressed, I will do so."

Ann Lightner-Fuller: Preaching the Gospel of Gender Equality

Until recently, one issue, the inclusion of women in positions of ministerial leadership, remains unaddressed by Walden and the largely male clergy within black denominations and within black ecumenism. Too often, patriarchal biblical precepts are employed to justify the exclusion of women. Ann Lightner-Fuller, an African Methodist Episcopal minister, has listened to her male colleagues' strong conviction that "Women should not preach. They take the Scripture of Paul and say a woman should be silent in the church. They make interpretations without any regard to its context and historical situation." In *Troubling Biblical Waters*, Cain Hope Felder challenges such beliefs, asserting that, "The patriarchal conservative tradition so evident over the centuries must give way to leadership patterns that are gender inclusive. . . . Too often being a black woman with ministerial aspirations has meant a triple-jeopardy experience, for racism, white feminism, and male chauvinism have all resisted efforts by black women to be accepted fully as ordained ministers."[12]

Ann Lightner-Fuller agrees that the church is still not only very racist, but also sexist. When women are ordained, they typically receive assignments at small churches and in remote outposts. Whereas men are more likely to see small, outpost churches as a crutch, she and other women clerics think of them as a challenge and as an opportunity to help them grow. Whatever the church's demographics, she maintains, women "want to make it a place to be worthy and to be an exciting place to worship. My first church had seven people, and we saw one hundred fifty converts in that church. When I moved to my present church, there were about seventy-five people. Over the past ten years, we put four hundred people on the roll. We are building a new four-hundred-seat sanctuary. It's what God will do when you do the work of the Lord." But, she adds, "Women work harder for the Lord. I preach harder, work harder, and study harder. I know I have to be the best because so many people out there are waiting to shoot you down, whereas brothers can do the least and get great applause from it." Although the patriarchal tradition is intrinsic to most denominations, the African Methodist Episcopal faith appears somewhat more flexible and progressive than others, especially since the 1960s, says Lightner-Fuller. This religious body was among the first to approve women's ordination in 1948 in the United States.[13]

As a prophetess, Lightner-Fuller feels that she must challenge the subordination of women in the church. "I preach a sermon in my book, *Desperate People*, called 'Desperate Women Pray Desperate Prayers,' and I talk about how people need someone to provoke them every now and then. Sometimes you have to be provoked to be your best ally." The acclaimed speaker is widely known for her work in developing female mentoring programs for the

African American church, and she speaks throughout the country on the issue of women and religion.

Lightner-Fuller, born in Raleigh, North Carolina, in the late 1940s, claims it was God's will for her to be called to the ministry. She grew up in a religious household of extended family members, which included her working-class parents, two siblings, and a maternal great-grandmother, the primary caregiver and "the stronghold in the family." Lightner-Fuller lived with her extended family in Raleigh until she was fifteen, when she moved to New York to live with relatives. After she completed high school in New York, she eventually married and returned to North Carolina. When her marriage ended in divorce, she entered Boston University, nine years after graduating from high school. She then moved to the Washington/Baltimore area to pursue her studies and majored in journalism. Fuller, now married to a Baptist minister, entered seminary in 1980 and finished at St. Mary Seminary in Boston with a master's in theology in 1984. She served as pastor of a small church in Maryland for two years before she was transferred to Mt. Calvary African Methodist Episcopal Church in Towson, Maryland, in 1986, where she has remained. She completed her doctoral degree in ministry at the United Theological Seminary in Dayton, Ohio, in 1994.

Lightner-Fuller has faced the limits of the stained-glass ceiling from the beginning of her ministry, but her strong faith, she says, has allowed her to persevere undaunted. "I was the first woman to preach a sermon at the main event of the one hundred seventy-fourth African Methodist Episcopal Annual Conference in Baltimore. Somebody told me they heard one of the brothers on the corner talking about how it was a sad day in African Methodism." Behind dark clouds of doubt, we catch glimpses of a silver lining. Lightner-Fuller became the first woman keynote speaker to preach the morning sermon at the 1996 Hampton University Ministers' Conference in its then eighty-second-year history. "The reception was God ordained from a predominantly Baptist conference," exclaimed Lightner-Fuller. She is reassured by the younger generation of clergy who seem more liberal toward women in the ministry. Al Sharpton affirmed her belief that the civil rights generation is more accepting of women and gays. "Older ministers did not have the exposure to gays or lesbians or it would have been unthinkable to admit it," he said. "It is not only a philosophical difference but a matter of comfort level. Women's rights had not come into fruition with the old guys. In my generation, we don't see it as abnormal, and we have to deal with it in a broader societal context to respect gay and lesbian rights and women's rights. It is based on the context and time you live."

While Lightner-Fuller is hopeful in this respect about the younger ministerial cohort, she is also disturbed because these clerics, especially males, are not as interested in pastoral care or as service oriented as she is. Rather, too many young clerics appear more preoccupied with individual and material success. When they boast about their financial packages or their churches, "It is a new term in the church for me. It's because of the caliber of people coming to the ministry. There are more doctorates, and they want to be compensated for their education. It's their mentality that 'I deserve this . . . if I were in the corporate world, I would be making this,' which they translate to churches," she remarks. The liberal Democrat added, "If the old ministers didn't start out with that attitude of the importance of the financial package, they have it now." Lightner-Fuller professes that women ministers are more service oriented than men and are more committed to the Lord and being a part of the church: "My father in ministry taught us that you go into the church and talk to the Steward Board, and you ask the salary of your last pastor and what can you afford, depending on your family, what your needs are, and whether or not there is a parsonage. But not, 'I can only come to you if you can pay me so and so.' My mentality is let's work together and we can grow together. I believe in ministry, and I've been taught that pastors should work with the church and its finances and that your 'package' will grow, and people will learn to give tithes and offerings."

MINISTERING FOR SELF OR SERVICE TO OTHERS

Robert Charles Scott and Al Sharpton: A Dialectic Within the Civil Rights Generation

Born at the end of the civil rights movement in 1968, Robert C. Scott, pastor of a 325-member Baptist church in Lexington, North Carolina, admits readily to Lightner-Fuller's allegations that his ministerial cohorts are more individualistic and materialistic and less committed to a life of service than their predecessors. "They bid for the highest financial package, so they can live and retire comfortably. The financial package is the first question on the mind of younger ministers, and even some are now asking for contracts—just like a business contract. 'I will stay here so many years,' and each year the minister will ask for an incentive," said Scott. "Old ministers feel the Lord will take care of me. The younger ministers feel the Lord will take care of me through this contract. The middle ones are between both worlds."

A carefully crafted financial contract allows younger ministers to better prepare for retirement and to avoid the plight of many older clerics who often ended their ministerial duties in destitution. Even though Scott acknowledges that the contract protects the minister and the church, he recognizes that it detracts from the spiritual bond that binds parishioners. He believes, like

Lightner-Fuller, a covenant should exist between the pastor and parishioners, not a business contract, to sustain the nurturing community. But this covenant, he posits, dissolves in the face of an ethic of materialism. "Young ministers want everything the older preachers have without having to put in the sweat, blood, and tears. They want the cars and big house, but it takes developing people's trust and faith that God will move people." Unlike John Peterson, the World War II generation minister in the earlier scenario who taught school so he would earn enough to be able to preach, Scott feels that congregants should pay their clergy a livable salary, so it will not be necessary for ministers to have two professions. "When they are biprofessional, it is usually the church that is on the side."

For Scott, who began preaching at age eleven in Monticello, Mississippi, neither the church nor the ministry has been on the sideline; both are central to his being. It was the place where he was born and reared; his grandmother, along with her brother, "started him in church." He thought "ministry was focused on preaching," but he didn't understand the essence of ministry until he attended divinity school at Duke University, where he received his master's. Under his mentor, the late Samuel Proctor, "the blinders were taken off," and he began to understand ministry as the "conveyance of God's love and compassion to people with myriad problems." Similarly, under Wyatt Tee Walker's mentorship, Scott, as a candidate for doctor of divinity at United Theological Seminary in Dayton, Ohio, has as his goal "to help find redemption and reconciliation among those who are broken in different facets of humanity—spiritually and emotionally."

Unlike Jim Hall's generation, where involvement with pastoral care was the essence of the ministry, Scott's peers are less concerned about the role of the shepherd who binds the wounds of the flock. This makes Scott somewhat atypical for his generational cohort. In reflecting upon other significant generational differences, he noted that ministers born in the World War I generation and in the earlier part of the World War II generation possess "an awe for God and a spiritual acumen that is not as present in my generation." They transmitted an oral black preaching tradition, whereas the civil rights generation wants to pass on a written legacy for future members. The older ministers are being replaced by individuals born later in the World War II generation and by older ones of the civil rights generation as the prototypes Scott's age cohort emulates. "They are looking at the ministry from a holistic perspective (mind, body, spirit). They have a theosocial, theopolitical, and theoeconomic perspective of the ministry," said Scott. He believes that theosocially, the black church has always been a catalyst for change in the black community. But the World War II generation of ministers who came of age during the civil rights movement are "concretizing lessons that have been shared with them from older ministers" and making them more apparent for his generation.

Some clerics concede that the social gospel of liberation and reform, which includes fighting for social justice and promoting economic empowerment, is one lesson being shared with Scott's cohort. Many younger ministers, therefore, are embracing the entrepreneurial ideals of creating collective wealth in the black community through investment and ownership of property, such as apartment complexes and schools. They also champion the causes of oppressed groups. Andrew Billingsley, in *Mighty Like a River*, notes that contemporary black churches retain a communal orientation. At least two-thirds of the churches in his survey of the Northeast and North Central had one or more outreach programs. Moreover, ministers with higher levels of education and larger churches are more likely to sponsor outreach programs.[14] Still, critics like Al Sharpton, who was born at the beginning of the civil rights generation in 1954 and who started preaching at age four, question if the younger ministers' creed is equal to their deed. He said, "I see a consciousness manifested in the younger generation in wanting to stand up and fight back, but I don't see this activism. The third generation is more committed to liberation in words and thinking than in their bodies. Whereas in the first generation, and even the second, they may have been more moderate in their thinking, but they marched, loaded the jail, and took the beatings. This generation wears African garb, quotes Afrocentrism, academic theories, even in church, but they are not out there. So you have a generation who can put together the Million Man March, but can't save the welfare bill or can't stop Medicaid from being cancelled. There is a wide gap between their rhetoric and reality. This third generation has black style and no substance."

Theopolitically, Scott maintains that traditionally black ministers employ the necessary devices "to help people become politically empowered through the church." While Sharpton recognizes that political empowerment should be a collective mission of the ministry, he is, nevertheless, wary that this sense of collectivity is being imperiled by an even greater individualistic ethos of the civil rights generation. "They are more oriented toward building their church and interpreting their individual ministry than being part of a convention or denominational group that interprets it for them," noted Sharpton. In earlier generations, "everyone was in the National Baptist Convention, the Church of God in Christ, or African Methodist Episcopal. Everyone followed the guidelines. Today, people build churches with two thousand members and say I want my ministry to be more individualized." Sharpton speculates that this growing phenomenon of megachurches is the result of the greater opportunities created by the civil rights movement: "Churches now can build school buildings and programs. But in the past they could not get bank mortgages, so they stuck together. Today, people can talk to bankers, chambers of commerce, and mayors, but in the past you were limited to a network of preachers." He added, "Young ministers may be more beholding to outsiders because they trade with more outsiders. Fifty years ago, the government would not have provided day-care funds, private school funds, and Head Start funds for churches. If government funds the church and has a partnership with you, it will dictate your political position. You don't bite the hand that feeds you." This new generation of ministers, he argued, "puts the traditional independent leadership of black ministers at stake because of their individualistic attitudes. In the past they might have been more powerful, because they owned their churches, and today they have access, but they pay a price for that access—political strength is diluted."

From the theoeconomic perspective, Scott acknowledged that many younger ministers "are looking at the church as an economic base to provide jobs and services for black communities. They are moving from being a Sunday morning esthetic experience and a Wednesday night Bible study to a seven-day-a-week operation that is much larger." Scott cited his mentor, Wyatt Tee Walker, pastor of Canaan Baptist Church in Harlem, as an example of this "megacorporation."

But has this trend toward the megacorporation affected younger ministers' view of pastoral care? Al Sharpton argued that many churches have expanded in the post-1960s, so that they are "no longer the refuge basis of the community." Instead, "in many cases they have become a megacorporation and do not necessarily deal with the daily and social needs of their members. They are like big warehouses—large buildings, large memberships, and large ministries." In the generations of World War I and World War II, the pastorate was more personal and generalized. "The pastor, no matter how prominent, would visit Sister Ann in the hospital and bury Deacon West," Sharpton lamented. In the 1990s, it is more impersonal and specialized. "The pastor has a staff who visits the sick, and you have people trained for the different ministries. It lacks the family ties we had in the earlier part of the [twentieth] century. It is a speciality, but an impersonal speciality. In the earlier part of the century, a pastor might not have studied ministry, but he had a personal effect— 'That's my pastor,'" he added.

Like others, Scott sees education as the major divide between the pre-1960s generation of World War I and World War II and the post-1960s civil rights generation. He noted the baby boomer clerics have "taken their education, their know-how techniques, and their administrative skills that have been applicable and advantageous to the corporate sector and have translated them into an ecclesiastical service." While the church benefits from greater efficiency, he admitted, "qualities that work at IBM may not work in the church." When Scott reflected on his generation, he said, "We find ourselves struggling with technology, since we have access to even more education and we live in the computer age. However, the church is stuck with a mentality that is afraid of technology. Many churches do not have computers, and having access to more information is pertinent."

For Sharpton, too, technology is apropos for the changing church, but it has its drawbacks. "In our growth, you give up some things and gain others. I think the tension is seeking balance, where you can modernize but not lose the personal, common touch of our people to survive all that we have survived. I think the trend is toward the large, impersonal, megachurch, but I think it is going to run its course. People are ultimately people, and you cannot computerize values. You can set up a more efficient way of preaching values and serving people, but it cannot be done out of a computer. It still comes down to human feelings."

Scott concludes that in his age cohort, ministers are now "wiser, but weaker," adding, "there has been a decrease in ministerial ethics—respect that goes into ministry and the person associated with it." In the African American tradition, it was the "sacred that affected the secular." But in the contemporary world, "we are picking up the secular and translating it into the church." In separating himself from ministers of his generation, Scott strives to be more like his mentors, the late Samuel Proctor and Wyatt Tee Walker. "They have been educated, have been through the civil rights movement, and have allowed that to mesh with their compassion, which is the essence of the Gospel. My generation can say it better, use polysyllabic words, but I don't know if we have the power of those older preachers, who have been touched with history."

Since Al Sharpton has been "touched with history"—the civil rights movement—he feels he can bridge the gap between the ministers of the World War I and civil rights generations: "Generation X heard about the movement and lives and enjoys the results of the movement. I am old enough to have seen the movement. I was alive when King was killed. For twenty-eight-year-olds, King is a distant story. I am old enough to know what has happened and what is happening now. A twenty-eight-year-old can only take for granted eating in restaurants and going to better schools. I am young enough to not have suffered segregation, but old enough to know what it was. I understand when young clerics say to older ones, 'I want to deal with computerized technology and move into the twenty-first century.' But I also understand the older ones who stress values, the civil rights marches, and the bloodshed. The sacrifice of older ministers made the access to opportunity possible. I do not think the [young] should disrespect the sacrifice, because they would not be in a position to enjoy the access to use many different things."

For Sharpton, "the sacrifice" must be that "thread that brings the generations together." And "if we don't deal with our continuity, and pass it on to
the next generation, we will repeat the same mistakes of every generation.
The idea is not to reinvent the wheel as each generation does, but to make it
turn more effectively. We must formalize ways each generation must pass on
its wisdom and the benefits of its mistakes," said Sharpton. Passing on the
legacy of ancestral sacrifice is not formalized in the black church and the
black community. Since it is not, Sharpton seeks out older mentors—like
Jesse Jackson who is a half generation older—because they can share their
knowledge with him on social activism. By the same token, Sharpton feels
obligated to share with someone a half generation or a generation younger
than he is: "It's about one generation's flow into another, because it is one un-
broken chain. Until we formalize that, we will not get to where we need to as
a people, not only in the ministry but across the board." Acceding to Sharpton, Scott reminds us that as the "black church goes, so goes everything else
in the black community." For the black church, in the words of C. Eric Lincoln, is and has always been considered the "most formidable bastion of black
solidarity." Thus, "care must be taken that the commitment to the spirit which
has defined the black church in the past must not be permitted to slide im-
perceptibly into the commitment to mammon when the Fortune 500 comes to
knock on a black church door that has stood open for two centuries."[15]

4

Black Physicians: The Community Healers

Traditionally, ethical oaths are administered to medical students. However, the Hippocratic oath, the most enduring heritage in Western medicine, has been the ethical guidepost for physicians since ancient Greece.

> I swear by Apollo, the physician, by Aesculapius, Hygeia, and Panacea, I take to witness all the gods, all the goddesses, to keep according to my ability and my judgment, the following Oath. . . . I will prescribe regimen for the good of my patients according to my ability and my judgment and never do harm to anyone.[1]

Robert D. Orr and Norman Pang, in a survey of deans of all 157 allopathic and osteopathic schools of medicine in the United States and Canada, found that of the 150 schools responding, 98 percent of the graduates took an oath in 1993, while only 26 percent of schools administered an oath in 1928. In examining the contents of oaths taken by medical schools, including the classical Hippocratic oath and its various versions, they noted that the contents of all the oaths pledged a commitment to patients.[2]

This ideal duty to patients has customarily cut across lines of race, ethnicity, class, gender, and age in Western medicine. Now earthshaking forces in the medical profession are challenging the patient-centered ideals embodied in the classical Hippocratic oath, the oldest known system of medical ethics. These changes in the health care system are captured in a contemporary parody of the Hippocratic oath.

> I swear by Apollo, the physician, by [Aesculapius], [Hygeia], and Panacea, and I take to witness all the gods and goddesses, to keep according to my ability and

judgment the following oath: . . . I will reveal to any of my offspring who aspire to join the profession the terrible pressures of the practices of medicine today, including professional liability, restricted freedom in the methods of treating illness and the use of hospitals and the prescribing of medications, and the hostile relationship with patients that has developed because of the insidious rationing of health care by DRGs, regulations of health maintenance organizations (HMOs), and so on. . . . I will prescribe regimens for the good of my patients according to my ability and judgments but never violate the rules of Medicare, Medicaid, HMOs, preferred-provider organizations (PPOs, and the like). I will never keep a patient in the hospital longer than the DRG allows or the HMOs and PPOs suggest, regardless of the inconvenience to my patient. I will always use generic drugs, even if I think the proprietary drug is more effective. I will always obtain a second opinion, even if I do not think that one is necessary and the patient does not wish one. I will try to ration the resources spent on my patients in line with federal, state, and insurance-company mandates.[3]

These tremors in the health care field, along with other aforementioned structural and cultural shifts, are contributing to generational fault lines in ways of thinking and behaving among black physicians, the missionaries of good health for the black community. The ensuing anecdotes of black doctors from different eras illuminate these fissures.

In 1935 William Harper, general practitioner, set up his solo medical practice in Atlanta, Georgia. After graduating from Meharry Medical College, he hung up his shingle and waited for black patients to show up. Segregation was the order of the day, so he like other black physicians of his era could serve only the black community, treating black patients in their offices, black hospitals, or in segregated wards. Doctors made house calls—day or night—and were intimately familiar with their patients and their families. Harper said, "When patients could not pay, they exchanged a sack of potatoes for service, particularly rural doctors." On a professional level, they interacted with their black colleagues in the National Medical Association (NMA), because they were generally not allowed to join the American Medical Association (AMA). But more important, black physicians were notable leaders outside the medical profession, serving as intellectual and economic resources for the black community.

In 1965, thirty years after Harper hung up his shingle, Frank Russo entered a tokenly integrated medical field. He attended a white medical school, interned at one, and completed his residency at white hospitals. He also practiced at a predominantly white hospital, treating both black and white patients alike, and he belonged to the AMA. Though his indigent patients could pay for his services through Medicare and Medicaid, he continued to serve those who could not pay in his office. House calls were virtually a bygone practice.

Being a solo practitioner was just one option in Russo's generation. Black men were slowly beginning to enter medical fields in academe, in public health, and in the corporate world as administrators, practitioners, and teachers. At the same time, their role as ecumenical leaders began to wane.

During the 1960s, black women were scarcely starting to increase their numbers and options in medicine at both black and white institutions. As the medical venue was changing, Minnie A. Stiff, pediatrician, was setting up a solo practice in the mid-1970s in Hampton, Virginia. For her, the most obvious transformations over the past twenty years or more include greater technology and specialization in medicine, along with its skyrocketing costs. "Now, with greater specialization, you are met by a stranger before you go into surgery," she observed. As a result, "confidence in doctors has eroded, so there is more litigation."

Lind Chinnery, who graduated from Meharry in the late 1980s, concurs with Stiff that greater specialization contributes to the abrading of confidence between doctor and patient. He noted that prior to the 1960s, all doctors needed when they graduated from medical school was a certificate from an accredited school and a license to practice medicine. But when he graduated, "board certification was an unwritten mandate to practice in a specialty. You have to finish a training program. Otherwise, you can probably practice in urgent care or as a general practitioner. But general practitioners are now dinosaurs. Doctors coming out of medical school in the 1990s have a certain number of years to become board certified before they can be accepted to a hospital staff."

In addition to the added requirements for doctors, Chinnery has seen the erosion of physicians' autonomy with the rise of HMOs and other managed care plans, and the loss of quality care as the field of medicine shifts from a patient-centered approach to a more profit-centered one. This change is creating an ethical crisis among doctors. The more committed young doctors find themselves in a catch-22 situation. He stated, "Either you maintain your integrity and walk away, or you let your integrity become compromised and play the game. I think the way medicine is going with HMOs and deselection, a lot of good doctors are leaving and the bad ones are staying, because the system is not geared toward medical excellence."

In the changing health care milieu, Craig Appleton, who graduated from a major white medical school in 1995, foresaw that doctors would have less autonomy over their medical practice because of HMOs and other changes in the field, so he chose the speciality of radiology. "I have spent so much of my life in school. I owe a lot of money, so I chose a speciality in medicine that would bring the greatest economic rewards and the best life for me. I certainly did not want to go into primary care, because it is considered the minimum wage speciality."

Along with the changes in the medical field from the time of William Harper's entrance into the profession in 1935 to Craig Appleton's arrival in 1995, there were major cultural and structural shifts. This chapter explores the impact of these alterations on three generations of black physicians and their historically important leadership role and responsibility in the development of black communities. In essence, it examines how these transformations have affected their sense of community, culture, and consciousness.

Carter G. Woodson, black historian, noted in 1934 that black physicians were the most portentous professional element in the black race,[4] although they appeared later than teachers and preachers. On the one hand, their importance is measured in terms of prestige ratings and the high esteem assigned to doctors by the larger society and by black communities, which also value their cultural and economic capital. On the other hand, the scarcity of black doctors providing adequate health care to communities has also contributed to their functional importance. Since black physicians make up only 3.7 percent of the total of all doctors in this country,[5] their absence impacts the quality of health care for black men and women in every economic strata.

A dearth of black physicians has always existed in the American medical profession. During Reconstruction and post-Reconstruction eras, the numbers increased significantly with the opening of seven black medical schools. In the early 1900s, the Carnegie Corporation for the Advancement of Teaching commissioned Abraham Flexner to conduct an intensive study of medical education in this country and Canada. While the Flexner Report of 1910 was extremely critical of both black and white medical schools, it was particularly severe for black ones. Except for Howard University Medical School and Meharry Medical College, the Flexner Report recommended the closing of black medical schools, which had a profound effect on black medical training and the supply of physicians serving black communities.[6] (Morehouse Medical College is the only black medical school opened since the early part of the twentieth century.) At the same time, most white medical schools were closed to blacks or enrolled only a few until the 1960s. Howard and Meharry, historically the top producers of black medical doctors, could not fulfill the black community's health needs. By the late 1960s, with the desegregation of white medical schools and the establishment of equal opportunity policies, an increase in the number of black students enrolled in medical school was evident. Nonetheless, in the mid-1980s, this trend started downward again.

The paucity of black doctors alters the distribution of medical services in the black community and the quality and quantity of health care. Infant mortality rates, low birth rates, maternal deaths, immunization rates, childhood tuberculosis, lack of dental care, childhood anemia, toxic lead levels, childhood deaths, strokes, and shorter longevity rates are major indicators of health status and the quality and quantity of care. Utilizing these health parameters, the data show that the incidence of afflictions is significantly higher for blacks than for whites.[7] Despite advances in technology, racial disparities also exist in diagnosis, treatment, and cure of diseases. In essence, the black population is disproportionately more ill and disabled. Blacks are more likely than whites to have a poor health status and outcome, to be indigent and uninsured, and to be dependent on underfunded, understaffed, and overcrowded public facilities for basic services.[8] The health status and outcomes for blacks, therefore, reflect discriminatory policies of the health care system in this country. While black patients face inequities in the health system, black doctors also encounter professional and income inequalities because they serve a black population that is disproportionately poor and sick.

But who will lead the way out of this health care imbroglio? Will it be the AMA, which has historically opposed universal access to basic health care, or the NMA, which has traditionally fought for it? Perhaps, as Frederick W. McKinney notes, "The paucity of black physicians practicing nationwide and the poor health status of blacks placed these physicians on the front line of the struggle for improvements in the health and social conditions of blacks."[9] In the 1960s, the NMA was the only medical professional body in the forefront of the passage of Title XVIII and Title XIX, which established Medicare and Medicaid during President Lyndon Johnson's administration.[10] The NMA has not only been in the vanguard of advocating access to health care, but it has taken a holistic approach to health rather than solely adopting a medical model, connecting health status to socioeconomic conditions that underlie illnesses, such as AIDS, hypertension, strokes, diabetes, cancer, and heart disease. This angle of vision does not see the causes of illnesses only in terms of bacteria and viruses but rather, in part, as a consequence of inequality in the delivery of health care and in the social system.

While the NMA has been a collective beacon for health care justice, Susan Smith McKinney-Steward, James McCune Smith, John Sweat Rock, Daniel Hale, and Eliza Grier are shining examples of individual foremothers and forefathers who pointed the way. In addition to practicing medicine, they were agents of change in the community. Contemporary advocates such as former U.S. Surgeon Generals David Satcher and Joycelyn Elders have brought attention to some of the issues facing minorities and poor people. Under the leadership of Louis Sullivan, former secretary of the U.S. Department of Health and Human Services, the white male as the ideal model for medical research was challenged. While these past and present voices harmonize in raising the health status of black communities, other voices have been heard in the medical vineyard, raising a similar tune of racial uplift. This melody is changing. Whether loudly or softly, the song of the World War I generation is sung in chorus, the song of the World War II generation is a solo with chorus, and the song of the civil rights generation is an aria. Despite generational differences, they all share a love of learning and new challenges, a passion for medicine, and a high level of self-confidence. Additionally, for most, being spiritually grounded and being an ambassador for the race is essential to their existence.

HEALING BEHIND THE COLOR LINE

William Harper: "When I Was Sick, He Administered unto Me"

Behind segregated walls, the chorus of physicians of the World War I generation like William Harper chanted collective tunes of racial uplift. Born in 1909 to a prominent black family in Atlanta, Georgia, the internist grew up on "Sweet Auburn Avenue," now the Martin Luther King, Jr. Historical Preservation District. He remembers this flourishing thoroughfare as the nucleus of prominent black families and the hub of thriving businesses, churches, and other social institutions. Growing up in this vital center of the black community and interacting daily in his home and community with black educators, bankers, businessmen, contractors, civic and social activists, poets, preachers, politicians, and physicians influenced Harper to believe that blacks could achieve, despite legal segregation. Although he was inspired by his community, his father, an educator and the first black member of Atlanta's Board of Education, and his mother, a social worker, were his greatest influences. They instilled in him and in his sister, also a social worker, a strong ethic of hard work and honesty, the importance of education, and the duty to uplift the race through service. His father was an exemplary black leader who fought for better educational opportunities for blacks prior to the civil rights era. As a low-key negotiator and mediator for political and civil rights, his father operated behind closed doors to achieve his ends.

Growing up during a period of racial accommodation in the early part of the twentieth century in Atlanta, Harper recalled that "there was not much hostile confrontation. People accepted their position, but they were never satisfied to do so." His world was colored black with specks of white. Rarely leaving the protected confines of the black community, he socialized at the black YMCA, watched movies at the black theater, worshiped at segregated AME and Baptist churches, attended black cultural events, rode segregated streetcars, patronized black businesses, and attended black private schools from kindergarten through medical school. After graduating from Fisk University with a BS degree in science, he attended Meharry Medical School. Harper graduated in 1935 and practiced behind segregated walls at black hospitals on black patients. While black doctors could administer only to black patients, white doctors could treat blacks and whites alike. In the South, black doctors could not practice at white hospitals and black patients were rarely admitted to white hospitals. Although public hospitals had segregated wards for black patients, black doctors could not practice in them. Moreover, they could not join the AMA.

Although being a doctor in a segregated community was prestigious, it did not necessarily bring economic prosperity. During the Depression, when Harper established his practice, unemployment was high and money was tight. "We didn't have enough black patients to go around to all the black doctors at that time. You came in and set up your office and waited and wondered where the first patient would come from," he said. To earn a decent income, he became the physician for the segregated Child Welfare Association and also administered anesthetics to patients in a black hospital. However, black doctors who practiced in urban areas were far more secure than the rural doctor in the 1930s. Though Harper was in solo practice, he worked with other doctors for their survival and the survival of the black community. It took time to build his successful practice with an overflowing patient load. During this era of segregation, he and his family, along with other blacks, lived out their lives in a world defined by race in an uneventful way.

While racial accommodation was the modus operandi of his life from childhood through his middle-adult years, Harper participated quietly in the civil rights movement, taking a moderate stance behind the battle lines. He worked to fully integrate the local white public hospital and the professional association. However, when the white medical society finally granted him the status of associate, he considered it an indignity and refused, because such a rank did not entail full membership rights and privileges. Although Harper, along with other doctors, was once arrested for picketing a segregated public hospital, his low-key style more often provided economic assistance to the students on the front line. While the civil rights movement represented an important milestone for blacks, it was not a life-altering event for him. "The movement came as a transition, but it didn't change my life," he said. He continued to practice medicine as he had since 1935.

Besides being happily married with three adult children, attaining economic independence, and having a sense of well-being, Harper believes that one component of his success is the need to give back to the black community by assisting youths, by providing health education, and by serving as an advocate for universal health care access for the poor. Harper, a gentle, self-effacing man, noted his likeness to his father. "If my father had a nickel, he would reach in his pocket and give the nickel to a child. Unfortunately, I am like that to a certain extent, treating the poor who can't pay."

Clinton Warner: The Race Ambassador for Collective Empowerment

Born in Atlanta, Georgia, in the early 1920s, Clinton Warner, physician, surgeon, and professor of medicine, desires like William Harper to improve the
quality of health care for blacks. Undoubtedly, he is more politically active
than Harper in the medical community, the black community, and the larger
society. His personal biography and coming of age in the political dynamism
of the 1930s and 1940s might account for this greater activism, his less-ac-
commodating attitudes about the limits of race, and his greater need to prove
himself in the white world. Spending most of his formative years between
Arkansas and a small town in Georgia, Warner, as Harper, grew up in a middle-
class Southern family in a segregated community. But while Harper was educated in private schools, Warner attended public ones. His father, a high
school principal and later a college professor, and his mother, a high school
English teacher, encouraged Warner and their two daughters to be successful.
They advised him that whatever career he chose, he should do it well, because
it was a matter of personal and racial pride. In the taken-for-granted segregated South of the 1930s, Warner's parents stressed racial pride as a mechanism for coping with and resisting racism. "They were always holding up
something that blacks should be proud of. We always listened to such musi-
cians as Wings Over Jordan and Nathaniel Dett, so I could not help but respect being black." Other prominent blacks, including George Washington
Carver, W. E. B. Du Bois, Booker T. Washington, and Frederick Douglass,
had an impact on his life. Through reading, he learned about these black heroes, but he was also able to meet Du Bois and Carver. He described his desire to find black heroes as "almost like the Jewish faith: people look for heroes within their faith."

As a freshman at Morehouse College, Warner was inspired by another idol,
its late president Benjamin E. Mays. Initially Warner did not take school seriously, so he dropped out of college and served in the army for four years. Although the army was the turning point for his motivation to complete his education, Mays was the decisive catalyst for his continuation at Morehouse. After
graduating from college, where he majored in biology, he entered Meharry
Medical College and graduated in 1951. He chose to go to medical school, not
because he felt doctors were highly paid but because of the limited options of
segregation. "You could only teach, preach, or go into medicine, and I did not
think I could talk good enough to preach. I decided to go into a career that was
considered an honored profession. I learned it was nice that you could make
money, then I decided if I do a good job, the other part will come."

For over forty-five years, Warner has been doing a "good job" practicing
medicine, although after graduating from a black medical college, Warner

was still not sure of "being good enough." He said, "I was determined to do my internship in a white hospital, so I could find out if I were as good a doctor as I thought." He wanted to match his skills against Yale, Harvard, and Princeton graduates, so he fought to gain acceptance into a well-known hospital in Chicago as the first black. After being accepted for an internship, he discovered that he was more capable than the others. As the only black intern, he led his class of one hundred. If someone had asked him when he was an intern if he supported black institutions, he would have responded, "I don't know. I had a sense of being inferior, or thinking I got an inferior medical education and nobody could tell me otherwise. I didn't know if it was worth supporting until I found out for myself." That year convinced him that he was as good as or, in most instances, better than his white medical colleagues.

Beginning in the 1940s, the NAACP advocated for inclusion of blacks in medical schools and equal access to educational opportunities. Twenty-six of the seventy-eight Association of American Medical Colleges' approved medical schools were closed to black students.[11] The color line in the medical profession was slowly dissolving in the 1950s and 1960s when Warner began his string of firsts. In the 1960s, he was the first black to be certified by the American College of Surgeons. In 1963 he was one of the twenty-one plaintiffs who filed the first suit to desegregate the public hospital in Atlanta, the white medical association, and the medical school. "I was the only black physician willing to sign my name," said Warner. "The other black physicians feared ostracism by the old line black establishment, who initially did not support the student movement." He also extended his interests beyond the medical community to fight for open housing. And despite threats, he became the first to cross the borders and move into a white community. Warner, a liberal Democrat, doesn't consider himself a radical, but he stated, "Sometimes I do some things I believe in, even though it may cost."

Even though Warner fiercely fought for integration, he chose to practice medicine in the black community and to teach and serve on the board of a black medical college. Warner feels strongly about the survival of black institutions and the need to strengthen them. His internship in an all-white hospital convinced him of the strength of his black medical school and black educational institutions in general. He champions the preparation of more black doctors, so the community can have better access to health care. For Warner, "a quiet national scandal is occurring and no one is addressing the state of minority health. Minority health should be a national priority. There should be a Marshall Plan for health, which looks at the health of all Americans, particularly those at the bottom." Though minority health needs to be emphasized, he thinks that "black doctors are powerless voices, not heard."

Warner believes that it is paramount for black doctors to have an active voice in the larger community to promote change in the health care system. Consequently, he serves on the board of a major health corporation. Again, he was the first and only black for many years. Though the "first is always lonely," he used his position as a token to "help enhance the collective interests of blacks." Describing himself as a doer, he serves on many medical and health boards, as well as boards in the black community and the broader society. He is particularly interested in black youths, so he serves on the board of a youth leadership development program. This is a group of high-achieving black male leaders who function as role models and as fund-raisers for scholarships. While the program is successful, he is critical of it because too many high-achieving and well-motivated middle-class students are selected at the expense of children of the poor. He also promotes economic development within the black community, believing that "successful blacks have an important role in this fight. It is inherent in being black. It is almost religious that you ought to do something. I want to do something good for the world."

Juel Pate Borders: The Ministry of Medicine and Doing God's Work

Juel Pate Borders, obstetrician/gynecologist and minister, also wanted to "do something good for the world," to provide black women with the best medical care. But when Borders, the daughter of William Holmes Borders, entered medical school in the early 1960s, few medical schools accepted women, black or white. After graduating from Spelman, a black women's college in Atlanta, she studied medicine at the primarily white (women's) Medical College of Pennsylvania, in Philadelphia. Following the completion of her residency in a white hospital in the North in the mid-1960s, she set up a solo practice as the first black female doctor in Atlanta, Georgia. Like her male predecessors, she came from a prominent Southern family and was educated in both private and public black schools from elementary grades through college.

Born in the 1930s in Chicago, Illinois, Borders spent most of her formative years in a black suburb of Atlanta. She grew up in a devoutly religious, comfortable, middle-class household with her parents and brother. She maintained that her father, the renowned Baptist minister and social activist whom readers were introduced to earlier, and her mother, a high school English teacher and director of her church's Christian education program, were the key ingredients in her accomplishments. "My family background and the insistence of my parents on academic and scholastic achievement and their constant demand for the best inspired me. If you had to stay up all night to turn in a book report, you stayed. You had to pass the course. You had to go to college. You had to do something that was acceptable." In the 1940s, the era of Borders's youth, parents had greater authority and control over their children. "Young people did what they were told. I believed very much in both of my parents, and if they felt this was the best thing for me, I didn't question it too much," declared Borders. Her father felt it was his duty to remind her that blacks had to work harder to get the same recognition. But he added that "though the color of your skin is different, there is no difference in your brain, heart, soul, body, and your ability to do." While both parents were supportive, her "mother quietly and continuously" pushed her forward. In the meantime, her black teachers reinforced her parents' prescription for success.

In the South in the 1940s and 1950s, the color line and gender line were overtly operative in the aspirations of black females. Like many black middle-class families, Borders's parents sheltered her from the color line by containing her within the black community. Yet racism did not completely elude her. She offered a war chest of stories, depicting the horrors of segregation that came from listening to her father who investigated lynchings in small towns in the South in the 1940s and 1950s. Borders described these events "as a horrifying experience from a distance." Her parents instilled in her a strong sense of race pride. "I've heard all my life—every Sunday and sometimes during the week—my father talking about the genius of the black race and what it would take to overcome the difficulties it faced."

Borders believed that one way to "overcome difficulties" was to administer to the health needs of women in the community. In the process of becoming a physician, not only did she confront the societal limitations of the color line, but also she encountered the gender line within her own family. While her father encouraged his son to go to medical school, he felt a career in medicine was not the place for a woman. Her mother believed it was a woman's place. "My mother never let you go backwards. You always had to push forward. My father would finance whatever the two of us decided to be the best [decision]," she added. When Borders could not attend a white public or private institution within her own state because of segregation, she accepted the board of regents' policy, which arranged for any black student who was accepted to an out-of-state university to be paid the difference between tuition at the state school and that of the out-of-state university. She spent a year at a white university in the Northeast, and based on her excellent record there, the Woman's Medical College of Pennsylvania accepted her. Although her grades were similar to what she achieved at Spelman College, the medical school simply assumed a black institution was inferior to a white one.

When Borders became a doctor, her father was very proud, so he constructed an office building for her and her husband, a dentist, and for her brother who also became a doctor. Stereotypes abound about women doctors, and Borders says, "It was rough initially." She had to prove her competency to black women patients, to her black male colleagues, to the black community, and to the larger society. In order to prove herself, she had to go beyond the call of duty, working harder and spending longer hours with patients. After only eight years of practicing medicine, her patients gave her a testimonial dinner. She built a successful practice, but eventually outgrew her space. She was initially denied a loan to construct a one-story building, the first of its kind for a black female doctor in solo practice in her city. Again, she felt the need to prove herself and other black women worthy of a business loan. "One of the reasons I am continuing to work as hard as I am now is because I want that good record established, so when the next black female with a moderate-sized venture applies for a loan, they will remember," said Borders.

Borders's primary purpose in life is not to prove herself to people, but to do "God's work" in the tradition of black women physicians of the nineteenth century, who saw themselves as "co-laborers in the work of the Lord."[12] "God is Supreme, Lord of all. I am His child; therefore, I am special. He has assigned me work to do and has blessed me with the capability for executing it, and nobody will stop me," asserted Borders. The ordained Baptist minister does not separate her two careers. She has always thought of her medical practice as a ministry—healing, teaching, and preaching. She feels that she has been "blessed with many opportunities," and that other blacks who are in a similar position have a responsibility to "help teach, uplift, and inspire and to make changes in the lives of others. You are morally and spiritually obligated to do so."

Borders lives and works in the black community, serving primarily black women, a large percentage who are professionals. She is particularly culturally sensitive to the issues of black women's health: the disparities in health status, health beliefs, health behaviors, and patterns of health service use, as well as the major social and structural factors that impede black women from realizing their full potential. The multiple jeopardies of race, class, and gender oppression create greater stress and thus more illness for black women and other women of color. Borders is acutely aware that to determine the etiology of illness, which may be culturally constructed, she must understand the context of black women's lives when counseling them on appropriate health promotion strategies.[13] Working through her church, social, and civic organizations and through her local black medical society as an officeholder, the moderate Democrat is on the front line battling issues of sexism, racism, and classism. Yet her ultimate calling is caring and healing in a holistic way, taking into account each individual's total physical and social environment.

With the changing health care system, Borders is concerned that the quality of care she gives as a solo practitioner is in jeopardy. "We've had doctors who've had to stop practicing because they can't afford it. Physicians have to deal with so many lawsuits, whether they are justified or not. You can't expect physicians to jeopardize home, savings, et cetera. You can't expect them to continue to keep their door open to people who can't afford to pay or won't pay, or insurance companies who will only pay one-third. The government will not allow us to claim deductions for money we can't collect, so we are doing charitable work. Some physicians do not think it is worth being under the economic stress, so they are going into real estate, computer science, and the restaurant business."

William Harper, Clinton Warner, and Juel Pate Borders, who entered the field of medicine during legal segregation, came from relatively privileged social backgrounds. The rhythm of the World War I and World War II generations' ethos expected doctors, despite upbringing, to sing and dance to the collective tune of uplifting the race. They were trained as primary health care givers to serve privileged and poor blacks alike, providing services at below cost or at no cost to indigents. They were also expected to be leaders. As Carter G. Woodson noted, black physicians' education and relative wealth gave them a pivotal economic and political role in the black community.[14] This was where they mostly lived and socialized, practiced medicine, and attended patients in black hospitals or segregated wards at white hospitals. By 1947 approximately 15 percent of all black physicians were graduates of white medical colleges.[15] Upon becoming doctors, they joined the NMA. Before 1960 black doctors were excluded from the American Medical Association and its affiliated bodies. To belong to the national chapter, blacks had to be members of a local white chapter, which excluded them. In the 1960s this policy was reversed.

HEALING IN AN INTEGRATED SOCIETY

A bevy of barriers in the medical system came tumbling down in the 1960s. White medical schools and hospitals previously closed to blacks were desegregated. By 1969 an increase in the number of black medical students enrolled in white colleges was evident, although Howard and Meharry continued to enroll over 61 percent of all black students.[16] In the late 1960s, more women also entered medicine; for example, when Minnie Stiff, pediatrician, graduated from Howard University Medical School in 1972, only 10 percent of her class were women. Her daughter, Leslie Renai Stiff Jones, an ophthalmologist, completed her medical degree in 1996 in a graduating class of 50 percent men and

50 percent women. The percent of first professional degrees awarded in medicine in 1993–1994 by race and sex shows that of the 923 blacks who received their degrees, 42.4 percent (391) were males and 57.6 percent (532) were females.[17] Although more blacks than whites are primary care specialists and general practitioners, a larger number began to specialize in the late 1960s.

In addition to more men and women of color and white women entering the medical profession, many other changes have occurred in the medical system that have impacted the quality and quantity of health care delivery for the black community and black doctors. The passage of Medicaid and Medicare legislation in the mid-1960s marked a turning point in health care delivery. And in the late 1980s, we observed the emergence of managed care, the loss of physicians' autonomy in the medical profession, and the shift from a patient-oriented approach to a profit-oriented approach, as well as an impending ethical crisis. In this context, I asked: Have these changes affected the values and behaviors of black doctors who entered the profession since the 1960s in relation to the ideology of uplift, reform, and liberation? If so, how have they changed? Do black doctors who graduated from historically black schools differ in commitment compared to those who attended white medical schools? Are there generational differences among those who were educated in or have worked in white milieus? Are there differences in the collective ethos versus individual ethos by class and family socialization?

Robert S. Rhodes: Opening New Frontiers for Collective Empowerment

Not only can Robert S. Rhodes bear witness to the many social shifts in the larger society and in the medical system, he can also testify to their impact on attitudes, values, and behaviors. For example, when Robert Rhodes, regional director of health services for General Motors Corporation, Eastern USA, and past president of the American College of Occupational and Environmental Medicine, was born in 1936 in segregated Orangeburg, South Carolina, his life chances of attaining his present status in white America were nil. Despite his lack of opportunities in a segregated era, his parents, teachers, and neighbors told him that "one day segregation was going to end, because it was illegal and morally wrong." Accordingly, they instructed him to "be prepared for the day when that would happen." He said, "You had to learn to speak well, to have command of the English language, and to present yourself well. I was always taught from childhood that no one in the world was better than I was, whether they were white or black. A person's skin color made no difference in whether you could achieve. But because I was an African American, I was going to have to be better than everybody else."

Notwithstanding the civil rights movement that broadened his opportunities in the mainstream, his social upbringing in the black community would have placed him at the top of its socioeconomic ladder. Traditional research supports that more physicians have come from upper-middle-class family backgrounds and tend to be more politically conservative. Moreover, the literature shows that the importance of family socialization plays a key role in the entry to the field. If professionals in the family are physicians, they can offer counsel and guidance throughout the long process of medical training. Aubrey Bonnett and Frank Douglas note three consequences: "One is the perpetuation of medicine as an upper-middle-class occupation with intergenerational links; second is the possible intergenerational continuity in the basic conservatism of the members of the profession at large; and third is the unlikelihood that many lower-class black children can seriously think about a medical career at an early age."[18] Considering that doctors in general have conservative outlooks, I wondered if black doctors who practice in white milieus, despite their age or class, differ in orientation toward service and collective uplift of the black community from those who practice within the community? If so, what are the larger implications for the health welfare of the black community? Perhaps the life history of Rhodes can offer some insights.

Growing up on the campus of South Carolina State College (now South Carolina State University), Rhodes was intellectually, emotionally, and spiritually nourished in a controlled milieu by extended-family members who were illustrious alumni and affiliates of the college and by a caring community of teachers and friends. His father, a chief steward and purchaser in the boarding department of South Carolina State College and an ordained Baptist minister, and his mother, a primary school teacher in the demonstration school at South Carolina State (which he attended), imbued him with a love of learning and the importance of education. His teachers reinforced these traits. His strict religious training—Baptist and Church of God—gave him a strong moral and spiritual foundation. "I walked away with a set of values in knowing right from wrong, knowing how to treat one's fellow man and knowing the value of love."

His father was the epitome of "doing good" and "knowing how to treat your fellow man." Rhodes said, "My father was the person that people turned to in our community if they had problems. I can remember many days that he gave up a bed at our house for a family of farmers that were broken down in town en route between Florida and New York and had no way to get there." His father, whose college degree was in auto mechanics, would fix their car, give them money, and send them on their way after a meal and a place to stay. When his father died, the title of his eulogy was "The Selfless Man." "He literally gave up almost everything in the world for people. It had a real impact

on me, so much so that if I had to point to anything that probably unconsciously made me not really turned on to the idea of being in medicine to
make money [it] was probably because of that influence," says Rhodes.

After graduating from high school, Rhodes yearned to become an architect,
but blacks could not earn a decent living at such an occupation in that era, so
he chose medicine. He completed his undergraduate degree in biology from
South Carolina State College and was commissioned simultaneously in the
U.S. Army. Like his uncle and brother, Rhodes chose Meharry Medical College and graduated from there in 1962. He completed an internship and a residency in pathology at Meharry from 1963 to 1967, and then left for active
duty in the army. He served as a medical officer in the United States Army
Medical Corps from 1967 to 1970, where he worked as an army aviation medical officer and aerospace pathologist. He also served as a researcher and as an
instructor in aviation medicine at the Armed Forces Institute of Pathology in
Washington, D.C., and at Fort Rucker, Alabama. He then left the army and
completed a fellowship in internal medicine and hematology, concentrating in
clinical hematology, laboratory work, and the blood bank at Vanderbilt University in Nashville. The fellowship, designed to increase the number of
African American physicians in academic medicine, gave him a chance to do
research on various blood disorders like sickle cell anemia. He returned to
Meharry as professor of internal medicine and pathology to head the hematology section in the Department of Internal Medicine, where he was involved in
developing a sickle cell disease research center at Meharry and a community
screening program. In that position, he initiated other innovative operations,
including the first presurgery donations of blood by patients in the 1970s.

After many years in academic medicine in hematology, and brief stints in
private practice in small towns in Tennessee and Baltimore, Maryland, he
switched to public health and occupational medicine. "I had an interest in this
area for many years, and it was an opportunity to do something different in
medicine. I have always been more challenged by doing things I found appealing to me, rather than just doing it with a purely financial motive in mind,"
Rhodes professed. After he was hired by General Motors as an occupational
physician, he did further study at the University of Cincinnati in occupational
medicine. Eventually, he obtained a master's degree in public health from the
University of Michigan. Rhodes progressed from an associate medical director to director of occupational medical services, with responsibility for all
health and safety activities for his division. In the meantime, he became very
active in the Michigan Occupational and Environmental Medicine Association
and eventually became its president. After serving on the board of directors of
the American College of Occupational and Environmental Medicine
(ACOEM), he was elected to its presidency in 1997.

Rhodes's medical career path has taken him in many directions: academic medicine, the armed services, corporate medicine, and private practice. While his interests have embraced larger issues of health and safety, education, and ergonomics that affect all workers in industries, his commitment or interest in matters affecting black communities has not diminished. He sees these issues as linked with the larger issues of health care, education, and economics in black communities. This is also his reason for maintaining membership in the NMA, because he can best advocate for blacks' collective health care issues through this organization. Rhodes believes that access to health care parallels the level of health problems in the community and is related to socioeconomic status. "If you practice in the inner city, the bulk of your patients are poor folks, and the bulk of black folks in this country are not wealthy people. And poor folks tend to get less health care in this country," argued Rhodes. "Because of the devastating effects on the black community, the NMA is unduly supportive of efforts to make significant changes in the health care system of this country." He thinks transformations in the quality and quantity of health care can begin with the removal of socioeconomic barriers, providing greater access to health care, and educating the public about prevention, diagnosis, and treatment of disease.

Even though a significant number of blacks have access to health care through Medicare and Medicaid, the quality of health care is uneven. White doctors may consciously or unconsciously hold negative stereotypes and expectations of black patients that affect outcomes. "The motivation on behalf of the patient by the physician providing the care, as well as the supporting structure in the hospital, is not always the same for an African American patient as it is for a white patient. The decision [by the doctor] to go the extra mile is often a personal decision," said Rhodes. He pointed out that, if a patient with high blood pressure had a stroke and survived it, the recovery of the patient is impacted by the extensive support of concerned professional staff members who motivate the individual towards rehabilitation. "If the physician has higher expectations and values a person's life as worthwhile, that person may recover all of his faculties and return to a completely normal life with almost no discernible difference in his quality of life. On the other hand, that same person who doesn't receive the attention and motivation of the physician and other staff may find himself disabled." While not castigating all white physicians, he believes that black physicians will have a greater interest in their black patients. This quality of care by race extends to both diagnoses and treatments alike. Several studies support Rhodes's claim of discrepancy between the quality of health care given to blacks and whites, including a major study published in *The New England Journal of Medicine*. In this study, black patients with heart disease were diagnosed and treated differently from white patients, that is, they were less likely to be referred for cardiac catheterization as an alternative treatment to manage chest pain. Another research investigation showed that black patients are more likely to be diagnosed and labeled with more serious mental disorders.[19] In treatment hypertension provides a good example of differences in the response of African Americans and other ethnic groups to health therapeutic modalities. Rhodes indicated that blacks tend to respond better to certain classes of drugs than others in the treatment of high blood pressure. "So people have to know these differences. I have seen [black] people going to white doctors, and they have them on medicine for white folks so they can control the blood pressure, but they didn't control the complications," he asserted. The white male as research model is a concern to him, because medicines prescribed to white women and men and women of color are based solely on a middle-aged, white male paradigm.[20] "Many major studies simply threw out data that came from black males and females and white females because there weren't enough of them to make a statistical difference," claimed Rhodes. While Howard and Meharry medical schools have addressed these issues for many years, as more blacks enter majority institutions, they are also beginning to have a discourse around these concerns.

Frank Russo [Pseudonym]:
In Harmony with Personal and Collective Empowerment

As a public health administrator, Frank Russo deals with such issues as the disparities in access, education and prevention, diagnoses, treatment, and cure in the public health care system. Since he entered the field of medicine, Russo has been acutely aware of these disparities in the health system. This physician and state health administrator was a direct beneficiary of the civil rights movement in the 1960s and its generation of doctors, like Warner, who filed suits and dodged bullets to erase the color line in the field of medicine. Without the movement, his life chances of being the first of two blacks to be admitted to a white public medical college in the South or to specialize in pathology, let alone being a CEO of a state health organization, were nil. He was born in 1943 and grew up in a working-class household in a small town in middle Georgia. He did not have an even chance to matriculate at Howard University Medical School or Meharry Medical College. His father, a menial civil service employee with a grade school education, worked at an air force base, and his mother, a basket weaver with a sixth-grade education, worked in a mill. Bonnett and Douglas conducted a pilot study in the early 1980s of the occupations of fathers of black students matriculating at medical colleges in the Northeast. They found that 35 percent of black medical students in their sample had fathers who were professionals or business owners, managers, or administrators, and 37 percent of the students' fathers were categorized as craftsman, operative, and unskilled.[21]

Although historical circumstances combined with Russo's personal history to create his chances of becoming a doctor, what social forces impelled him to reach for goals beyond his humble beginnings? Russo's parents created a nurturing and supportive spiritual milieu for "learning and building positive self-esteem" for Russo and his siblings. This was reinforced by his maternal aunts and uncles. In the 1950s in a small Southern town, the community was an extension of the family. It was the expectation for teachers to motivate and push their students. They had especially high hopes for Russo. Sports also played a significant role during his formative years in "promoting discipline and teamwork." Participating in sports also had an unexpected consequence of aiding him in fighting the color line, which had begun to alter in his adolescence. When he was younger, he was "afraid to go to town because older white teenage boys or adults would jump on you." Emulating the aggressive role of sports as a coping strategy helped him physically, as well as boosted his confidence to choose fight over flight. With the wheel of fear turning on the axis of anger, he searched for an altercation with white youths to test and defend black manhood against white manhood.

Although his parents rarely discussed race, Russo absorbed the atmosphere of black inferiority, subordination, and disrespect. Observing how black people, the heads of their households, were treated in their menial jobs, particularly the treatment of elderly black men by young white boys of thirteen or fourteen years, made an impact on him. Their passive response he understood, but he was angered by their plight. From his elders, he learned early "the valuable lesson of having options and being economically independent." While dating a young woman who baby-sat for two white doctors, he caught a glimpse of "their lifestyle and their sense of independence." He visualized being a doctor as an option for himself, resolving that it did not matter how hard he had to work, at least he could set his "own hours and not have to answer to anyone." Education would provide that option for Russo, who attended black institutions through graduate school. The money for his education came primarily from work and combined work/scholarship, along with the paltry sum of three hundred dollars contributed by his parents to his total postsecondary education.

After receiving his undergraduate degree in biology and master's in physiology, he was the first of two blacks admitted to a medical college in Georgia. Fortunately, he had the support of the dean of his medical school, which was the one bright spot that loomed over the lonely dark path to success. He could have exercised his option of flight, but he chose to fight the everyday overt racism of faculty and students. The onslaught of everyday racism was taxing on his psyche and affected his studies. On the other hand, he realized that the president of his black alma mater, the medical school dean, and his friends and relatives were telling him he was representing his black college and its community. "So, I didn't have a choice but to do well," he declared.

He turned to his mother for spiritual comfort from the racial assaults and financial woes that assailed him. While in medical school, his personal condition became a vehicle for social change to create greater options for others. "I was hell-bent on changing things in medical school. When they didn't recruit any black students in the next class, I went to the local newspaper and published articles and had them quote me about their [poor] treatment of black patients," said Russo. When he complained about the admissions committee, he was also appointed to it. Russo proved to be the change agent and a race ambassador by proving that he could succeed and open doors for other blacks.

After leaving medical school, Russo served as a general medical officer in the U.S. Air Force for two years in Germany before entering an intern program in pathology in Texas. He spent four years training in his speciality in pathology at a primarily white university in the South before he became a state commissioner of public health, directing the public medical laboratory and community health section. He was also a doctor for the state's Department of Corrections.

While Russo's major aim is to work toward a collective goal of improved public health for all citizens of his state, he is sensitive to the needs of poor black constituents who are overly represented in the system. He advocates for qualified black medical directors who can meet their needs. His efforts are often undermined by "racist medical policies and practices," and he is constantly fighting them. Married with two children, the liberal independent knows it is in his personal and collective interest to remain steadfast in challenging the color line, whether in the local or national medical societies or on medical boards. With racism so rampant, Russo sees black collectivity as a means of survival, and he feels that blacks with greater resources have a special obligation to empower others. "As a minority that does not have control, we always represent each other, and to some extent we cannot get away from each other. Therefore, we have an obligation first to ourselves and then to others. I don't think the two are incompatible."

Colbert Miller [Pseudonym]:
In Conflict with Personal and Collective Empowerment

Unlike Russo, Colbert Miller does not feel blacks have an obligation to uplift. But he believes they should support the collective effort for personal gains. Miller is also from a working-class background and a beneficiary of the civil rights movement. Like Russo, he was educated in black schools from elementary school through college. With a biology degree in hand, he attended a white, private medical college in the South as one of its first blacks. Miller continued his specialty in internal medicine at the same university. After spending two years in the army, he received a fellowship in cardiology and went into private practice in 1980. In contrast, Russo chose public service. What influences might account for their different orientations?

Colbert Miller, born in 1946 in a rural county in the South, was influenced by his father, a mom-and-pop restaurant owner with a grade-school education, and his mother, a domestic worker, also with only a grade-school education. They held high aspirations for their son and instilled in him a strong work ethic, a sense of commitment to personal goals, and a belief that he could achieve them. The message he heard from his parents was, "You are better than everybody else, and you can do what you want to do. I am not going to tell you what you cannot achieve. We might not be rich, but we'll find a way to get you what you want." Hearing their echoes of self-belief was self-fulfilling for Miller, despite the fact that he lacked professional black role models like lawyers and doctors to emulate. With his parents' encouragement that he could achieve anything he wanted, he expanded his horizons about the realities of those possibilities in his physically isolated rural community through reading.

Although his world was severely constrained by race, class, and geography in the rural South of the 1950s, Miller dreamed of becoming the president of a company. When he told his teacher about his aspiration, she could not visualize that possibility and discouraged him. Her response was, "Unless you were born into a company of presidents, you'll never become one." He answered, "I'll be a doctor."

Like many of Miller's generation, the civil rights movement and the black power movement had a profound impact on the chances of a life dream becoming reality. Miller's dream was to become a successful doctor. He had the option of attending Howard University for his medical schooling but chose a white medical school instead to give himself a chance to compete in the white world. "It came to me at the last minute that if I were going to work in this world, I needed to think like the white man, know how he plays his game, and know how he deals with business," said Miller. Playing the game successfully in medical school involved learning the rules. For Miller, it meant one of two ways: being independent and learning to study on his own or "playing like you were white." He and the other three black medical students devised means to beat the system. "We decided that we would join a fraternity and [one of us would] become the secretary to get all the files [laugh] and the old tests that the white boys or Jews passed along. We became white and assimilated to play the games the way [whites] played them. I joined a Jewish fraternity, became secretary, and had all the files. I copied them and passed them on to other blacks," claimed Miller.

Miller learned, much to his chagrin, that playing white is not equal to being white. When he completed his medical school training in cardiology, job opportunities did not await him. "You see, one of the things about training in a predominantly white program is the lack of opportunities. Your white colleagues get offers to go all over the country, but your choices are very limited to nonexistent," he noted. Rejecting "a last minute" offer of a professorship at Howard University in 1980, he opted to go into private practice. Since few blacks were in the practice of cardiology and many white doctors did not want to go into practice with a black doctor, he set up a solo practice. Despite the rejection, he continued to play the assimilation game and chose a white business manager and a white lawyer to assist him in setting up his business and in obtaining a bank loan of $150,000.

His successful downtown practice in a thriving Southern metropolis has a patient load of 30 percent blacks and 70 percent whites, of which 80 to 85 percent are referrals. Miller obtains white patients through lecturing and involving himself in medical politics and black patients by supporting the black hospital and organizations. He practices at six hospitals, but most of his black patients are at a black hospital. Miller castigates black doctors who refuse to practice at the black hospital in his city. Such hospitals were the primary source of black care before the 1960s. According to one authority, "more than four hundred hospitals have been identified during the twentieth century as having been established by black and white founders to serve a black population."[22] When integration occurred, along with the advent of Medicare and Medicaid programs, black doctors and patients had greater options, and the already marginal hospitals suffered economically and disappeared from major cities. Today less than three traditionally black hospitals still exist. Most of Miller's patients, black and white, are middle class; he has a few Medicare and Medicaid patients. By having middle-class patients he has a more profitable business.

A political independent, Miller, who is married with three children, is ambivalent about his and other more privileged blacks' obligation to the less privileged. "I don't think successful blacks have an obligation to help others, although they should. Successful blacks work hard to achieve, and other blacks should go to school and work hard and achieve. *You* can't tell me I *should* give to the NAACP. If *you* tell me that, I'll tell you to go to hell, but I think I *should*. I am a life member," he said. Though he feels the majority of professional blacks are concerned with their own advancement, he believes they also should be concerned about uplift, reform, and liberation of the poor solely out of a sense of personal expediency. "If I go higher on the totem pole, not only am I going to have to worry about the white man doing it to you, but if I am leaving you behind, then I got to worry about you doing it to me. So if I'm moving, I got to worry about your coming too. Because if I am not, I will be isolated, and the white man will be 'shorting' me."

Mary Louise Patterson:
Bearing the Collective Responsibility and Empowerment

In contrast to Colbert Miller, Mary Louise Patterson, the daughter of Louise Thompson Patterson, would probably not say the "white man is shorting me." Her ethic, ideologically and behaviorally, is clearly a collective one. She believes like Frank Russo that blacks have the responsibility and obligation to help one another. Her strong service orientation is also reminiscent of Juel Pate Borders's. The two women are alike in some ways and different in others. Both Borders and Patterson come from prominent, educated families. Notwithstanding the contrast in their social upbringing, it still led them to a collective ethic. Borders comes from a Christian religious background, while Patterson was reared in a politically oriented family whose functional equivalent was communism. On the one hand, Borders was educated in the segregated South of the 1940s and 1950s and studied medicine at a women's medical college under a capitalist economy. When Juel Pate Borders entered the medical profession in the 1960s, few women were in medical school in the United States, although women started to increase their entry by the early 1970s. On the other hand, Patterson was reared and educated in the 1940s and 1950s in an integrated setting in the Northeast and did further study under a socialist economy in Cuba and in Russia, where she obtained a medical degree from Patrice Lumumba University in the former Soviet Union in the 1960s. In Moscow, numerous women were studying to become doctors. Unlike Borders, who has a solo private practice serving black female patients, Patterson, in a private partnership with ethnically diverse doctors, serves children from different backgrounds.

In spite of their disparate social backgrounds, Borders and Patterson are both grounded in a philosophy of service to others. While Borders's belief system is more religious—she feels her destiny is determined by God—Patterson can be described as a humanist; she said: "I do not believe in a superior being that has determined our destiny for us. I believe we are responsible to ourselves, our children, and their children. We are responsible for the planet and other living things on it. It is a philosophy of peaceful co-existence. Everyone should live in peace and harmony and the absence of oppression and discrimination of any kind, with the ability of each individual to develop himself or herself to the maximum potential and to have all basic needs for sustaining life met. We must respect each individual for what they can contribute as human beings. We must learn from the past and pick up the mantle of those who have gone before us in the struggle for liberation. That kind of dedication and commitment to others is what the purpose of life should be!"

While Borders is committed to serving women, Patterson, a pediatrician, is dedicated to healing children. Born in Chicago in 1943, Patterson grew up in Brooklyn, New York, in a predominantly Jewish neighborhood. Patterson's father, a lawyer and social activist, and her mother, a teacher, social worker, and union organizer, encouraged their only child to be "committed to the struggle for black liberation." Since her parents were social activists, success was measured for them not as an objective status, but rather as "assuming leadership positions of responsibility and involvement in the community." She said, "My parents never discussed the problems of blacks in terms of making it if you are talking economically. We talked in terms of sociopolitical problems of blacks and racism and class oppression. There was a need for me to side with those who were oppressed." In addition to her parents, their friends, who were artists, intellectuals, and political activists, also influenced Patterson by the examples of their lives.

Through her medical career, Patterson has chosen to continue the battle to improve the welfare of the black community and all poor and oppressed people, particularly children. "In an era where affirmative action, civil rights, unions, working people, and women are under attack, and where too much emphasis on greed causes abandonment of education, lack of recreation for youth, homelessness, unemployment, and elderly neglect, the confluence of issues is an imposing struggle," asserted Patterson. She upholds the belief that "all blacks have a responsibility and obligation to help each other and have a commitment to the struggle." For the civil rights generation, who share an ethic of expressive individualism, her message is: "Success in the American society is meaningless and often self-destructive. It is not committing oneself to a development of a people. Self-aggrandizement and self-indulgence is a very empty kind of existence. That is not making it. It is a false dream. It is a nightmare." For Patterson, success in this society means extending oneself beyond one's own individualism and identifying with the collective oppression of others. Now living in New York, Patterson, married with three adult children, continues to identify with oppressed groups and to take up the banner of her parents' struggle through her community health programs and as an officeholder and member of numerous medical associations.

Mary Louise Patterson, like many doctors of her generation and those of the World War I generation, is concerned that the traditional culture's collective ethic of service, the credo of extending oneself beyond one's own individualism and embracing black uplift, reform, and liberation, is less important to doctors in the civil rights generation. This value alteration is reflected not only in their medical practice, but also in their lack of leadership in black communities.

Lind Chinnery: The Challenges of Continuing the Service Tradition

Lind Chinnery, born in the late 1950s, is in accord with the sentiments of his predecessors. He postulates that the objectives of doctors of previous generations were more humanitarian than pecuniary. "They went into this particular profession for very noble reasons, and they wanted to help mankind. They had all these dreams about doing the right thing, stamping out disease and pestilence, and wanting to improve the value of life and happiness. I don't think the reason they went into it was so much monetary. Our society has slowly evolved into a less morally conscious society and into a more political society. So right now it's going to involve dollars and cents with the new generation—the 'New Jack.'"

"I don't consider myself a New Jack. I'm more of the baby boomer type," said Chinnery, an internist, who was born in St. Thomas, Virgin Islands. While growing up, he moved back and forth between St. Thomas and New York City. What influences affected his personal success and social consciousness? It was his father, a small-restaurant owner with a high school education, who instilled in Chinnery the importance of education. He encouraged his son to pursue science rather than music, so he could earn a living. After graduating from the historically black Virginia State University, Chinnery taught high school science before matriculating at Meharry Medical College in 1978. He graduated in 1982 and completed an internship and a residency at George Washington University. He then entered the medical profession in 1985 as an internist in primary care.

Chinnery believes the process of his medical socialization at a black medical college was critical in affecting his social consciousness and the way he practices medicine. He feels strongly, too, that despite the value change to a more individualistic ethic among black doctors of the civil rights generation, differences still exist between those doctors who trained at black medical schools and those who trained at white ones. "[In] black schools I think there's more camaraderie among physicians. I think there's more dedication to the race, more dedication to their particular population." In addition, he thinks the role of technology plays a key part in the socialization process in patients' care. "I think black doctors from black schools are better clinicians when it comes to being able to look at someone and diagnose them than those who came from white schools. They may not be as sound theoretically, because they have to work with less equipment and deal more with intuition, more sensing, more seeing and touching. They may not have had access to a CAT scan or lots of technology, so the clinical diagnosis is what they depend on," asserted Chinnery.

In fact, Chinnery, along with others I interviewed, attributes some of these differences to a more humanistic tradition of black medical schools. Similarly, Robert Rhodes, whom we met earlier, noted such differences when he taught at the medical schools of Vanderbilt and Meharry in the 1970s. "In the years that I taught at Vanderbilt, the educational background of, say, over half the students at Meharry—even though most of them had a science background—tended to have much more of a liberal arts bent to it. One of the feelings expressed at Meharry was the need to combine academic skills in both science and the humanities, as well as in English. The combination of skills made a good physician and developed a certain spirit of humaneness in the individual." According to Chinnery, this tradition may have waned over the years, but it is still evident. In addition to his medical socialization, "watching the civil rights movement and watching the 1970s with all the flower power" influenced Chinnery's collective ethic of giving back to the community. "We were more for going out there, fighting for rights and justice," he asserted.

Having his social consciousness raised by the black power movement and honed by his medical socialization, he sees himself in striking contrast to the younger age cohort of his generation, those born in the late 1960s and 1970s. "The guys a little after me—those in their early thirties—are of the same mentality. But the ones now—those between twenty-six and thirty—still in training and getting ready to come out, have a whole different attitude. They want to know, 'What can you do for me?' They were born into a situation where the struggle had already materialized. It's not only that they don't have the commitment of the older ones; we had different training in school. When we were in medical school, it was all about science and medicine. Nobody told you [that] you were going to have to be a businessman and know about contracts and all of this. We never had any financial classes or management. The new doctors are getting some courses in financial management and different things aside from pure medicine. They're not going into the specific parts of medicine for anything but monetary gain, so if they say, 'I'm going into training,' they are not going into it for any reason to help anybody. Theirs is about what's the best thing for me that I can make a living on without having to work as hard. That's why I see a lot of the primary care slots not being taken, because people are not going into primary care. It's a big problem."

Craig Appleton [Pseudonym]: What's in It for Me?

The dearth of primary care doctors may pose a collective concern for our health system. But it is no big problem for Craig Appleton, whom Chinnery would probably call a "New Jack." Appleton, who was born in the early 1970s and admitted to medical school at age twenty, was strikingly candid enough to say he chose radiology as a speciality in medicine because of its lucrativeness and for the maintenance of regular hours. "My goals are no different from most doctors my age: most of us do not want to be in primary care," he acknowledged. Such an attitude is not surprising for Joy Robinson, an ophthalmologist. She was also born in the civil rights generation but completed her medical training at Howard University a decade apart from Appleton, in the 1980s. Noting that the medical graduates in the 1990s are very different from her own age cohort, she conceded that this later cohort is "more selfish and money-oriented. It has a 'me-first' attitude. When residents are given night calls, they make excuses or call in sick. It was unheard of when I was in training. They are more rebellious and are not accepting of things in the past."

Doing something strictly for humanitarian motivation is a lofty ideal. However, it has never been part of Appleton's consciousness. While he was growing up in a predominantly white upper-middle-class community in the Midwest, his parents taught him "to first look out for self, not others." His father, a general surgeon, and his mother, a corporate manager, always encouraged economic independence and self-sufficiency, and they stressed that if he worked hard, he could overcome any barriers, including race, which was deemphasized in his home. He thought of himself as an American first and that meant "having money, material success, and prosperity."

Since Appleton, who practices at a major white suburban hospital, was educated in white institutions from primary grades through medical school, his contact with other blacks was practically nonexistent. At his premier medical school in the Northeast, his medical socialization differed considerably from Chinnery's. His training was characterized more by "cut-throat competition than camaraderie between students." One study has documented that students' attitudes and values change over the course of their medical socialization. They alter from "idealistic, humanistic, and compassionate to hedonistic, cynical, and judgmental"[23] as a result of the competitive, compulsive, and depersonalized milieu of their training. Certainly, this competitive socialization has been exacerbated by the emergence of the medical industry as a major business over the past thirty years and the incorporation of a business ethic into students' training. In addition, changes in the funding of medical education occurred in the 1980s. Accordingly, the majority of students are forced to take out mammoth loans. They leave medical school heavily indebted. When

I spoke to Olanrewa Adeyiga, a professor of medicine at Howard University, about the cost of medical school and its impact on students, he indicated it is "like going to jail. With the guaranteed loans from the government, you are mortgaging your life. So students want to know if they are going to make money." The increasing focus on the costs and benefits of medical school becomes a decisive factor in influencing students' speciality choices, which contributes to the declining low-earning speciality of primary care. It is the reason why Appleton chose radiology.

Not having a connection to a black community, Appleton never felt a shared collective consciousness that giving back was a part of his social responsibility. "I have a responsibility to myself, to be the best I can and help myself. Although my parents helped me with my medical training, I have loans to pay off. The whole medical field is changing. It is a big business, and like any business [person], I want to maximize my profit," claimed Appleton.

Indeed, as Craig Appleton exhorts, the medical institution is undergoing major transitions. In *The McDonaldization of Society*, George Ritzer offers the perspective that medicine, like many other domains in society, is increasingly adopting the paradigm of McDonald's. The fast food chain is a model of efficiency, quantification and calculation, predictability, and "control, especially through the substitution of nonhuman for human technology."[24] Some factors contributing to McDonaldization are: the rise of investor-owned corporations, like Columbia/HCA, which is interested in medicine as a for-profit enterprise; the increase in managed-care organizations, such as HMOs and PPOs; the push by federal government and private insurance companies to cut costs; the increasing competition in the medical marketplace, highlighted in part by the oversupply of doctors in specialties; and the increasing specialization and advanced technologies in medicine. The introduction of managed-care groups, for example, raises portentous new issues about the quality of health care for the black community, as well as questions about the impact of managed-care regulations and stipulations for patient treatment and for the survival of black doctors.

Many doctors see their autonomy slipping away with respect to making the best decisions for their patients, because they must be concerned about utilization and cost containment. "It forces you to ration care you give to patients, which impacts the quality of care. It also increases the fragmentation and impacts people with minimal resources. Poor women must go to a certain clinic for lab work, despite lack of transportation or a babysitter," says Olanrewa Adeyiga, who graduated from Howard University Medical School in 1979 and who teaches obstetrics and gynecology at his alma mater, as well as practices medicine in Washington, D.C. The managed-care organizations also contract with a select network of doctors, hospitals, or other types of health care providers. One of the many effects of this new phenomenon has been the shift from solo practice to partnerships. Doctors in solo practice have found that it is becoming increasingly difficult to continue. Moreover, the selection criteria for joining the networks of doctors, hospitals, and other health care providers in managed-care organizations are negatively impacting them. Board certification becomes a criterion with respect to managed-care organizations selecting doctors, and Lind Chinnery, like many black doctors, asserts "it is used behind the scene to weed out minority doctors." Since black doctors have cared for a disproportionate number of black patients, the overall quality of health care for black communities is imperiled by these emerging changes in the health care system.

5

Black Entrepreneurs:
Mixing Mission with Making Money

There is not much race independence for the race that cannot speak its mind
through men whose capital can help or harm those who would bring oppression.
We need capital to dictate terms. This notion is old enough, but bears repetition.[1]

John Hope, president of Morehouse College in Atlanta, Georgia, spoke those
words at the fourth conference of "The Study of the Negro Problem" held at
Atlanta University in Atlanta, Georgia, in 1899. Joshua I. Smith, former commissioner of Minority Business Development under President George Bush
and CEO, chair, and owner of the Maxima Corporation, agrees that such a
time-tested message bears repeating in the early twenty-first century. Smith
believes like Hope that "economic rights ensure civil rights." Both men view
the creation of wealth through black enterprise and economic development as
paramount to the progress of the race.

While Smith regards material wealth as the key measure of the highest development of a people, Hope sees the moral and spiritual key as preeminent.
He indicated that inasmuch as

this development is dependent on the material foundation, the man who lays that
foundation is as great a benefactor to the race as that man or generation that will,
in the end, present that final gift, which shall yield the rich, ripe fruit of the emotions and the soul—the consummation of those aspirations that look beyond material things to the things that are abiding and eternal. In some such noble form
as this the vocation of the business will present itself to me; and were I a vender
[*sic*] of peanuts or an owner of a mill, I should feel that I, along with preachers
and teachers and the rest of the saints, was doing God's service in the cause of
elevation of my people.[2]

Whether one believes that material or spiritual wealth is the test of the highest development of a group, the historical reality of black enterprise and economic development has been a triumphant and trying experience. Black entrepreneurs of Durham, North Carolina, were an example of such victorious enterprise and economic development at the turn of the twentieth century. Joshua Smith jokingly summed up the contemporary trials and tribulations with this quip: "A minority business person in America died and went to hell and realized it was six months before he found that he was not in his own office." After President Bush appointed Smith as commissioner of Minority Business Development in the late 1980s, Smith held hearings throughout the country on the status of minority business affairs. His conclusions were the same as those reached by Hope at the dawn of the twentieth century. Black businesses are underutilized, and they lack capital, exposure to growth industries, expertise, and market access. Though his committee made recommendations to strengthen the role of minority entrepreneurship, such as promoting international trade and opportunities for minorities and strengthening minority set-asides like the 8(a) Program, they were ignored by President Bush.

Despite black entrepreneurs' continual nightmarish obstacles, they are "in a very real sense, the personification of the American Dream," says Paul Lindsay Johnson.[3] They possess a pioneering spirit and are risk takers, innovators, and leaders. They are energetic as well, working long hours to challenge the system on its own terms and to succeed in overcoming odds as entrepreneurs, as creators of capital, as generators of employment, and as investors in the economic development of black communities. From emancipation to the present, black entrepreneurs in this country have been bound by this tradition across time, milieu, and the cycle of growth and decline. A. Wade Smith and Joan V. Moore viewed the ascent, descent, and renewal of black enterprise in this country as taking place in three cycles.[4] These cycles overlap with the time periods during which entrepreneurs of the World War I generation, World War II generation, and civil rights generation commenced their businesses. The first cycle began roughly around the Civil War and lasted until the end of legal segregation. The second cycle emerged during the post-World War II desegregation. In the third cycle, a new breed of assertive and well-educated black entrepreneurs surfaced after the civil rights movement of the 1960s. These cycles, Smith and Moore noted, are affected by such market dynamics as inflation, energy, science and technology, international interdependence, business management and productivity, and industrial policy. They are also influenced by entrepreneurial effectiveness, which includes "such elements as management and technical skills, market knowledge, capital availability, government policy awareness, cooperative links with government agencies at local, state, regional, and national levels, and a cooperative relationship with the civic, financial, and business community."[5]

ENTREPRENEURSHIP BEHIND SEGREGATED WALLS

In the first cycle, black entrepreneurs seemed less affected by these market dynamics, since their businesses developed behind segregated walls during post-Reconstruction. The political, social, and economic restrictions of that era curtailed black business activities, limiting them to the black consumer market. Despite the forced economic detour to "develop separate enterprises and to sell in a restricted race market,"[6] blacks made significant gains in business, particularly in the South. Such diverse black leaders as Booker T. Washington and W. E. B. Du Bois encouraged self-help and racial pride among blacks and urged them to establish businesses as a way of maintaining freedom and empowerment. In fact, it was Washington who organized the National Negro Business League in 1900. He became its first president and the catalyst that promoted the entrepreneurial missionary spirit.[7] Increasingly, during the World War I era and during the nationalist movements of the 1920s, blacks started their own businesses, largely as sole-owner proprietorships or family-owner proprietorships in service and trade, and in mom-and-pop grocery and retail stores. Myriad businesses evolved out of the slave society. Du Bois argued that the "barber, the caterer . . . the restaurant keeper were the direct progeny of the house servant, just as the market-gardener, the sawmill proprietor, and the florist were descended from the field hand."[8] These sectors of the economy did not compete with whites. Moreover, they required less capital and management expertise. Progress of black businesses was very rapid between 1900 and 1940, cresting to new heights following World War I. Catering to the unmet needs of the community, black businesses developed to serve black consumers, particularly in the areas of personal services and public accommodations. Beauty and barber shops, restaurants and hotels, insurance, banking, and retail stores were types of businesses blacks operated. Some businesses were completely along new lines, though in strictly segregated markets. In the 1920s black businesses expanded, and "banks, insurance companies, real estate agencies, import and export houses, chain stores, steamship lines, stock exchanges for dealing in securities" of African American corporations, and other "wildcat" schemes were conceived to solve economic problems.[9] In the 1930s, however, the entrepreneurial spirit was dampened with the onset of the Depression. Still many black businesses were successful in the era before and during World War II, because segregation served as a protective tariff for black entrepreneurs.

James Paschal: A Fighter for Economic and Civil Rights

James Paschal, Atlanta restaurateur and hotel operator, began his enterprise behind segregated walls, which acted as a protective tariff when he joined in partnership with his brother, Robert, to open a small restaurant in 1947. Working as a Pullman porter, he acquired enough start-up capital and equipment to operate a thirty-seat restaurant that sold sandwiches and sodas. Like most black business owners of that era, he and his brother worked as cooks, janitors, and waiters, along with two helpers. When the Paschal brothers started receiving requests for brunch, they had to prepare it at home. "We didn't have a car, so it had to be brought up by cab." When the brunch became successful, customers inquired about dinner. The brothers rented a house and converted it into a restaurant with a kitchen and additional seating capacity. Since chicken was reasonably priced, it became their specialty and number-one seller. A year after their expansion, the brothers started a catering service, preparing six thousand chickens daily for a local firm. Soon the business outgrew its space, and the brothers needed larger accommodations to expand. In 1959, with financial backing from a black bank and insurance company, they purchased additional property and constructed a restaurant, which included a coffee shop and dining room that could accommodate 225 people. Their labor force expanded from two helpers to forty. Eventually, the restaurant became internationally renowned, especially for its fried chicken. In 1960 they opened a popular modern jazz club on the lower level of the restaurant. Many of the patrons were white. Business was booming, so the Paschal brothers began to negotiate for additional property to build a hotel. In 1967 James and Robert opened the Paschal's Motor Hotel with 120 guest rooms.

What was the driving force behind the pioneering spirit of James Paschal? One of seven children, he was born in a small community in McDuffie County, Georgia, in the early 1900s to hardworking parents. His father, a hotel worker, and his mother, a housewife and domestic, had only grade-school training. They taught him that hard work and self-sufficiency are the road to success. So when his father became ill, Paschal took over his responsibilities at the hotel where he worked and learned how to operate the business. He remembered the hotel's white owner saying to him, "You are going to have a large business of your own." As a child, he was "always interested in business and in knowing how it operates." The encouragement of the hotel owner inspired him to greater achievements.

Indeed the young Paschal was a Horatio Alger, a self-starter who showed entrepreneurial acumen. At the age of twelve, he constructed a number of shoe-shine stands and placed them on street corners. He shined shoes on weekends, along with other young black men whom he hired to assist him.

He also had a paper route and sold beauty products while in high school. When he accumulated sufficient capital, he purchased a grocery business in his community. When the store proved profitable, the black property owners wanted the business for themselves. Since he didn't have a lease, he had to give it up. This did not dishearten the adolescent, who took comfort in the success of his previous businesses. While one door of opportunity closed, another one opened. The black owner of a local funeral home was so impressed by Paschal's energy and willingness to work that he constructed a building for Paschal's business that was more spacious than the previous building. "We were able to sell groceries and sandwiches and provide a place for dancing. We had slot and race machines, which helped generate revenue." Although race constrained the location and clientele of Paschal's business, it did not confine his vision. "We were living in a segregated society at the time, and there were laws one should respect. But as far as my thinking, I had no limits. I always looked forward," he noted.

After graduating from his segregated high school in the 1930s, Paschal went into the army. Upon his discharge in 1944, he moved to Atlanta. He wanted to continue his entrepreneurship but was unable to obtain equipment and start-up capital. To earn a living, he worked with the Pullman Company in New York and traveled from coast to coast. This gave him the opportunity to observe a variety of businesses. He was especially interested in "operating a hospitality industry—a hotel and other related businesses." No doubt his interest heightened because during his coast-to-coast travel he found no room in the inn for black Pullman porters in the 1940s. Being a Pullman porter was not, however, his calling. "Business was in my system. I wasn't satisfied until I came back into it again," Paschal said. "Back in 1947 when we opened our restaurant, our investment was $500. We tried our black institutions, and they said we couldn't make money. We were able to have $5,000 financed through another corporation. When we returned later to the same black institutions that denied us, we were able to do the remainder of our financing through them. It was pretty difficult fifty or more years ago to borrow $100,000 unless you had a projected income." With patience, dedication, and hard work, he and his brother carefully built upon each success.

Although Paschal, a moderate Democrat, is a bottom-line, profit-oriented businessman, he has an ardent social consciousness. As a player behind the scenes, he became a formidable supporter of the civil rights movement. Paschal's Motor Hotel and Restaurant was a regular meeting place for Martin Luther King, Jr., David Abernathy, Joseph Lowery, Andrew Young, Hosea Williams, and other civil rights leaders. "One of the bloodiest marches in Alabama was planned here," Paschal noted. He and his brother gave support to the student demonstrators in the early 1960s, offering bail money and food. The restaurant's reputation as a place where people could plan strategies for civil rights and politics was the result of segregation. It was the one place black leaders could meet in Atlanta.

Paschal's Motor Hotel and Restaurant remained a comfortable tradition until the mid-1990s. James Paschal remarked that since the civil rights movement, "things have not changed that much. All the leaders still meet at Paschal's in the morning." The restaurant has been dubbed "the place where morning politics get started." It has been frequently stated that "when election time comes, any politicians who don't meet at Paschal's in the morning can rest assured that they won't be elected." It was a political center, where candidates have included council members, mayors, governors, and even former president Jimmy Carter.

Paschal and his brother gained and lost as a result of the civil rights movement. Once blacks could eat and sleep anywhere by law, they lost some black clientele. While losing some customers, James Paschal acknowledged that expanding opportunities in a larger market also brought more diverse customers. As business ventures diversified and enlarged in the 1970s, Paschal, too, was able to benefit from his support of the civil rights movement and move beyond the segregated economic walls. When more blacks gained political power, such as former mayor Maynard Jackson in the 1970s, they fought to have greater participation by minority businesses in city contracts. In 1978 James and his brother formed a joint venture with the Dobbs House in Memphis, Tennessee. The Paschal brothers submitted a bid to the city of Atlanta to service principal concessions at the Atlanta airport. "We were the highest bidders. We won the contract," he said. "Since then, we have been serving as a principal concessionaire. That started the Dobbs-Paschal Mid Field Corporation, which controls all retail outlets at the terminal. We have another corporation—Paschal's Concessions, Incorporated. We also operate a number of vendors at the terminal, separate from the concession." His enterprises at the airport cater to an international clientele. He concluded the story of his successful operation by noting, "Our plans are now to do another one hundred room hotel in our parking area."

Perhaps time will not allow for the execution of those blueprints. Gail H. Towns reported in *Black Issues in Higher Education*, "In one transaction, Clark Atlanta University has acquired a legendary black business, a new dormitory and a world-class chicken recipe. Paschal's Motor Hotel and Restaurant, an establishment elevated to folklore status in many circles because of its role as the birthplace of civil rights strategies that changed the nation, has been purchased by the university for $3 million."[10] For Paschal, business and economic development means the political, social, and educational uplift of the community. He remarked, "We just feel that we should make a contribution. There is nothing that gives us greater satisfaction than to help."

The Paschal brothers sold their business to Clark Atlanta University in 1996. Robert Paschal, who worked in the restaurant's kitchen for over fifty years, retired that same year and died in early 1997. While Robert preferred working in the kitchen, James, married with one adult daughter, always enjoyed the administrative aspects of the work. At the time of the interview, the energetic and youthful-looking septuagenarian continues to work "twelve to fourteen hours a day, seven days a week." It is not out of economic necessity anymore; it is because he believes the business is "in my system." He said, "It helps keep me going, and I feel like it is what I want to do." A successful symbol of black business in the Atlanta community for over a half century, he encourages young people who want to start their own business. But he cautions them, "Know something about the business you want to operate, because it will influence how much time you'll have to get it off the ground. By all means, have working capital to support the business until it gets off the ground. Any business you start is not going to be successful immediately. Be patient."

James and Robert Paschal commenced their entrepreneurship in the first business cycle, but it was clearly altered by the second one. The post-World War II years brought an expanded market for black businesses and greater diversity in types of businesses. Banking and insurance were the fields in which blacks made the greatest strides in cycle one. They were also a vital force in the black community in terms of lending money to black consumers and businesses. However, with the advent of desegregation, nationwide manufacturers, retailers, and financial institutions began to recognize the potential of the black consumer market and commenced to compete for it. In addition, many middle-class blacks moved away from the central city and left once-thriving black businesses behind to the lower-income segment of the market. Given the changing milieu, the protective tariff of such black-owned businesses eroded rapidly. While many could not compete, other black businesses were left to vie for a dwindling black consumer market. At the same time, racism and undercapitalization constrained their participation in broader markets.

BLACK ENTREPRENEURSHIP IN THE INTEGRATED SOCIETY

In the late 1960s, the urban rebellions and the thrust of black-power advocates to achieve community control through economic and political spheres raised the specter of the many dilemmas facing black businesses. Whether motivated by concern for black economic progress or more likely by the wish to avert economic upheaval, the response of the public and private sector was to step in to provide more assistance to black businesses. Further impetus was given to expanding black entrepreneurship when President Richard Nixon, a strong advocate of black capitalism, appointed the Presidential Council on Minority Business Enterprise and established the Office of Minority Enterprise in 1969. This office coordinated all federal government assistance programs for minority persons seeking to establish or expand businesses; it also linked the efforts of the private sector and local and state governments with those of the federal government. Other federal initiatives that were particularly important included the establishment of the Minority Enterprise Small Business Investment Company, the Community Development Corporation, and the set-aside programs, such as 8(a). Such programs were designed to increase the contributions of black men and women, other men and women of color, and white women to the economy through ownership of businesses, and to create capital, employment, and economic development.

Although these programs helped some black entrepreneurs, there were many problems. They lacked provisions for expansion of black businesses, lacked commitment from the administration, and lacked capital. Moreover, many so-called black businesses were under the control of whites. In addition, some critics challenged the notion of black capitalism; they believed that it would lead to insensitive blacks who would enrich themselves and forget about empowering the community. Roy F. Lee noted, "The voice that calls for allowing minorities to share in the nation's progress is the same voice that encourages hatred for black Americans and encourages dissension along racial lines."[11] Despite these concerns, the 1960s and 1970s, like the 1920s, witnessed a renewed interest in business ownership as a solution to empowering the black community.

A smattering of success stories did emerge with the assistance of public and private initiatives in construction, manufacturing, information and computer services firms, automotive products and services, transportation, retail trade, and wholesale trade. Benson Robinson, in automotive products and services, and Joshua Smith, in information and computer services, are notable examples of entrepreneurs in these selected service industries that cater to a broader market.

Benson Robinson [Pseudonym]: A Black Horatio Alger

In contrast to James Paschal and his brother, whose business was launched in the protective segregated market of the pre-1960s, Benson Robinson's business was established in the 1970s to serve a broader market. His successful enterprise was a direct beneficiary of assistance from the private sector. Unlike James Paschal, who became an entrepreneur in grade school, Robinson's entrepreneurial activities did not begin until he was in his early forties. After serving in the armed forces, he was employed as an IBM operator at an air force base and as a car salesman before purchasing his auto dealership. Robinson gave the following account of how he got started in business: "I worked for a liberal [white] fellow, and he always saw more qualities in me than I saw in myself. I was perfectly happy working for this gentleman. I thought I was making a good living. I lived in a very nice neighborhood. I was happy and comfortable. I think that's what happens to a lot of people. They get in what is called a comfortable zone."

His boss saw entrepreneurial qualities in Robinson and pressured him to go into business for himself. "I told him I didn't have the money, and if he wanted to give me the money, I'd [go into business]. I didn't have money and my folks didn't have money. He told me, 'I will help you in every way, but I will not give you any money. You have to get out there and work for it.'"

In 1972 General Motors was starting a minority program to encourage and train blacks for ownership of dealerships. Robinson remarked: "I was approached in '72 to be a part of this program, but I turned them down. Several people convinced me that this was the thing to do and the way to go, so I decided to do it, and I am glad I did. But at that point, I didn't think it was a good idea. When I started the training program, I was counseled to stick it out and that one day I would be the largest black car dealer in the country. I graduated from the program in 1974 and was able to purchase a business."

For the first four years Robinson was in business, the country was in a recession. But his business was still profitable. In 1979 he expanded his business into another state. "I didn't have the money to buy it," he said, yet he took the risk and was extremely successful. His business remains at or near the top of *Black Enterprise*'s list of 100 Top Businesses. Unlike Paschal, who believed in his entrepreneurial acumen, Robinson stated, "I never thought I would achieve all of this in a lifetime. I am proudest of what I've been able to do." Like Paschal, he believed the long working hours devoted to his businesses contributed to his success. While the two men share much in common, they differ in their business philosophy. Paschal, a moderate Democrat, feels comfortable operating business ventures in the black consumer market and the larger market. Besides being profit driven, he knows it is important to be a business role model, to create employment, and to contribute to the economic development of the black community.

In contrast, Robinson maintains a low profile in the black community and does not like being a role model for anyone except himself. "The role model of Benson Robinson is Benson Robinson," he exclaimed. He also does not think it is profitable to have his business in black neighborhoods. Though some branches of his businesses are in mixed communities, his headquarters is in a primarily white community. "I like my business exactly where I am," he said. "It used to be an old adage [that] if you had my type of business, you would put it in a black neighborhood, and that has proven not to be good. Back in the 1970s, you put a dealership in black neighborhoods and that failed." Robinson, a political independent who usually votes Republican, employs mostly whites in his business, even though he acknowledged, "I still do a good job in black business. For black people to do business with me, look how far they have to travel. When people travel that far, I'd say I have a lot of support from them." He added, "Blacks think I should hire more blacks, but I don't hire a lot of them. It's a business decision, since 80 percent of my customers are whites. It's not what is good for Benson Robinson, but what's good for his business. My basic philosophy is, if I run my company the way it is supposed to be run, then I am successful." Although his staff is largely white, Robinson gives contracts to black vendors or contractors. He is supportive of other blacks who own franchises in the parent company and advises them on how to be successful. He serves on advisory boards of major corporations and advocates for more black businesses to be placed in white communities, where there are "prime opportunities and not failing opportunities." He also served on an advisory committee for small business affairs in President Jimmy Carter's administration.

What catalysts influenced Robinson's business philosophy? We can look to his background for some hints. Robinson was born in the mid-1930s in a white lower-middle-class community in Indiana. He was reared and educated there through high school, along with his three sisters and two brothers. Robinson's father, the first black police officer in his town, had two years of college, and his mother, a housewife, had a twelfth-grade education. Robinson attributed his strong motivation to "a drive from within." He pointed out that "seeing how others lived and wanting to live that way" prompted him to see "that the only way you'll get it is to work for it," although he admitted hearing his parents, particularly his mother, tell him to work hard. They would say, "I will give you some of your needs, but your wants are elsewhere, and if you want them, you have to work for them."

Many black entrepreneurs of Paschal's generation and those educated in the 1950s, like Robinson, did not go beyond the twelfth grade. But Robinson doesn't apologize for not attending college. He thinks working hard and having goals were more crucial to his success than any formal training. Not only does Robinson think a lack of higher education is not a hindrance to his success, he also does not see his race as an impediment. Although his parents did not have a race discourse with him, they clearly imparted that hard work would overcome any obstacles. Growing up in a light-complected family in a mostly white community, he remembered his mother saying, "You must treat people as people." He said, "This is the greatest thing she left with me." He learned also "to take people as people." He admitted that his light complexion is an asset in his business, because his white customers do not identify him or his business as black.

Robinson, married with two adult children, is a complex and conflicted man in his racial ideology and action. While he advocates for minority ownership of businesses, he hires few blacks. Similarly, Robinson expresses a class orientation more than a race orientation. However, he sometimes behaves differently. For instance, he makes certain that minority subcontractors receive a share of his business. Interestingly, he perceives himself as black first; yet, he deemphasizes the importance of race. He also maintains that the double consciousness does not present a problem for him. On the one hand, he stereotypes blacks as lazy and indicates that whites treat him with respect. On the other hand, he reports racist attitudes of whites toward his business success. For example, when he opened a new business in another city, one of his white business contacts, whom he had regarded as a friend, made these disparaging remarks to another white business associate of Robinson: "Why does that black son-of-a-bitch need another store? He got more money than he can spend. Why does he need another one? Why doesn't he let one of us have one?"

Despite Robinson's sundry psychic discontinuities, he wants the next generation of black entrepreneurs to know that important ingredients of their success include hard work, dedication, and an investment in human resources. "I make a point to say nobody works *for* me. Everybody works *with* me. It is this management style that has made me successful," noted Robinson.

Joshua Smith: Success as Wealth and Power

Whereas assistance for Benson Robinson's business emerged from affirmative action in the private corporate sector, Joshua Smith was the direct beneficiary of the Small Business Administration's set-aside program, which helps small, minority businesses to obtain government contracts on a noncompetitive basis. Smith, the CEO of Maxima Corporation, was a successful graduate of the program in 1986. Later his company was hailed as the Republican flagship in black capitalism. Vaunting his accomplishments, he said, "I must have been a reincarnated cockroach from the Rockefeller office." Starting out as sole proprietor with fifteen thousand dollars in 1978, Smith parlayed his investment into a multimillion-dollar operation, becoming one of *Black Enterprise*'s 100 Top Companies. By 1988, Maxima Corporation, an integrated information management products and services firm, had over 1,350 employees in forty-six offices in thirteen states. In 1986 Maxima was selected as *Black Enterprise*'s Company of the Year; in 1985 it was chosen as the fastest-growing black-owned company in the United States and picked as one of *INC* magazine's five-hundred fastest-growing, privately held companies in the United States. Smith's mid-size computer service business in Lanham, Maryland, is an example of how black businesses are expanding to a broader market in the post-1960s.

The company has had its upward and downward spirals. After Smith competed in the mainstream for a contract with Prince Georges County, Maryland, and the U.S. Department of Defense and won, he was no longer eligible for the federal 8(a) program. His business suffered because the 8(a) program allows small, minority-owned businesses to receive contracts on a noncompetitive basis. Believing in himself and his dreams, Smith used the opportunity in the 8(a) program to show that he could compete in the mainstream by delivering a good product and by seizing opportunities. Moreover, his leadership skills of tapping into the strength of his employees, of motivating them to work hard, and of giving them a stake in the company contributed to his recovery.

For Smith, becoming a successful businessman was the process of observing, assessing, and learning from people with specific strengths, and then putting this into his own spheres of understanding. Those realms of understanding were derived from significant life events and life experiences, melded with an obdurate personality. Smith related, "I was a maverick at an early age and different from my other brothers and sisters. When I was sitting in a highchair, my mother told me, I threw a plate off and broke it. She spanked my hand. I was told I said, 'I'll break this plate.' She put another plate down and I broke it." Afraid to spank him again because she saw welts, he declared, "I won that battle. She would spank me, and I had decided not to cry. It is the way I came into this world. I never got into any trouble, but I did what I wanted to do and was headstrong."

Smith sees his family as the foundation for those realms of discernment and molding the maverick, recalcitrant traits for success. Born in 1941 in Garrett County, Kentucky, he grew up in a large, tightly knit Baptist family in the small town of Loveland, Ohio. His father, an educator, received his BA in education and sociology from Kentucky State College; his mother, a housewife, did not complete high school. Though his father was initially employed as a high school principal in Kentucky, he worked as a common laborer in Loveland to support his family. Because of discrimination, he could not find a job as an educator.

Smith was strongly influenced by his father and attributed his achievements to him. Smith's father, a bright, determined, charismatic man who was a powerful speaker, stressed the importance of education: all six of his children completed college. He inspired leadership qualities in Smith, encouraged family solidarity, enforced strict discipline, and instilled a strong work ethic and the importance of maintaining obligations. "At seventeen, I cleaned and cooked in a restaurant, as well as played in a jazz club, and still graduated the first black valedictorian in Loveland, Ohio," Smith asserted. "He taught me how to deliver the valedictory address and saw a lot of potential in me." Other values that Smith's father imparted were instrumental in his success, especially in business, for instance, having a sense of balance and thinking through what you are going to say. "He told me no matter how bad a situation gets, never burn a bridge. You learn how to leverage things. You learn to absorb and you don't always spout off because someone upsets you. He taught me how to be tolerant, but not to back off your goals." From his mother and sisters, he learned the valuable lesson of how to assess his surroundings and to judge people. Their important lessons of working hard, assessing one's environment from the perspective of the female consciousness, and developing leadership qualities were treasured gifts and the life line for his triumphant enterprise.

After graduating from high school, Smith earned a BS in chemistry from Central State University, a historically black institution in Wilberforce, Ohio. He did further advanced study at the University of Akron School of Law and Central Michigan University in business management, but he did not receive another degree. He considers the following life experiences as crucial to his success in the world of business: serving as an instructor on the secondary and university levels; working in manifold segments of the information industry, including publishing, consulting, and association management; and serving as the executive director of the American Society for Information Service.

For Smith, success is centered "around power and how to acquire power and wealth in an economically dominated world." The lifelong Republican views the intertwining of business and politics as a way to increase his influence and affluence, so in 1987 he became extremely active in the Republican Party. Smith, an eagle in the party, required sponsorship; and it was George Bush, then vice president, whom he met in 1986 after Maxima was designated the *Black Enterprise* Company of the Year, who sponsored him. Though he describes himself as a fiscal conservative with a liberal bent toward human rights, he views the Republican Party as more aligned with his planned goals and objectives of creating black wealth through ownership of businesses. Working diligently to assist with Bush's election, he was chair of the Task Force on Entrepreneurship; member of the Republican Finance Committee; member of the 100 Black Americans for Bush Committee; member of the Republican Presidential Trust; honorary chair of the Maryland Bush/Quayle Committee; chair of the Maryland Black Businesses for Bush; chair of the Maryland Blacks for Bush/Quayle Committee; and cochair of the Maryland

Bush for President Finance Committee. Smith, who also worked with the Republican National Committee, wanted the party to become more sensitive to black entrepreneurs' priorities. Accordingly, he encouraged Bush to seek the black business-person vote and avoid "the pulpit or civil rights vote," because Smith felt, "they'll ask you where were you and why weren't you there. You'll be rendered artificial and not have any sustenance. If you go after the vote, black business is there."

When Bush was elected president, Smith was told he would be the number-one black person for a cabinet post. But he responded: "I can't be in that position because my wealth is not secure. Wealth is where I want to be. I believe in living on the interest and not on the principal." "I know you are not ready, but you can get into a commission," he quoted Bush as telling him. Eventually, he accepted a post as chair of the Commission on Minority Development, because he believed in 1989 that Bush was committed to minority-owned business development. After his appointment, Smith traveled around the country, speaking and holding hearings. In his final report to the president, he said,

> It is the charge and challenge of this commission to take the lead role in conveying directly to the President, the Congress, and the American people that a strong minority business segment of the economy creates a stronger country. Minority businesses are vital to the American economy because minority business people locate their businesses within neighborhoods, revitalize communities, create jobs and train minorities, and serve as role models.[12]

Smith played an influential role in recommending policies, but his recommendations were ignored by Bush, his friend. This led Smith to become disaffected toward Bush and the party. He vowed to become more committed and determined in directing his energy toward helping blacks after bumping his head against the glass ceiling and getting caught up in the trappings of power politics. Smith said, "Energy is everything. But it is up to us how we expend it. I make a conscious decision based on the allocation of energy. I am frugal and conservative, and you can't do anything to me to make me use up my energy."

Empowering Blacks Through Economic Development

Smith differs from Benson Robinson when he speaks on behalf of the black community by encouraging economic development. While Robinson advises a few entrepreneurs in his industry, Smith speaks to a broader range of constituents and concerns. Smith asserted, "Everyone recognizes that economic development is going to change the fate of black people." In his articulation of the need for black economic development and businesses, several themes emerge: the need to be producers rather than consumers, the creation of wealth through business, and the need for alternative leadership models. For him, wealth is a means to individual and collective empowerment in the black community. Smith, who is fond of quoting Frederick Douglass, said, "The history of civilization shows that no people can sit for a high degree of mental or even moral excellence without wealth. A people who is uniformly poor and compelled to struggle for barely a physical existence will be dependent and despised by their neighbors and will finally despise themselves." Smith says, "It is all about wealth." In his striving to achieve wealth, he claimed, "You can find it under a rock, win it in a lottery, steal it, inherit it, earn it through business, or the old fashioned way—marry it." Having wealth, blacks can build their communities through self-help and employ other blacks. (Smith said that 60 percent of his company is white.) He noted that, too often, black people think "wealth is for white people [and] welfare is for black people," and he wants to change that perception, which he thinks is grounded in a religious orientation that poor people are closer to God. "God loves rich people, too, and not just the poor. He loves people who sow the seeds and reap the harvest to help others. We need to quit eating the seeds before they hit the field." He also thinks "we need wealth to feel good. When we feel good within ourselves, then we feel good for our neighbors, and feel proud of the successes of our millionaires and billionaires and want to learn from them."

While he argued that blacks need wealth, he said, "We need more wealthy people doing something with that wealth. If more wealthy people brought something back to the community, less hostility among the poor toward the wealthy would exist." For Smith, giving back is prescribed by his "time and resources," but, he noted, "community service is never ending, and you are always asked to do more."

Smith constantly reminds blacks that wealth is also a stepping-stone that fuels the economy, and "we should pool the resources of nearly $[6]00 billion we consume." In castigating blacks for not having real assets, he argued: "We have not developed our measures of success in the black community. We buy fancy cars and glitter. Our perception of wealth is characterized and reinforced by glitter. Wealth is not a manifesting event, but a lifestyle based on secure principles." A recurrent admonition in his speeches to the black community is: "If you are wearing it, it doesn't belong to you. If you are flashing it, it is not working for you. If it is on your back, it is not in the bank. If it is on your ass, it is not called an asset. You need to trade the Rolex for a Rolodex of investments. You need to trade that Gucci bag for a real money bag. People have Gucci bags worth more than the contents. You need to trade that BMW for stock in IBM, before the IRS gets you."

While Smith's criticisms of blacks may have some grounding, Melvin Oliver and Thomas Shapiro found in their study, *Black Wealth, White Wealth*, that systemic discrimination causes blacks to have difficulty in obtaining even the most commonplace forms of wealth, such as housing, and this results from structural discrimination.[13]

Smith wants black leaders to stop talking about the problems of economically undeveloped black communities and start solving them through economic strategies rather than continuing the politics of the civil rights approach. "Politics is economically driven. When we talk rights as black people, it starts in politics from dollars," said Smith. Since he thinks leadership must be viewed in the context of an economically dominated world, "Black leadership must change. We've had our preachers, and I think the day of civil rights leaders or preachers has passed, and their battle armor is won." Their strategies are "like going up against a nuclear weapon, using a bow and arrow. It doesn't work anymore. They don't have the equipment to fight tomorrow's battle." It does not follow that because "they were leaders, they can be leaders for the current era or future." At this point in the interview, he mused about the civil rights movement, paying it a double-barreled homage: "I wouldn't be sitting here today or have this successful business." Then, reversing this position, he maintained, "People tell me this, but I take issue with them." He thinks the older civil rights leaders "perpetuate that thinking, because they have nowhere else to go."

Smith envisions himself taking up the banner since he has "developed that credibility to lead." Coming from an arena of high-tech business and management, he feels he has a different role to play and can act as an alternative role model. But since blacks "have not seen business play a role in the community, it is therefore not regarded in the same light as in the white community." Smith believes successful black business persons need to show others how they have done it. "I am an example of what I talk about. If I can convey the message in an oratorical manner, that is better because it is what people need. I advocate a new kind of leadership that is driven not by civil rights but by economic rights."

He always reminds his audience, "Black people are at a critical juncture in America's history. We've been led out of the forest and jungle through civil rights. We are now at the river, the economic river. We got to swim. If I am drowning and you can't swim, leave me the hell alone. Let me be on my own. If we can't swim, we can't cross that river. We got to do what the flight attendant tells us, 'Put on your oxygen mask first, then you can help others.' We got to swim to put on our oxygen mask to create real wealth. When you boycott, you don't deal with control. You make them [whites] go from Plan A to Plan B."

For Smith, who is married with an adult son in business, "it's time for blacks to face up to the realities of a capitalistic society and understand what economics is about. Economic rights assure civil rights. Business and social programs don't mix. There may be social efforts to achieve business opportunities, but we can't mix business programs with a social agenda. We must benefit society through participation in the process of business."

Self-help and the importance of economic empowerment are the legacies Smith would like to leave to future generations. He wants young people to know "success is not absolute, but a never-ending journey." In the quest for success, he reminds young people, the only things that will show up on their doorsteps are "mangy dogs, other people's troubles, or someone else's opportunities." Unfortunately, in recent years, other people's troubles have landed on his doorstep. A protracted legal battle has ensued between Joshua Smith, the company's founder, and his son, a former vice president at the company until he was fired by his father in 1993. The feud has been costly. The company's declining revenues, from $60 million a decade ago to $5 million, forced Smith to file for reorganization in bankruptcy court. Since 1998 he has served as the managing partner of The Coaching Group. As a first-generation business person, Smith always learns from his mistakes and keeps moving forward, "looking at the glass as half full rather than half empty."

Black Enterprise's 100 Top Companies differ from the majority of black-owned businesses; they are in the high-growth industries of communications, information services, health care, biotechnology, computer products and services, and electronics. In 1992 black-owned businesses were 3.6 percent of the nation's businesses, and most of these black-owned companies were small. Between 1997 and 2002, black-owned firms increased from 4 percent to 5.2 percent of all U.S. firms.[14] These firms are however disproportionately in low-growth retail or service industries. The rate of minority companies entering the more lucrative manufacturing or financial and insurance industries is only half that of white companies.[15] But with the advent of a new breed of more educated black entrepreneurs, the business landscape is changing.

While there is an upside of change in demographic characteristics of black entrepreneurs and the growth in types of industries in which they participate, one change that will have a downside effect for future entrepreneurs is the cut-back or policy change in affirmative action set-aside programs. For example, in *Richmond v. J. A. Croson Company*, the Supreme Court struck down municipal and state set-aside programs that required 30 percent of each construction contract be awarded to minority business enterprises. This decision had a negative impact on black businesses. In Hillsborough County, Florida, for instance, minority business awards dropped by 99 percent after the county's program was eliminated.[16] These programs benefited the Benson Robinsons and the Smiths in the second cycle, but are not as available now for those in the third cycle.

THE EMERGING GLOBAL ENTREPRENEUR

The third cycle of entrepreneurs, according to A. Wade Smith and Joan V. Moore, is armed with "survival instincts from the black experience and business background savvy incubated in white institutions."[17] In this cycle entrepreneurs, now including more women, are knowledgeable of technological advances and government policy. While they actively contribute to civic and social activities, they are members of trade associations and chambers of commerce, nationally and sometimes transnationally. In the face of discrimination, they design a course of action and execute it. They seek a broader market—from financial services, information and communications technology, radio and television broadcasting, data processing, chemical and specialty manufacturing, and business services to manufacturing and distributing food products globally to developing products for the public and private sectors. They also use creative financing mechanisms to acquire companies and to increase the value of their holdings. They develop business through mergers and acquisitions, joint ventures and partnering, and innovative marketing.

Vincent Carpenter: The New "Freedom Capitalist"

Vincent D. Carpenter, entrepreneur and owner of a financial service, is exemplary of this cycle, as are of those who were born and who came of age in the civil rights generation. Born in 1963 in Ahoskie, North Carolina, Carpenter knew at an early age he wanted to become an entrepreneur. When he was seventeen years old, he passed the Virginia real estate agent licensing requirement, but had to wait until he was eighteen years old to obtain his license. While attending a predominantly white university, Carpenter worked as a part-time realtor, as a salesman in a department store, and as owner of his own janitorial service. As a financial services and communications major, his ambition was to become a stockbroker. After passing the qualifying exam, he met resistance from numerous financial services. A vice president of Dean Witter asked him, "How can you cut it as a black youth?" Another indicated that he would not be smart enough to pass all the qualifying examinations necessary to become a full-service stockbroker. Undaunted by his age and color, he said to the vice president of Dean Witter after his third interview with him, "Your loss is somebody else's gain." Eventually, a financial services organization that he had consulted about career opportunities when he was a high school student hired him. This company provided Carpenter with experience as a registered representative, and he passed all the qualifying examinations for certified financial planner. Prior to establishing his own company at age twenty-two, he was a financial planner and the vice president of operations for another firm. His own firm, Chesapeake Financial Services, was the first full-service African American financial planning and investment advisory firm in his locale. Initially, when his clients see that he is black, they are astounded. For both his black and white clients, 60 percent and 40 percent, respectively, an initial attitude of underlying mistrust exists, a sense that blacks cannot be good managers. His game plan is to no longer try to convince them of his competence; instead, he relies mostly on client referrals. In the meantime, he is starting other enterprises. He is also actively involved with many civic organizations and has political aspirations.

What propels Carpenter to run so fast? Money and mission energize his engine. He wants to be rich, but he also wants to create wealth for others. Still, there is something more deep-seated that drives him. A life-altering event at the age of seven that almost caused his death sets him apart from his peers. He understood at a tender age the importance of making use of opportunities given to him.

Carpenter moved back and forth between his birthplace, Ahoskie, North Carolina, and Chesapeake, Virginia. While visiting his grandparents' farm in Ahoskie, he was kicked by a pony. "An infection from the kick disintegrated the ball and socket of my right hip," recalled Carpenter. He spent months in a body cast and braces, enduring the taunts and teasing of his peers. He wanted to run and play basketball like his classmates to prove himself and to fit in. But the injury continued to afflict him, even after more than six corrective surgeries. For most of the two years following his illness, he was tutored because he was unable to attend school. Carpenter, always inquisitive and industrious, learned to enjoy the world of books. He became proficient in such diverse subjects as astronomy and Greek mythology. Returning to school, he was above average in performance. His academic achievements were reinforced by his parents, who had high expectations for him.

The second turning point in his life occurred in high school when his father, a career military man with an eleventh-grade education, and his mother, a housewife and laborer who completed her GED, were divorced. As the oldest, he had the responsibility for taking care of his brothers and chauffeuring his mother to work. Oftentimes, he would dress up in a suit and make a detour on the way home, stopping at a business to inquire about the requirements and qualifications for getting started in that business. This was the way he became interested in real estate and financial planning.

These significant events helped to shape his perception about the precariousness of life; one should make hay while the sun is shining. Although he wants to make millions before sunset, it is equally important to have "a legacy of documented accomplishment of improving the lives of others." "I have a business of mission and one is just plain business-money," he asserted. Carpenter believes, like the other entrepreneurs discussed here, that capitalism will contribute to the economic development of the community. But this can only happen when we spend money and time with one another, he said.

Carpenter concludes that his generation of entrepreneurs is the "product of the older ones' dreams, hopes, and struggles, but also the product and realization of their worst nightmares. Older ones had their hotels, restaurants, and banks in the community. These businesses provided jobs and economic development. When integration came, these businesses suffered a huge trade deficit. We traded freely with others but did not make that same demand on them."

Cindy M. Walters and Deidra Sutton, business analysts for the Hampton Roads Minority Business Development Center, told me that many young, enterprising, highly educated black clients in the 1990s "don't want to identify with the black community," they "want to move up and out of the community." They are in technical fields like computer services and want to start their business in a more open market and to be players in corporate America. Such young upstarts are different from their forebears. They start out with the belief that no "barriers exist if you apply yourself " Walters and Sutton maintain that if these entrepreneurs have an idea, "they expect to leave college, obtain the start-up capital, and make a million dollars immediately without understanding the time, obstacles, and commitment one must invest to achieve their ends." Victor Ellington, owner of a computer services firm, is an example.

Victor Ellington [Pseudonym]: On the Net—Beyond "Roots"

After graduating from an Ivy League school with an M.B.A. and an undergraduate degree in engineering, Victor Ellington worked in corporate America for two years. Then he started his successful business in product design and service. He used his personal savings, a minority business loan, and a loan from his parents for start-up capital. Both of Ellington's parents were managers in major corporations, but they encouraged him to become an entrepreneur because of the constraints of corporate life. When he started his company, he never doubted that he would succeed.

Unlike Carpenter, Ellington is interested in only one mission and that is "making money." Born in 1971 in a suburb of Boston, Massachusetts, he is typical of an emerging breed that has no strong interest in "identifying with the black community." "I only deal with the color of money, and I don't see a market potential in black neighborhoods. It is a savvy business decision," said Ellington. His attitude is not surprising, because he has always felt more comfortable in a white milieu. "It is where I was born, grew up, went to school, attended church, and worked. So it is natural for me to have my business in this community," he responded. When I asked if he felt any obligation to give back to the black community, his response was simply, "No." I inquired further if he perceived a contradiction in obtaining a minority business loan and his expressed lack of obligation to the black community. Appearing somewhat uncomfortable with the question, he replied, "Not really. I feel I got the loan because of my skills and my strong ambition to achieve success in business." While that may be partly true, the minority business opportunity programs were the result of the collective efforts of the civil rights era. In contrast to Carpenter, Ellington did not express an interest in sharing with other small black companies how to obtain that success, even though their failure rate, similar to that of all small businesses, is about 80 percent.

Armed with more technical and knowledge-based skills and more understanding of high growth industries, the new breed, like Ellington, finds that technology can serve as a source of business opportunities, particularly home-based ones that need limited start-up capital. According to a survey by Dun and Bradstreet Corporation, "minority business-owners are more likely to use Internet than their nonminority counterparts" and "20 percent more likely to see an increase in profits."[18] The Internet, an ingenious marketing tool, allows those "with technical know-how like Yasmin Shiraz to reach the global marketplace.

Yasmin Shiraz: On the Net—Reaching Back to Her "Roots"

Born 1970 in Wilmington, Delaware, Yasmin Shiraz, an up-and-coming magazine publisher, writer, and lecturer, utilizes the Internet to market her business. According to the National Foundation for Women Business Owners, she is among the growing number of women of color who own businesses. These businesses increased by 153 percent between 1987 and 1996, when "the number of black women-owned firms more than doubled (135%)."[19] These young, highly educated women are likely to embrace the Internet to pursue new business strategies, estimate the competition, recruit qualified personnel, and market globally. Shiraz is enthusiastic about the possibility of Internet-based entrepreneurship for black men and women. It became one medium of advertising and marketing for her hip-hop magazine, *Mad Rhythms*, which reached the age cohort of seventeen to twenty-five. "It levels the playing field for blacks and nullifies stereotypes. We won't be judged by our presentation as it relates to color or gender. When individuals order a magazine, they don't ask if it belongs to someone black or female," maintained Shiraz. She also uses the Internet for her advertising campaigns for major corporations like Reebok and for developing partnerships with them. Shiraz fears however that many potential entrepreneurs who are young, black, and poor are being left behind in the technology and information age. Working with other entrepreneurs, she would like to be instrumental in changing this predicament and to employ this technology as a tool in the creation of wealth in black communities. She believes the Internet is great for networking with other black entrepreneurs. She finds that enterprising blacks who use it are rediscovering community and assisting one another. Pooling their resources, they have the potential for linking black communities' interests with larger corporate ones in the developing field of communications and technology.

Shiraz, who grew up and was educated in predominantly white suburbs of Delaware and Maryland, graduated from Hampton University. Here, at this historically black institution, her racial consciousness was heightened while she majored in sociology. After completing her master's in sociology, Shiraz, who is married with two children, worked briefly as a community college instructor and in the publishing industry before striking out on her own to fulfill her personal and collective dreams.

One of her dreams was to counter the negative portrayal of black youths in both black and white media. This was her reason for creating an urban entertainment college publication in 1994, and this venture also led her to believe that the Internet could be a potent weapon in deconstructing such hegemonic cultural images. Shiraz remarked: "*Mad Rhythms* was created to produce a hip-hop/youth culture medium that does not reinforce negative images. You can read an article on the same artist in other magazines, but *Mad Rhythms* leaves out the expletives, leaves out the glorification of negative behavior, and ends up producing an article that is better for the reader and the artist. Hip hop was created to bring the culture down, and it's about time magazine publishers realize that. Unfortunately, entertainment entities have consciously decided to focus on the most negative aspects of hip hop, which ultimately paint the picture that all of hip hop is negative. Well, when you're looking in a hip-hop pool, whose reflection do you see? The reflection is that of you, black American. And, all of young black America is not negative. Where is the responsibility of entertainment critics to the images that they are putting out on the black youth culture? Many business owners cower under the guise that they have to make a profit, but you can make a profit without selling negativity on every magazine cover, every video, and every single on the radio. You can make money and be responsible for the black culture at the same time." Young hip hop moguls such as Sean "P. Diddy" Combs, Damons Dash of Rocafella Records, Kevin Liles, former president of Def Jam Records, and Chaka Wilson of Enyche Clothing were supportive of her magazine, as well as other fledging hip hop entrepreneurs. As an aside, such savvy young entrepreneurs have created multimillion-dollar empires that are not only interested in selling the black experience to the black community but to white America and to audiences around the world.

Though Shiraz relinquished her most-widely read urban entertainment college magazine, she launched other enterprising ventures, such as her own publishing company, her marketing and publicity agency, and her college entertainment tour, one of which is titled "The Politics of Hip Hop Culture." Here Shiraz says that she exposes the "racism, sexism, and capitalism within the hip hop culture." As an author of several books, including *Blueprint for My Girls*, she lectures across the country. Shiraz's Blueprint for My Girls Network creates tailored workshops and seminars designed to empower youths.

Such knowledge-based industry, as Shiraz's, is separating this generation of entrepreneurs from their predecessors, not only in how they conduct their businesses, but also in terms of their global market outreach. While most black entrepreneurs are still dependent on the market of the black community, in a knowledge-based economy they have the potential of reaching a more color-blind market through new technology and communications. Consequently, technology may be a leveler for black entrepreneurs in the twenty-first century. Will this new equalizer be used solely as an individual mission to make money or will it be used, like Shiraz's venture, in the collective mission of service?

6

Black Politicians:
The Bellwethers of the Post-Civil Rights Era

Freedom's doors swung open to diverse occupational opportunities in the late 1960s and early 1970s for a new generation of blacks. No longer confined to being teachers, preachers, doctors, lawyers, or entrepreneurs, young blacks could now become accountants, corporate executives, mayors, and scientists in the private, public, and not-for-profit sectors. These "children of the dream," as identified by Audrey Edwards and Craig Polite, were the first wave of the integrated generation. "Affirmative action, equal employment opportunities, set-asides, mentors, networking, training programs—these became the buzz words of a generation who grew up possessing something no generation of blacks before had ever experienced: a sense of entitlement, a belief in the right to have access."[1] The previous edition of this work, which focused on the aforementioned occupations in the pre-civil rights era, found noteworthy generational value shifts among those individuals who came of age before and during the civil rights movement and those who came of age after it.

The swinging of the pendulum from collective consciousness and group mobility to individual consciousness and individual mobility is one such example. In addition to the assimilation of the dominant group's worldview of individualism, this value transformation has occurred within the context of structural and social changes such as globalization, deindustrialization, black suburbanization, retrenchment in affirmative action and other public policy priorities of the 1960s and 1970s, as well as the more politically conservative climate of the past twenty-five years. Additionally, within the black community, increasing fault lines are occurring along class, generation, and political orientation. For instance, the Joint Center for Economic and Political Studies found that among black professionals, "Younger blacks are more optimistic, self-confident, and positively oriented toward corporate America than their elders."[2] In general, despite class, younger blacks are also more favorable toward smaller government. As blacks have entered diverse careers in a more politically conservative and market-driven, consumer-oriented post-civil rights era, do these generational patterns continue to prevail? With the bevy of professional opportunities for African Americans from archeologists to zoologists, it is impractical in these new chapters to answer this question of generational changes by looking at the myriad of occupations. Hence, to assess if these patterns continue to hold true of post-civil rights professions, I have chosen the politician and the visual artist as representatives of the post-civil rights professions.

Perhaps the assertion of the late politician Jessie Rattley, whom we will meet later, that "everything involves politics and it governs everything you do," provides a persuasive rationale for my choice of elected officials as the bellwether of the black community. Moreover, since the masses tend to mirror the opinions of partisan and ideological elites,[3] the black elected official seems a logical choice. According to the Joint Center for Political and Economic Studies, for example, in terms of partisanship, black elected officials and the black public identified themselves as overwhelmingly Democratic, 76 percent and 67 percent, respectively. While black elected officials were less likely to identify themselves as Independent than members of the black public, younger black elected officials, between eighteen and forty years of age, were more likely to be self-identified as Independent. A similar pattern was evident among the younger population in the general public.[4] Another raison d'être for selecting elected officials is the phenomenal growth of this profession among blacks. In 1964 approximately three hundred blacks were in public office, including only three in Congress. Only a few blacks were elected in the South.[5] Today, according to the Joint Center for Political and Economic Studies, approximately 9,500 black elected officials are in office, including forty-three members of Congress. A final reason for choosing politicians is that by the very nature of the occupation, they are ideally expected to serve the public and not to be self-serving. These four rationales provide the basis for my choice of black elected officials.

PUBLIC SERVANTS OR SELF-SERVING?

Prior to the passage of the Voting Rights Act of 1965, as previously noted, few blacks were elected to public office. Since its passage, along with the court-ordered creation of black majority voting districts, black elected officials have steadily increased. From 1970, when the Joint Center for Political and Economic Studies began to track black elected officials, the figure rose from 1,469 in 1970 to approximately 9,500 in 2006, a meteoric rise in representation just over forty years after the passage of the Voting Rights Act, at all levels—municipal, county, state, and federal. With this astounding growth of black elected officials, how have black communities benefited from these changes in the post-civil rights era? Do generational differences exist among black elected officials with respect to their obligation to the black community?

According to the Joint Center for Political and Economic Studies, some noteworthy divergences exist among generational cohorts in life experiences and in public policy issues. For instance, black elected officials age sixty-five or older are more than twice as likely to have attended segregated high schools as those in the youngest age cohort between eighteen and forty years. Likewise, older black elected officials were more likely to attend a historically black college or university than the youngest cohort, 68 percent and 37 percent, respectively. Not surprisingly, since the civil rights movement occurred in the 1950s and 1960s, older black elected officials, those sixty-five years and older, were more than seven times as likely as the youngest ones, those between eighteen and forty years, to have been involved in the movement. Although generational differences are more pronounced with reference to involvement in the civil rights movement, differences in membership in the civil rights organizations are more moderate. Interestingly, while racism is still problematic among all generations of black elected officials, older black elected officials are likely to identify racism as the nation's most important problem, while the younger elected officials consider education as the most pressing problem. Moreover, the younger black officials are not as pessimistic about racism as the older generation. The two youngest legions of black elected officials, those between the ages of eighteen to forty years and forty-one to forty-nine years, were more than twice as likely as the sixty-five years and older to have been reared in families where their parents were also active in politics, and where they were also more likely to have parents who held an elective office. Similarly, the older groups of black elected officials were less conservative in their political views and differed from the youngest cohort in terms of their support for vouchers and the Social Security system. In other words, they were less favorable toward these issues than those between eighteen and forty years of age.[6]

Although younger elected officials, like the general black population between eighteen and fifty years, are more supportive of vouchers, they do not march in lock step with their generational cohort. Take, for example, Kwame Kilpatrick, mayor of Detroit. He does not believe that the voucher system would work in his city. "I just never saw it as a good idea. There are just not enough slots for everyone to take a voucher of public money and go to a private school. So really what you'd be doing is underfunding the majority of kids that would be left in public schools, and the last thing we need right now is for more dollars to be taken out of classrooms. I don't support it at all." Similarly, he adds,

> I don't agree with privatizing Social Security. I do believe, however, that there needs to be a real discussion about Social Security in a nonpartisan light. When President Bush proposed it, some people automatically shut down. I just don't believe that everything he says is necessarily stupid. I don't believe that privatization of the whole thing might be the answer, but we know that there is going to be an issue with Social Security because there are not as many people working and putting into the system. We need to really have a discussion on how adequately it will be funded through the years, when will we begin to see a real problem with it, and what should we do as a country to address that emerging need."

As one of 160 black women in the nation who had been elected to a political office in 1970, the late Jessie Rattley would have also been opposed to vouchers and privatizing the Social Security system.[7] Her formative years of eking out a living in the red clay of segregated Alabama during the Depression, a pivotal marker in her narrative, would have been in contradistinction to her very being and to her stalwart social consciousness of easing the pain of poverty and injustices for the less privileged. Let us turn to her story on why the political trailblazer might have differed from the youngest elected officials.

Jessie Menifield Rattley: The Political Trailblazer

> You hear every day somebody ought to do this. We look at the plight of our children. We look at conditions under which people live. We look at the political system and we see people who are ignored and abandoned. And it just seems to me that somebody is supposed to be there to call attention to these things. So I do it. . . . Something inside of me keeps pushing me to do something . . . I should be very pleased about what I have accomplished, but I find myself, with this inner voice, still pushing, and if I had no involvement or nothing to do, I would not be happy at all. And I guess throughout my whole life, I've said that I am that somebody.—Jessie M. Rattley

The late Jessie M. Rattley's words capture her quintessential life of service to others and sum up her politics in motion. What life forces and inner voice propelled this first black and first woman to be elected to serve as president of National League of Cities; this first black president of Virginia Municipal League; this first black and first woman to serve as the mayor of Newport News, Virginia; this first black and first woman elected to the Newport News City Council; this social activist and educator to keep pushing? Perhaps it was the voices of her mother and grandmother whose strength and faith taught her life lessons about self-reliance, hard work, and responsibility for self and others. By their examples, directly or indirectly, she could envisage that where there is a will, there is a way, and that she could make things happen.

This unwavering public servant was born in Birmingham, Alabama, in 1929, to Altona Menifield, a hard-working housewife and a washerwoman for whites, and Alonzo Menifield, a Pullman porter with no more than a fourth-grade education. Her father was frequently absent from the family because of his work. In fact, Rattley's first recollection of him was boarding a streetcar to depart for Texas, where he made his runs as a Pullman porter. As the youngest of four children, she remembered wailing and holding onto her father to prevent his leaving, while simultaneously clinging to her mother. She did not see him again until he returned from one of his runs just in time to enroll her in the first grade. So Rattley, along with her two older siblings, was primarily reared by her mother and grandmother (the oldest brother had died at birth). As a child of the Depression, the face of poverty was omnipresent. She recalled that her grandmother, who worked in white people's homes, would bring them food that had been left on top of the garbage cans. "My sister doesn't like for me to tell that story. She doesn't like me to tell that we ate a lot out of garbage cans. The folks wrapped the food up. Rather than just keeping it and saving it for my grandmother, they would wrap it up and put it on the garbage can. And she would pick it up for us to eat. That's embarrassing to her. But that was my life and I'm not ashamed of it," said Rattley. She was also not embarrassed to share one of her most histrionic moments in elementary school. "I didn't really have adequate shoes. I was always large, as they would say—big-boned with big feet and it was difficult to find shoes. We just couldn't afford them and I had a pair of shoes where the soles had come off. And I had to flip and flop and put it down, so it wouldn't curl up on you. I had decided I couldn't be bothered with that, so I just went to school without shoes. And when Mama found out, she hit the ceiling because it was winter time." Though lacking material resources, poverty did not mark her identity; therefore, neither Rattley nor others in her family or her community viewed themselves as poor and incapable of human agency.

Everybody knows about the stock market crash. You can tell just from that bit of history that in a sense we were all poor regardless of race. But yet, we didn't look upon ourselves as being poor because nobody was telling us that we were poor. I have never felt poor. We didn't really have that many material things. Most other people lived under the same conditions and we lived so much better than many of our neighbors, and that was because we worked hard and kept things clean. My mother and grandmother always grew flowers and we found beauty in the splendor of them. We learned how to innovate.

Her formative childhood influences included sitting at the knees of her blue-eyed paternal great-grandmother, the offspring of a slave mother and white master. Here Rattley learned firsthand about the horrors of slavery, the struggle, survival, resiliency, and politics of being a poor black female from her great-grandmother who lived to be over one hundred. From her maternal grandmother and mother, Rattley was imbued with a strong work ethic, "the can do spirit," the value of homeownership, and the ability to define her own destiny.

We lived in my mother's mother's house, a woman who had Indian blood and black skin as smooth as silk with beautiful hair and high cheekbones. We had one side of the house and she lived in the other side. We didn't have electricity or telephone. We had an outdoor toilet. Our home was always clean and organized with a flower garden. We had a large vegetable garden and we raised hogs. I learned how to feed hogs and how to pick the crops. We worked in the earth a lot, and we were never hungry, but we never had a lot of anything. It was obvious that my grandmother, a determined, hard-working, faithful Baptist woman who attended Sunday school every Sunday, could outwork any man. Every morning she would leave before daybreak to go to work in white homes.

From Rattley's outgoing mother, she learned the importance of a strong work ethic, kindness to others, and indirectly how to stand up for herself. "She taught us to do good deeds, to give respect, 'to do unto others as you would have them do unto you,' and we fully understood that. And although we didn't have anything, if we heard of a family in need, we would give to them. We gave clothes and most of the time we would try to do it anonymously. But that was the way we grew up. We shared what we had," recalled Rattley. It was an era when neighbors looked out for one another and shared their meager resources. Such acts were the unspoken code of conduct and the faith in the caring community. Her soft-spoken mother had this faith. "[My mother] had a saying that still stands out in my mind. She used to say it all the time. 'You know we don't have any food. But I'm gonna put on my pot and let the water boil, because somebody will give us something before the day is over.'" In her close-knit, caring community, someone would inevitably stop by and say, "Menifield or Altona, you want some greens, or I have some peas I just picked." Rattley's mother's strong faith was grounded in the Bible verses that she often recited. "Yea though I walk through the valley of the shadow of death, I will fear no evil, for Thou art with me. Thy rod and thy staff they comfort me," was one of her frequently cited verses that would eventually become Rattley's own mantra in treading the murky political waters.

Although her mother was a woman of steadfast faith who read scriptures daily with her family, she rarely attended church. Nevertheless, she sent her children to a nearby Baptist and Methodist church for Sunday school and youth programs. At times Rattley seemed to suggest that religion was her mother's opiate.

> Mama thought in terms of God as her Savior, because daddy was not very kind to my mama. As we matured and looked back on the relationship, that was hurting. She was timid and wouldn't fight back. No man could treat me the way my father treated my mother. It wasn't all the time, but he would get pretty angry sometimes and he would hit her and say mean things to her. And she would take it. She never stopped cooking for him, or cleaning, or washing. She stayed right there. You see I would have been gone. And I think that attitude came from the fact that I saw her as very submissive, although a very talented person as far as working with the hands, being faithful to her marriage and her children, and staying home.

Plainly, while Rattley's mother influenced her, she developed an oppositional framework to the interior of her mother's subordinate gendered role, coping behavior, and worldview. She learned to stand up for herself and others. But most of all, she learned to find a way to have her own. She had clear memories of her mother, who had a third- or fourth-grade education, sitting in a window and repeating her favorite topic: "I wish I had stayed in school, and I wish I had this or that." Her mother's yearnings strengthened her resolve for autonomy and her sense of self-efficacy. "It is very significant, because somehow from that I developed this determination that I would never want for anything, that I would make it happen. I would work for it. I would never sit around and say I wish."

Making Things Happen: School as a Building Block

Obtaining a good education was one of the key building blocks in her political stepping-stone and in making things happen in her life, so she worked assiduously and performed well in school. "I wanted to go to school," she asserted. "I was anxious to learn. I did everything that was asked of me. I didn't have a lot of things other kids had. But I worked hard." Throughout her schooling, she maintained high scholastic standing and was one of only four students in her high school who took rigorous academic courses instead of vocational ones. She also was involved in extracurricular activities, playing basketball and performing with the band as a drummer and as a majorette. In addition, she worked in the principal's office as a typist, where she was first introduced to business administration. In his office, she felt her calling to serve as a marshal. "A marshal in that high school was like a truant officer. This was not for any pay. It wasn't really for recognition I don't guess. It was for making sure that our students got to class on time; that the halls were silent when they were supposed to be; and that if those white folks came over, the superintendent and his board, that school would be *A* #one. Everything had to be right." And for some reason, Jessie thought that she had to do part of this. Even then, her emerging leadership skills were evident. "Everybody in the school knew me. I cleared the hall and students obeyed me and behaved."

Rattley, known as the principal's pet, honed her leadership skills under the high school principal, one of the mentors who strongly influenced her by reinforcing excellence and discipline. "Our high school principal was very demanding. He wanted the Fairfield students to have the highest grades. We had strong guidance there. He came to visit our homes. We also had other teachers in different subjects that took an interest and made a great impression on me." She was especially inspired by one woman teacher and mentor who taught her chemistry and physics in high school, and who eventually joined the faculty at MIT. In addition to the supportive teachers, she and her siblings found an educational resource in their next-door neighbors who were teachers and professionals.

While most teachers stressed excellence and maintained high expectations for all their charges, Rattley, who thought of herself as dark for most of her formative years, believed some teachers internalized racism of the dominant group and catered to students based on their skin color and other physical features. "At that time we had a lot of segregation within the black community. It was all based on color and the texture of your hair. And the light-skinned kids were always recognized. They were the kings and queens who participated in the school activities. It was so blatant. I had a friend who was light skinned, with beautiful long black wavy hair, and she didn't have to put forth much effort. I don't recall any feeling of jealousy. I simply felt that I would have to work harder."

When one of her teachers assailed her ability to speak, she knew that she had to work harder. "If you tell me that I cannot do something, I'm going to do it. I had an English instructor to tell me at one point in high school that I would never be able to speak, and I said, 'Damn you—I would.' Because I had difficulty pronouncing words, I was determined. And yes, I ended up giving the speech for graduation. And this teacher came to me and said, 'I didn't believe that you could ever do it.' She was talking about public speaking and really expressing myself and pronouncing words. I did a lot more before then. I even wrote a play. I don't think you should ever tell a student you will never be able to do something. Just tell me I can't do something and I make it happen."

Rattley's Racial Resistance as a Building Block and Proving Ground

Just as Rattley had positioned her stance as a youth against the color complex and other destructive divisions within the black community, she also situated herself against the color line, another significant building block in her political grounding and racial resistance. Growing up in segregated Alabama in the 1930s and the 1940s, Rattley knew too well the confining familiarity of segregated spaces. "You lived in a separate community; you went to a separate school; your church was separated; and if you had a park, that was separated. There was absolutely nothing that you could do that you would intermingle with whites."

Like so many others of her era, she wanted to disprove the stereotypes and assumptions about black inferiority. She recalled how the white superintendent of schools and board members would inspect her black school to see if the principal was performing his duties. As a marshal, Rattley remembered doing her part to help keep the building clean and the students orderly. "We were all about proving to the white folks that we could excel. Every day we had to prove that we were not the way they said we were."

Proving herself was a proactive means of surviving the Jim Crow of Alabama. When she encountered overt racism, she resisted its domination. She offered these accounts of her defiance within the context of that time. In order to travel by streetcar, she had to walk a short distance through a white neighborhood. Inevitably, someone would call out, "nigger, nigger, nigger,"—and at an early age, she and others would say, "cracker, cracker, cracker," and run. On the streetcar, Rattley and her friends would sit behind the prescribed colored sign, but they would scratch it out and color it red. "We didn't want to sit behind it, but there was nothing we could do about it. There were some young people bold enough to throw it out the window when they knew the driver wasn't looking, so we had ways of showing our resentment. Now a lot of people just took it passively, but I didn't. I did anything I could do and thought I could get away with to show resentment. If they called me a name, I called them one right back. 'You poor cracker,' and they hated the word cracker. I wasn't going to take it. I didn't see why I had to take this at eleven years old."

At eleven, Rattley started working as a domestic for a white family that had previously employed her grandmother and mother. After school, she cleaned, cooked, washed, and ironed, and on Saturday, she worked all day.

For her services, she was paid $2.35 a week. She understood the order of the day, so she did not resent her working condition; rather she viewed it as an opportunity to acquire needed goods for herself and her sister. This family had a daughter named Ann, and she had heard her peers discuss the "colored people." One day she said to Rattley,

> "Jessie, [this is a girl calling me Jessie] you're black and I'm white." "No Ann, that's not true. Who told you that?" "Yes, it is true," said Ann. I took out a piece of black material and said, "What color is this?" She said, "Black." "What color is this?" She got upset. I said, "You see, I'm not black." But keep in mind, I told you I thought I was dark. And I said, "Ann, you're not white." "I am white!" So I took something white and put it next to her and asked, "What color is this?" "White," she responded. "What color is this?" She left the room screaming at the top of her voice and ran in her mama's bedroom. Her mama called out, "Jessie Menifield, what did you say to my Ann?" I told her. And she just stood there. She had to laugh. The child was so upset. I was not going to permit her to think that I was black and she was white. I wanted her to think about this for awhile.

Whether whites spoke to her in a patronizing manner or spat on her or called her nigger, she stated, "I got the feeling that many whites referred to me as arrogant, because I don't scratch when I'm not itching. And I didn't drop my eyes, and I tried to be informed and tried to know what I was talking about, and I would let them know I resented this treatment."

The Hampton Experience: A Building Block for Life

In 1947, after graduating from high school in Alabama, Rattley continued to make things happen. She always wanted to attend Hampton Institute (now Hampton University), even though several black colleges offered her a full scholarship and Hampton did not. Her years there tested her mettle, which was another significant building block in her political foundation. "I had been told that Hampton University was the best school for blacks in this country. And I would have an opportunity to find out if I was as good as my teachers thought I was in high school. Because they said if you didn't do your work at Hampton, you would be put on the train and sent back home after the first semester. I was told it was very difficult, but if you graduated from Hampton University, you would get a good job and your education would have value." Since she didn't have any money to attend the university, she worked for a semester as a secretary at Jones Valley Finance Company, a black firm in Birmingham, as well as other part-time jobs, including an insurance company owned by black millionaire A. G. Gaston, to earn money to enter Hampton

Institute in the spring. After earning enough money and being accepted to Hampton, Rattley remembered buying a vintage trunk and painting it green with black trim for her worldly goods. "I bought two dresses and I got the things that I needed and at the end of that semester, I got my train ticket and I went to Hampton. I was a little bit short in paying my tuition, but of course, they let me register."

Three days after her arrival at Hampton, her connection with A. G. Gaston helped her to obtain employment in the business office. The financially strapped student also waited tables at Langley Air Force Base on weekends and worked some nights as a switchboard operator on campus, despite taking a heavy course load (upward of 24 hours a semester), to pay her tuition, room, and board. In her last semester, Rattley moved to a professor's home off campus to save paying room and board. During this time, she existed on a diet of franks and beans. In spite of her financial woes, she succeeded against difficult odds, graduating with honors in three and one-half years.

The Building Block of Activism and Empowerment

After Rattley's graduation from Hampton Institute with a degree in business education in 1951, she was hired to teach at a high school, where she successfully started its first business department. While enthusiastic students filled her classroom, a clamor by individuals in the community to teach them her trade did not go unheeded. After a brief stint of teaching, in 1952 she opened her own business school with only ten students and ten typewriters. It was the first postsecondary institution to offer business education and preparation for black men and women on the Peninsula. Of course, it was against the advice of naysayers. But Rattley had learned during her seminal development that the word "can't" was not in her lexis. "When I hear someone say I can't do that, I want to know why. You may not be able to do it today, but if you work hard, you will be able to do it. And I understand a lot of people give up because it's easier that way, and they don't have to withstand the opposition or the possibility of failure. But I was determined that I was going to do it even before I listened to what others had to say. My attitude was, I never had anything, if it's a failure, I just have to fail."

The same year she started her school, she married Robert Rattley, a civil service supervisor and a supporting mate, and they had two daughters, Robin and Florence. In her role as wife, mother, and educator, she was strengthened by her obstacles and by all the negativities of the dream sinkers. She succeeded in operating her business school full-time, both day and night. Although she faced the dilemma of training black students for positions that were limited in the segregated labor market of the 1950s, she was plainly resolute that they would be well prepared and that employment would be available after completing her business college. Rattley affirmed, "I was training black women and men for careers in business and nobody was hiring black people. No blacks worked in the shipyards; no blacks worked in the banks; no blacks even worked in the supermarkets; and no blacks worked in any of the department stores. None of the legal or professional people would hire blacks, even doctors or lawyers. Therefore, I had to open up job opportunities for these students. That's when I got involved in everything."

As Rattley reflected upon her activism, she remarked: "I think what is significant about my life is that I started these movements here in Newport News before the civil rights movement actually started. That's a little hard for some people to understand because they thought that what I did was just what King was doing, and I was imitating him. But I was doing it out of necessity. I didn't plan to do it. I did not do it in 1952 to start a civil rights movement." Admittedly, she acknowledged that the civil rights movement enhanced the work that she had already begun.

When the first students graduated from her business college, she sent two or three students daily to apply for a position at the shipyard. "When they finally decided to test them, they didn't even have a standardized test. They would just pick up a letter off the desk and dictate it, and tell them to transcribe it. They didn't even know how to grade it, so we finally got them to have a personnel office. It was the same thing at city hall, where not one black clerk or office person worked. I got really excited about a lot of things that I was able to accomplish." She even met with the Joint Chiefs of Staff and other officials in Washington to make sure her students were hired with the federal government. Eventually, she proudly proclaimed, "They were hired all over the country." She also organized economic boycotts against businesses that refused to hire blacks, integrated public accommodations, advocated for better housing, and championed the voice of the voiceless in her community. "But as far as people knowing about it, they don't. Of course, today, everybody's taking credit for it. But it was rough. It wasn't easy but it was something that needed to be done."

For her activism, Rattley was labeled crazy and a troublemaker by whites and some blacks who believed race relations were good and she should "stay in her place." However, when she succeeded in opening doors for those blacks who begrudged her courage, she sardonically characterized their behavior this way. "Once I opened the doors, they benefited. Someone even called me and asked if it was all right to carry his wife to dinner at such and such a restaurant." Another asked, "Have you integrated that one yet, so I can enjoy it?" To lead, Rattley always knew she had to do her research, check and double check her information in order to have a sound basis for action. It is the way she began her leadership and the way she ended it. Likewise, she cautioned other leaders to do the same. In 1970, she parlayed her grassroots activities into elected politics.

Getting Into Elective Politics

For nearly two decades Rattley battled racism in business, in housing, and in city services and employment from outside the system. The turning point in her life came in 1969, when Rattley gathered her family around the kitchen table, at a time when few women were in politics, to discuss her interest in running for city council. According to the Joint Center for Political and Economics Studies, from 1970 to 1975, there were 4.5 black men elected to office for every black woman elected.[8] On her first attempt, she won a seat on the city council in 1970, becoming the first black and first woman to be elected in Newport News and one of the few at that time in the nation. Rattley provided this rationale for entering elective politics.

> I never planned to go into politics. Certainly, I had no background and I was not in politics in Alabama. I would attend every city council meeting. I was speaking before the council, and was trying to open job opportunities. I was trying to get better housing conditions, better education, and better human relations among races. I discovered that everything involves politics and it governs everything you do—everything! In order to get the federal government to recruit for my school, I had to meet with the Chiefs of Staff. Well, how did I get that meeting with the Chiefs of Staff? It was through a friend who had a political office in Washington that I happened to know. To get resources into Newport News, I had to get them through political action. But if you look at it, and I think everybody should think about it, politics governs the food we eat, the clothes we wear, what type of house you will live in, what type of community you will live in, what type of education we will receive, even how long you must go before you can qualify for a position and what type of job you can hold. Even now, politics controls what God has given us. It controls the air. So that was my reason. When I found out that the only way to get jobs, housing, better roads, better parks, better recreation, or better anything, it was through politics. If I was going to do anything, I had to be involved in politics, I had to understand politics, and I had to understand how to play the game. It's not about money, except some politicians know how to make money doing it—illegally, most times. But it's about service.

Politics as Service

After Rattley initially won her seat on the Newport News City Council, she was again reelected in 1974, 1978, 1982, and in 1986 with the highest vote totals. During her fifth term, she was appointed as the first black and first woman mayor of Newport News, serving until 1990. During her twenty-year political career, she was elected as the first black and first woman to head the National League of Cities and served as trustee on the Executive Committee of the U.S. Conference of Mayors and as president-elect of the U.S. Conference of Mayors. In 1980 President Jimmy Carter appointed her to the Intergovernmental Advisory Council of the U.S. Department of Education. During his administration, she led a throng of delegations to various countries, such as Africa, China, Cuba, Hungary, Japan, and Panama. She became one of Virginia's best-known politicians. In fact, she was known by her actions from the streets of Newport News to the hallways of the state capitol and the East Room of the White House.

In the twenty years that Rattley served, this political pioneer, working with the city council and state and federal governments, brought over a billion dollars into the city of Newport News. In cooperation with fellow council members and federal and state agencies, she helped to change the face of Newport News from a blue-collar town. The construction of the Continuous Beam Accelerator Facility, known today as Jefferson Lab, is an example. It brings in leading scientists and researchers from all over the world, which has led to economic growth and job opportunities. Major corporations, like Canon, also relocated their headquarters to the area. In encouraging economic growth and development for her city, she never forgot her core constituents. She championed economic and educational opportunities for poor people and blacks, helping to improve housing conditions, recreational and educational opportunities, and the infrastructure. Her proudest accomplishment was the implementation of a new drainage system in the low-income neighborhood, putting an end to many decades of flooding.

> In this community when it rained, it flooded, and there were a few people who could not get out of their homes. We had no drainage and our sanitary sewers and water went together, which would mean our children were playing in the water. It was in the southeast community and every white politician would come over at election time and say if you vote for me I'm going to do something about the flooding. Nobody did anything. When I was elected, I did something. I got them separated. So then the question, how did you do it? I found the money to pay for it. I educated people that this is a sanitary health problem, aside from the inconvenience of not being able to get to your automobile if you have one, or of getting to a bus stop to get to work. During the slightest rain, it would flood. There were certain streets in the southeast community you couldn't ride through after rain because you car would be stalled. Most people said the improvements would never happen, but I made it happen.

Politics of Race and Gender

Making things happen as the first black and first woman elected official of Newport News was not a painless procedure. Every action of her being was dissected and scrutinized for public viewing and consumption. From the on-set, she indicated that,

> Many white folks thought the whole city would go to pot, and there were some who refused to call me mayor. But I was able to deal with all of this and I got the respect of many white folks, and, of course, black folks, too. But the strug-gle has been my whole life and it's dangerous out here. And when you hear of these conspiracies, even though they sound like a fairy tale, much of it is true. I was in the FBI files, and I was checked and double checked. They tried to find something on me.

In experiencing the double standard and double jeopardy of being both fe-male and black, her phone was tapped. "Oh, Jesus, they found the tap," she exclaimed. She was followed, threatened, and her guests' license plates were recorded and checked out. Even news reporters would stake out her house to observe visitors, and she felt much of the media canard was unwarranted. Once when her taxes were delinquent, the media "played it up for a week," despite the fact that she was away on official city business to bring revenue to the community and despite the fact that other members of the council were also negligent in paying their taxes. At another time, she bought two lots of property owned by the city and her actions were assailed as a conflict of in-terest by the media. Rattley noted that the city attorney had arranged the le-gal papers for her. Moreover, the transaction was done in open council, where she had asked for a ruling on the legality of purchasing the two lots. To illus-trate the double standard, she cited a later mayor who advertised for an auto-motive dealer, in which she believed was unethical and represented a conflict of interest, as well as favoritism, since other dealers also pay city taxes. How-ever, no one assailed him. For Rattley, the emotional and psychic memories "were too numerous and too emotional to relive. It was constant harassment." When asked how she coped with the tough game of politics with the added ingredients of gendered racism, she responded:

> As long as I am doing what I think is right, I tend to be able to withstand the criticisms, the obstacles, and the blocks that individuals throw down for you to fall over. It's about being knocked down, but getting up and kind of shaking yourself off and starting again. I had studied black history during my early high school years and I have always felt that these people were able to overcome slavery and the degradation of that time and I should be able to do the same thing. And if someone says I can't do something, I'm going to do it. You resist with knowledge. You must have goals and determination and commitment. And you cannot do these things with a personal objective in mind because I know of benefits that I have brought to citizens of Newport News that I have never got-ten credit for and probably never will.

As far as the racism and sexism, she answered, "I can't change my black-ness. I can't change my sex, and I don't desire to, so I decided to learn all I could, and to devise ways to fight them at their own game."

In 1970, when it became apparent that she would win her election as the first black woman, she offered this illustration of how she played the political game.

> When it was conceded that I would win, the former chief of police who was a friend of J. Edgar Hoover and not a lover of black folks said he was going to run as an independent to keep that nigger in her place. He ran and won, so here's the Chief and here's Jessie Rattley. I served and I gave him the respect he was due. [Of course, he liked black women behind closed doors; he was that type of Southerner. I was used to them after living in Alabama.] I tried to get a glue sniffing ordinance passed banning the sale of airplane glue, un-less you could prove that the glue was being used to put together airplanes. Young kids were squeezing this glue into a brown paper bag and getting a high. He fought it. I got a lot of empty glue tubes that kids had been snorting and carried them to city council, so they could see how serious it was. Be-cause he couldn't support anything that Jessie Rattley was pushing, he still fought it. I knew it was right. I knew we had to do it because a lot of kids were dying. I called his son, a well-respected neurosurgeon in the white com-munity, and asked him if he would share with me the effects of glue sniffing. He wrote me this paper, telling me just how detrimental it is to the children. I thanked him. So the night I brought it up for a vote, I explained why I was so interested in getting this ordinance passed because of the effects it has on our children. And I said, "I have one good authority, an expert in the field and a well-known neurosurgeon, who has written a statement as to the harmful ef-fects of glue, especially on young children. I will just pass it down so each of you can see it."

The ordinance passed unanimously. After the meeting, the chief rode home with another member of the council, and the chief said to this member, "You know what. That damned black bitch really scored one on me tonight." She claimed: "I didn't call his son's name publicly. I just passed the letter down, and there was the chief's son's stationery and his signature."

Rattley believed that,

> You had to be proper and you had to turn the negatives into positives. And I met a lot of people across the country, who, when I had a question, and I needed some facts, some knowledge, I would call, I would research it, and I would get my proof. Another one I pushed through, and everyone is talking about it now, is lead poisoning. I tried to get an ordinance through on that point and had dif-ficulty there too because the paint people didn't want to hear it, and I had to do a similar thing to get that passed.

In Rattley's twenty years in political office, she always prepared what she referred to as a report card of documented accomplishments. She claimed, "It was enough for me to just stay there for twenty years. I could have done that by just licking asses. But I stayed there because of what I was able to accomplish." It coincides with her definition of success. "I define it as what you have been able to accomplish for others and you want to hope that it's lasting. I believe you should help yourself, but I just feel as though that is not sufficient. The only way you can be successful is to do something that will help somebody else and that is why I believe anybody can be successful by my standards."

The price for successfully serving others can exact its emotional tolls, particularly when it comes from one's primary constituents. As mayor, Rattley was paid only four hundred dollars a month, which she used for clothing, food, and travel. However, some of her black supporters saw her position as a means of benefiting themselves. "You know most people expect money. A lot of people feel that they are going to get some personal benefits, and what I am upset about is I hear enough about trying to get some permanent benefits for the community, yet some of the constituents feel that if you are in public office then you can do favors for [them]. And they literally mean that. They want you to give them money, give them gifts, get them a job, or do this, that, or the other. That's what they see it as. One man came to me and said, 'Will you let me have ten?' I said, 'I don't have any money.' 'Oh, you know you have money. You own everything in the city. You're the mayor.'"

She added,

I am just afraid that some of our young people who are contemplating going into politics really don't understand what they need to know, and enter it for the wrong reasons. And, of course, there have been so many casualties out there that I think it is going to turn a lot of people off. So every day, people get the image that blacks should not be in politics because they are incompetent or they are criminals. And I feel it so deeply that I become emotional, because of the view that so many people have of politics and politicians. I look at some of the newcomers to politics and their views are so different from mine. It appears that all it is giving is social status. And they really can't tell you anything that they have done to help anybody. I would be ashamed. I can't say what makes the difference, but much of it is just for show and for a feeling that this will put them in a powerful position. And if they would really look at the history, especially for black Americans, you will find that there were many politicians of the view that you had to help the community. Many of the people who had a real purpose for running and really wanted to do something helpful had to leave office in disgrace.

After twenty years in elected politics, a bitter defeat ended her career in public office in 1990. But she kept on pushing to serve others. She taught as a senior lecturer at Harvard University's School of Government and as a senior lecturer in political science at Hampton University. When she died in 2001, she was finally recognized with much fanfare and accolades. Her body was the first to lie in state in the Newport News City Hall. In recognition of her dedication to the city of Newport News, Jessie Menifield Rattley Center, which contains City Hall and the surrounding buildings and grounds, was named in her honor on July 13, 2004.

Political Lives in Context

Jessie Rattley's political career, like black elected officials of her generation, emerged from her struggles in the civil rights movement, which is in accordance with the findings of the Joint Center for Political and Economic Studies. She, as other elected officials of her age, held membership in various civil rights organizations, and in spite of the organization's mission, a common thread of core issues such as housing, jobs, education, criminal justice, and an expanded federal government's role in eliminating racism united each of them. Moreover, those who came of age during the civil rights movement understood the importance of ethnic bloc political and electoral mobilization to bring about change in the African American community. Even though Jessie Rattley, a staunch Democrat, served in public office for twenty years in a city of over 100,000 with a white majority population, she never failed to advocate for her core working class and poor black constituents.[9]

Next, we shall turn our attention to James W. Holley III, self-identified liberal, Independent mayor of Portsmouth, Virginia. The Joint Center for Political and Economic Studies' national telephone survey of eight hundred black elected officials in 1999 reported that those politicians sixty-five years and older identified themselves as 77 percent Democratic, 15 percent Republican, and 7 percent Independent.[10] Like Rattley, Holley was also involved in the civil rights movement prior to being the first black elected councilperson for Portsmouth. Unlike Rattley who towed the partisan line, he is frequently criticized for "playing a hole card." To the critics who accused him of acting politically expedient, he responded, "I represent a 'whole' card." Hence, he is apt to support a liberal Democrat or a conservative Republican, depending on the direction of the political winds. This was the case in Senator George Allen's senatorial campaign of 2006. He offered this explanation, "Actually, a lot of astute politicians recognize that I am going to work with whoever will work with me. And so, I'll go into a black church and tell them that I think George Allen was a good governor. Now you may not like him because he's white but that has nothing to do with what he has delivered." For Holley, if you deliver on your promise, "There will be jobs for Afro-Americans, that will be progress for this community and the quality of life will be raised for everybody. When Allen was the governor, he could have said, 'Stop!' on my project to dredge the port. And he could have hurt us, but he helped us."

Though Holley differed somewhat from Rattley in political partisanship and behavior, both shared a similar formative social background and time period of World War II, the Great Depression, and Southern Jim Crow that shaped their values of racial uplift and individual and collective empowerment and the importance of spirituality, education, and a strong work ethic. However, unlike Rattley's working-class origin of personal poverty and struggle, Holley had a more privileged background. In fact, he was from a well-established, fair-complexioned family, which he said made whites more comfortable with electing him and other blacks in the late 1960s and 1970s throughout the South. "I will be the first to admit that the white community ultimately concluded that if this thing [integration] has to be imposed on us we want first everybody that looked like us—white people—and the first wave of politically successful black elected officials throughout the Deep South were the fair-skinned brothers and sisters. Whites would say, well they are not black, they are part of us some way by blood transfusions. And for the long time it was difficult for African-looking Afro Americans with thick lips, big noses, big feet, and stuff like that to get elected." Portsmouth has a population of 100,000, with a nearly equal representation of blacks and whites. Certainly the centrality of race in politics is still a reality. It manifests itself through skin color, as some studies have supported that white voters are more likely to support light-skinned black candidates than dark-skinned black candidates. Interestingly, when this question was posed to Kwame Kilpatrick, mayor of Detroit who is darker than Holley, he said, "I think that was still an issue when I came in [2001]. It is definitely an issue with the Hispanics and Asians, and definitely in the larger white community. Unfortunately, people are still color struck when it comes to who is smart and who is not, who is violent and who is not, who is more threatening and who is not. Yes, I think it still plays a tremendous role—who's beautiful and who's not. I think the standards of beauty are skewed in a different way. Unfortunately a lot of people make prejudgments based on skin color." Since the centrality of race remains a crucial feature in the lives of black elected officials, how has Holley negotiated it?

JAMES W. HOLLEY III: SAILING WITH THE WIND

As did Jessie Rattley, James W. Holley III, mayor of Portsmouth, Virginia, started his political career fighting for civil rights. First elected to the City

Council of Portsmouth in 1968, Holley, under the tutelage of his mentor, Hugo Owens, a black dentist, had caught the political fever, particularly after winning eleven federal court battles. When the Portsmouth public library refused to admit African American citizens, Holley and others took the battle to court. The judge ruled in the plaintiffs' favor, and the library opened its facilities to all. Holley was also a plaintiff in the litigation to permit African Americans unrestricted use of Portsmouth's city golf course. Again, the court ruled in favor of the plaintiffs. In addition, Holley spearheaded the desegregation of public housing and most of Portsmouth's restaurants, as well as a myriad of other color barriers.

What personal and social forces fueled his passion for politics and public service? Seemingly, a religious underpinning to improve the quality of life for himself, his family, the black community, and the larger society motivated him. For Holley, born in 1926, religion was that center of his middle-class family life while growing up. "Being exposed to the religious life was the centerpiece for all of our hopes, dreams, and aspirations. So I was impressed by those persons who embraced religion, in whatever form, to improve the quality of life not just for their own family, but everybody around them." His mother, an elementary school teacher and graduate of Shaw University, was a primary influence in the formation of his value system. She stressed religion, excellence, education, and listening skills, which was buttressed by his father, who served in the military for thirty years. These familial values were reinforced by church members and prominent role models within the church—the physician, attorney, and minister. "If you were in a church setting that was like circling the wagons around you to encourage you to do well," said Holley. Indeed, the World War II veteran did well. He earned a bachelor's degree in science from West Virginia State College and a degree from the Howard University College of Dentistry. Married with three adult children, he has served the community of Portsmouth as a dental surgeon in his private practice for over forty-five years.

The affable, easy-going dentist and mayor of Portsmouth, Virginia, was the first African American mayor elected to head that city in 1984 and has served twice. Prior to becoming mayor, he served on the city council from 1968 to 1984. His occupation as a dentist, serving a black clientele in the 1950s and 1960s, afforded him more leverage to speak out against the racial injustices of his community and to improve not only his family's life chances, but also those of others in his community. When I asked what made him a fighter, he replied: "I was intelligent enough to realize what the Constitution of the United States said, so I did not want these human rights taken away and I did what I could. Although I was already up, I was a doctor and I could have just said, 'I ain't going to worry about what happens to the rest of the niggers, I got a chicken in the pot and I got my car.' But I wanted to light a spark so others would come forward. In a sense, I thought that I was starting something for others to emulate, and it did."

In the late 1950s, what started out as a neighborhood cookout in his newly developed subdivision became the bonfire that ignited his political path. When the event concluded, a concerned woman neighbor wanted to address an unsightly problem regarding an open drainage ditch that crisscrossed the subdivision's property lines. She implored him to act as the representative on behalf of the inhabitants to speak before the city council and request the body to correct the problem. Since his property was also affected, he readily agreed, knowing that he had the support of the group. "We thought it was an issue that needed to be addressed, because it would transfer some private property; it was not safe; and it was incumbent upon the municipality to address the concerns and correct it because we were freeholders or taxpayers. And so that council took it under advisement and sometime later they did fix it. I had in a sense garnered some notoriety because sometime later I understand there had been a number of efforts to adjudicate that, but it never came up. After that, every time there was some considerable issue in the community, I had different groups ask me if I would speak." During this time he even fought for public-housing developments to become desegregated, even though he would not personally benefit. Not only did he feel a collective and personal responsibility to assist less privileged blacks, it was also partly because of self-interest as well. "If [poor blacks] feel as if you are gaining and they are losing, they become hostile and they will attempt to vandalize property as well as attack you personally. So I took the position early on, and mine is one of logic, they are not going back to Africa, and so the best possible way for us to grow is to reach out and work together." Eventually, after serving as campaign manager for his mentor, he decided to run for political office. "No Afro-Americans were on the council. And so after maybe 10 years of being everybody else's campaign manager, I ultimately was imposed upon to run, and I was the first to win."

As mayor, Holley has been instrumental in bringing opportunities to the city for youth, revitalizing neighborhoods and downtown Portsmouth. During his entrance and exit in public life, he has encountered many obstacles. When he was first elected to public office as council member, segregation was so overt that white council members refused to sit next to him, because they thought maybe he didn't take a bath. With dogged determination and being a skilled listener, he made his white colleagues feel comfortable with his blackness. Holley attributes his success to being a good listener. "I will hear you out. I will make you cognizant of what I think on a very succinct matter, but I won't impose that on you. I will hear what you have to say. And if it becomes a judgment, I will weigh that carefully." In 1982, after running unsuccessfully for mayor, he parlayed his diplomatic skills into changing Portsmouth's city charter. He offered an amendment to the charter, asking the state to change those elected officers—mayor and vice mayor—so they can be elected by all the people. Although he held little hope of its passing, it did. In his first bid for the mayoralty race, he lost; eventually, he won in 1984. In 1987 he lost his post in a bitter recall election over allegations that he sent hate mail, overspent the city's travel budget, and extensively used the city phones to make long-distance personal calls. "They contended that I did some inappropriate things that a mayor wasn't supposed to do. The mayor was not supposed to have dinner on a trip, wasn't supposed to travel first class, or anything they could think of. They also questioned whether I needed to go to all of the conferences. I took the position that I wanted to learn as much as I could from other mayors and other cities, whether large, small, or medium, to see what they were doing. I was able to bring back some ideas, but they didn't think it should cost them anything."

With friends rallying around him and encouraging him to stay in politics, in 1996 Holley reentered the political arena and has continued to serve for over a decade. At eighty years of age, the seasoned politician would like to be remembered as a man for all seasons. As one who unites people, he believes that if you can get along with all people, you can solve problems. As noted, Holley created some political sparks and backlash from black supporters when he endorsed Senator George Allen of Virginia. The senator had used racial slurs during his campaign in 2006 and was defeated in the congressional midterm election. In a press conference, Mayor Holley endorsed George Allen with this statement, "I would be remiss in friendship and responsibility if I did not endorse George Allen for his reelection to the Senate." The conservative senator had supported the federal Project Hope VI grants for Holley's redevelopment project in Portsmouth. When a reporter asked why a mayor for peace would support the senator who has wholeheartedly supported Bush's Iraq invasion and Bush's plan to attack Iran, he stated, "I was only looking at Portsmouth, and what's good for Portsmouth." To be politically astute, Holley advocates that an individual should never burn a bridge. "If an individual gets to the point where he burns bridges, he is no longer useful to the community because when you burn that bridge you leave some people back. As long as the bridge is there, those that did not get as astute as you can catch up. Where you went, they can walk in your footsteps. If you don't have that, they'll even forget about you and they will say, 'Where is he?' But when the bridge is still there, they will say, 'There he is. He's not that far, we can catch up with him.' You can make amends with that so they'll say, 'What happened?'" He is perspicacious enough to know that the storm will blow over, for Mayor Holley is guided by his political philosophy, "When sailing, let the wind die down, and the boat won't go anywhere."

Political Lives in Context

In the 1950s and early 1960s, Holley, a dentist, and Rattley, then a teacher and founder of a business college, were firmly ensconced in their careers in their respective segregated community while fighting in the civil rights movement. In contrast, John Lewis was coming of age as a high school and college student during the movement. His age cohort, born during World War II, shared a similar communal value system of social uplift as Rattley and Holley. He was symbolic of the energetic and impatient youthful cohort of the World War II generation from working-class and middle-class backgrounds who was determined through nonviolent means to overthrow Jim Crow. While Holley and Rattley were bruised in the civil rights battle, Lewis was bloodied and bowed in marches, in freedom rides, and in sit-ins. Not only was he a major participant in the movement, he is one of its giants and a living legend. Though half a generation older than Lewis, Holley and Rattley stand on his back, since they, as well as most black elected officials, particularly in the South, were elected within a short span of the Voting Rights Act of 1965. The nonviolent 1965 Selma to Montgomery march that he, along with Hosea Williams, organized to dramatize voting inequities, turned violent when the peaceful protesters were beaten by state troopers. This defining event became the impetus for the 1965 Voting Rights Act and it would set the stage for the thousands of blacks across the nation to enter the political arena. In 1964 only three African Americans were in Congress. In 2007 forty-three members are in Congress. John Lewis, who suffered the battle scars in the march toward freedom, was elected to Congress in 1986 and has served from 1987 to the present. While his story has been retold many times, his courage reminds us of our possibility as change agents.

John L. Lewis: In Search of the "Beloved Community" in America

"My life has been sailing against the current," aptly depicts the verve of this freedom fighter and public servant, born February 21, 1940, outside of Troy, Alabama. John L. Lewis, the son of sharecroppers, rose from poverty and working in an Alabama field to the halls of power on Capitol Hill. Frequently unopposed for over twenty years as the congressman of the Fifth District of Georgia, Lewis, formerly one of the Big Six leaders of the civil rights movement and one of the lead organizers of the 1963 March on Washington, has been the recipient of numerous awards, including the John F. Kennedy Profile in Courage Award for

Lifetime Achievement, the Ford Theatre Lincoln Medal, the National Education Association Martin Luther King, Jr. Memorial Award, the Golden Plate Award given by the Academy of Excellence, the Preservation Hero Award given by the National Trust for Historic Preservation, the Capital Award of the National Council of La Raza, the Martin Luther King, Jr. Non-violent Peace Prize, the President's Medal of Georgetown University, the NAACP Spingarn Medal. In honor of John Lewis, the Timberland Company has established an award that honors humanitarian service, as well as the John Lewis Scholarship Fund. Lewis has also received numerous honors and honorary degrees from colleges and universities throughout the United States, including Princeton University, Spelman College, Duke University, Morehouse College, Clark-Atlanta University, Howard University, Brandeis University, Columbia University, Fisk University, Williams College, University of Texas, Georgetown University, and Harvard University. Lewis has written an autobiography, *Walking with the Wind*.

Social Background and Influences

John Lewis grew up in a supportive household with parents, siblings, and extended family in segregated, rural Alabama. Somehow his folks knew there was something very special about him. As a child, he always wanted to preach about the "beloved community," sometimes extending it to all living things. "This may sound strange or crazy to you," said Lewis, somewhat self-effacingly when I first interviewed him in the late 1980s.

> I grew up with the idea of wanting to be a minister, and one of my uncles had Santa Claus bring me a Bible for Christmas. So the family started referring to me as "preacher." I lived on a farm, and I had the responsibility to take care of the chickens. I used to preach to the chickens, and on one occasion I tried to baptize one. When a chicken would die, we had a funeral. My younger brothers, sisters, and cousins were the mourners. We had a chicken cemetery and a chicken burial ground, and I would preach the funerals. I would also preach to the chickens at night when we closed them up.

Lewis eventually went on to get a degree in religion and philosophy from Fisk University in Nashville, Tennessee and, while there, he also graduated from the American Baptist Theological Seminary. Although he never became an ordained minister of a church, he has been called the "conscience of the U.S. Congress."

Significant Events and Racial Experiences

At Fisk, Lewis became an activist and leader in the civil rights movement. As the only member of his family to become involved, his parents were initially very frightened for young Lewis. Yet they were also fiercely supportive and proud of his participation. In the movement, he worked directly with Martin Luther King, Jr., and learned about the discipline and philosophy of nonviolence, a momentous turning point in Lewis's life.

> It created for me, like so many people, a new sense of values, and that's what I think happened to many of us. There was a revolution of values and ideas. You come to that point where you could see people as human beings. And you even forget to a significant degree about race, color, and whether someone was born on this side of the track or the other side of the track. Seeing people as people, you could try to move and create what Martin Luther King, Jr. called the Beloved Community—the open society and the sense of family—and that's what we are, the extended family.

Lewis has spent his life working toward building the Beloved Community. It has not been easy. There were always skeptics, black and white, who claimed it could never happen. "People said we couldn't talk the talk; we couldn't walk the walk. Governor George Wallace said we would never make it on our march from Selma to Montgomery, but we made it. We got a Voting Rights Act. We ended the era of segregated public accommodation." Lewis is referring to the 1965 march from Selma to Montgomery, Alabama, one of the most decisive moments of the civil rights movement, which he spearheaded along with Hosea Williams, also a prominent civil rights leader. They led over six hundred peaceful, orderly demonstrators across the Edmund Pettus Bridge in Selma on March 7, 1965, to demonstrate the need for voting rights in the state. In a brutal confrontation that became known as "Bloody Sunday," the marchers, including Lewis, were viciously attacked by the Alabama state troopers. The media coverage, in highlighting this merciless cruelty, accelerated the passage of the Voting Rights Act of 1965. Earlier, in 1964 John Lewis had coordinated efforts of the Student Nonviolent Coordinating Committee (SNCC) to organize voter registration drives and community action programs during the Mississippi Freedom Summer. During his civil rights activities, Lewis was arrested more than forty times, was physically attacked, and suffered serious injuries, yet he continued to practice nonviolence, seeing it as a way toward equal justice as a means to help build the Beloved Community. Lewis embraced the belief that, "through creative effort, by sticking together, and by developing a sense of solidarity, we could overcome."

When he left SNCC in 1966, he continued his commitment to the civil rights movement as associate director of the Field Foundation and his participation in the Southern Regional Council's voter registration programs. He later became the director of the Voter Education Project, and under his direction, the organization changed the nation's political milieu by adding nearly 4 million minorities to the voters rolls. Before entering the political arena, President Jimmy Carter appointed Lewis to direct more than 250,000 volunteers of ACTION, the federal volunteer agency. When he first ran for the Atlanta City Council in 1981, some people told him he couldn't get elected. His opponent was "too well known and had too much money." But Lewis understood his "life has been sailing against the current." This same current was present when he was told that he couldn't win his congressional seat in 1986. "I drew on my inner resources and inner strengths. It was the only thing I really had. I say to young people today, 'You can make it. You can do it. Don't sit back and say you cannot make it. If you believe in yourself, you can do it.' I've been blessed by coming under the influence of Martin Luther King, Jr. and the influence of the discipline of nonviolence," Lewis remarked quietly and assuredly.

For a younger generation who did not experience the influence of a man like Martin Luther King and who did not come through the same kind of struggle, there is remorse. In an interview with Seth Goddard, he lamented, "We don't have that sense of what I call moral urgency. There are different battles. It's a different period and it's not as simple. We saw those [public] signs [of segregation] and they were very visible, and today many of the signs are somewhat invisible. We have a different leadership. I think too many of us in the late '60s, '70s, the '80s, and even during this period, got caught up in getting 'my piece of the pie,' getting 'my piece of the action.' We'd become too concerned about mine, mine, mine, rather than being concerned about all of us. We are all in this thing together."[11]

Since his civil rights days, this bright candle of consciousness has steadfastly worked for world peace and social and economic justice in his search for "the beloved community." Lewis has never lost his faith in this ideal. It is no wonder that he is regarded by his colleagues as the moral conscience of Congress.

Political Lives in Context

In 1987, when Lewis took his seat in Congress, the country had shifted to a more conservative political climate. Not surprisingly, blacks like Clarence Thomas, Shelby Steele, Walter Williams, and Ward Connerly became outspoken advocates of both political and social conservatism. They opposed the social policies of liberal Democrats that came out of the civil rights movement and the public policy priorities of the 1960s. In general, these conservative black Republicans have rejected the use of governmental intervention as the potential solution to the social problems that persist in black communities. Instead, they advocate self-help programs and strict adherence to the traditional American values, such as individualism and hard work. But Lewis never wavered. In 1993 John Lewis, who represents Georgia's majority black fifth district, received a 95 percent rating from the Americans for Democratic Action for his legislative actions, while the American Conservative Union gave him a rating of 0 percent. One year earlier, Gary Franks, who represented Connecticut's majority white fifth district, was given a positive rating of 80 percent by the American Conservative Union and a 20 percent positive rating for his legislative positions by the Americans for Democratic Action.[12] Interestingly, in 1992 the Congressional Black Caucus (CBC) wanted to oust the only black Republican from the CBC because of his opposition to the section of the 1965 Voting Rights Act that created the majority-minority congressional districts. That year many new Southern CBC members had been elected from the newly drawn majority district. [Gary Franks agreed to extend me an interview in December 2006, but later declined because of extenuating circumstances.] Both men and women in various levels of government benefited from the creation of a black majority district.

According to the Joint Center for Political and Economic Studies, in the mid-1980s, black women elected officials had begun to increase their numbers. Beginning in 1990 new black elected officials were disproportionately women. This trend represented a dramatic change from the early 1970s when about 82 percent of newly elected black officials were men. In 2001 women comprised 35.4 percent of all black elected officials. In 2001 there were 15 women in the Congressional Black Caucus and 194 black women state Senators and representatives across the country. In 2002 there were eleven women serving as mayors in cities with populations of more than 50,000. Shirley Franklin, mayor of Atlanta, for example, was among those who were elected in 2001, the Year of the Woman. Franklin, unlike Rattley and Holley, held no elected office prior to becoming mayor. However, when I interviewed her in the late 1980s for the work on *The Black Elite*, she was a readied apprentice-in-waiting, having served as a major player in the administration of two mayors—Maynard Jackson and Andrew Young—who had come out of the civil rights struggle. Franklin, also a businesswoman, differs from the aforementioned politicians in that she was born and reared in the North and educated in diverse milieus. She was a part of that first integrated generational cohort that Edwards and Polite referred to as the children of the dream who had educational, economic, and social options available to them.

When Franklin was born in 1945 during the prosperous post-World War II years, the Great Migration of blacks from the South to the North was in full swing. Detroit, Michigan, was considered one of the black meccas of the North. Some twenty-five years later when Kwame Kilpatrick, mayor of Detroit, was born in 1970, a reverse migration pattern had begun from North to South. Atlanta, Georgia, was the mecca for blacks. When Franklin's generation came of age during the civil rights movement and the events of the 1960s, the economy was still booming, and it was a time of hope and racial progress for African Americans, as well as blacks throughout the Diaspora as newly independent countries gained independence from formal colonial powers. The idealistic youth of the 1960s heard President John F. Kennedy's clarion call to service, urging them to "Ask not what your country can do for you, ask what you can do for your country." In contrast, Kwame Kilpatrick's generation's coming-of-age took place in the increasingly conservative political era of Reaganomics. Unlike the youthful idealism of the 1960s, this generation heard a different clarion call, to paraphrase Kennedy, "Ask what your country can do for me, ask not what I can do for my country." Kilpatrick's era was a time of rising crime rates, exploding epidemics of crack-cocaine, and rising black prison-population rates, familial disruption, unemployment, and racial profiling, particularly in poor urban black communities, like Detroit, known for its auto industry. This city, as other major urban cities in the North, was undergoing rapid deindustrialization as more corporations, like the auto plants, left Detroit and relocated to surrounding suburbs, to the South, and offshore. In major cities of the North and South, middle-class populations were abandoning the cities for surrounding counties, leaving behind an eroding tax base.

As big-city mayors, both face similar major problems of an aging infrastructure, an eroding tax base, crime, drugs, poverty, and high unemployment. However, Atlanta has a more vibrant economy to meet the challenges of these urban problems. While Kilpatrick believed he was destined to lead by becoming a politician, Franklin described herself as "an accidental politician and an unintentional mayor." At age twenty-six, Kilpatrick began his political career when he succeeded his mother in the Michigan State House of Representatives and later became the youngest mayor of a major city in America. That was in 2001, when both Franklin, at fifty-five, and Kilpatrick, at thirty-one, became big city mayors. Now both in their second term, Franklin won her second term by an overwhelming margin, whereas Kilpatrick staged one of the 2005's greatest political comebacks. Interestingly, Franklin, in her first term, became the darling of the media and was described by *Time* magazine as one of America's best mayors, while Kilpatrick was dogged by the media and labeled as one of America's worst mayors by *Time*.

Unlike Franklin and other older politicians discussed here who came out of the civil rights tradition, Kwame Kilpatrick represents a new generation who was born after the movement. According to the Joint Center for Political and Economic Studies, younger black elected officials are more likely to be businesspersons or lawyers as opposed to ministers or civil rights leaders. They are also more likely to be college educated and to hold an advanced degree, and they are less likely to have attended a segregated high school or a historically black college.[13] The parents of black elected officials in Kilpatrick's generation are more active in politics: 33 percent of the black elected officials between eighteen and forty years of age had parents who held an elective office; between forty-one and forty-nine years, 49 percent held elective office; between fifty and sixty-four years, 23 percent held elective office; and sixty-five years and over, only 14 percent held elective office.[14] Younger, black elected officials are also less likely to have been active in the civil rights movement or to hold current membership in the civil rights organizations. In addition, while older black elected officials are more likely to emphasize a civil rights agenda, the younger ones' emphasis is on economic rights. Perhaps this is because younger black elected officials are less likely to consider racism the most important national problem than older black elected officials.

Younger black elected officials are also likely to be more conservative and nonpartisan than their older counterparts. With different experiences, one is likely to have different worldviews and priorities. In essence, these younger elected officials share similar attitudes as their cohorts in the general black population. Seemingly, they are losing touch with their elders, as there appears to be a latent discontent with the old guard. In recent years a new generation has risen up to challenge the old guard, such as Newark's mayoral race between Sharpe James and Cory Booker in 2001. Booker lost his challenge in the first campaign, but won in the second political round.

Born after the assassination of Martin Luther King, Jr., Booker was raised in the suburbs of New Jersey. He studied at Stanford University, became a Rhodes Scholar at Oxford, and graduated from Yale Law School. Booker, a Democrat, supported vouchers and faith-based and private sector initiatives, which are opposed by the older generation, like James, and is seen by many as contrary to the traditions of the Democratic Party. Interestingly, Booker carried 40 percent of the black vote to James's 59 percent, 57 percent of the Hispanic vote to James's 42 percent, and 62 percent of the white vote to James's 37 percent. Moreover, Booker, who had a well-funded campaign, used paid workers in his 2001 campaign to get out the vote operation, while James relied more on volunteers from the city workforce, labor unions, and some paid workers to get out his vote.[15]

In the 2004 election, the Democratic Leadership Council pushed forward a new generation of black party leaders like Barack Obama and Harold Ford, Jr. with more centrist views. These Democrats have also promoted a centrist view of civil rights, incarceration, education, and the employment issues, as well as international issues such as genocide in the Sudan and AIDS in Africa. They were reluctant to confront the social and political issues addressed at the hip-hop political convention in 2004, or Congressional Black Caucus agenda meetings or the national black agenda gatherings. This generational change is even reflected in the Republican Party. When Askia Muhammad, a columnist, compared the themes of Representative J. C. Watts's speech to the speech by General Colin Powell, he commented that it "shows me the difference between what it means to be young, Republican, and black, and to simply be a Republican, and it's more than just words. Gen. Powell's speech, emphasizing his concern for the poor, [the] disadvantaged, the 'least of these my brethren,' (so to speak), reflects the 'old view' of black politicians, service to the 'black constituency' and its disproportionately more desperate position in the American society and economy. Rep. Watts's speech, on the other hand, reflects that new 'post-Me-generation' mentality of blacks entering politics which emphasizes service to self and family, ahead of service to race and community . . . Unlike Gen. Powell's more 'traditional' approach, Rep. Watts also says exactly what anti-black white Republicans want to hear coming from a black person . . . that the suffering and miserable conditions from which so many blacks in the under class suffer is a result of their own poor lifestyle choices, not the result of white racism, or the legacy of slavery."[16]

How does Kwame Kilpatrick fit into the perspective of this new generation? Let us turn to his story for further insights.

Kwame Kilpatrick: A New Generation

Born in June 1970 in Detroit, Michigan, Kwame Kilpatrick, mayor of Detroit, is the sapling from an old, politically active family tree, which is firmly implanted in the politically charged church community, the Shrine of the Black Madonna, a Pan African Orthodox Christian Church. For Kilpatrick, his family, church, and community are the taproot of his political being. "I came out of a politically organized, community organized grassroots, very pro-active Garveyite mentality of blacks having their own everything. It was a nationalistic type of environment." This native son of Detroit denotes the new breed of politicians born after the struggle of the civil rights movement, whose parents enjoyed its first fruits and thus had the opportunity to become more active in politics than the older generations of elected officials. Both of his parents were members of the Shrine of the Black Madonna, an organization with a politically active network, and the driving force behind the first mayoral race of Coleman Young, the first African American mayor of Detroit. Kilpatrick's mother, Congresswoman Carolyn Cheeks Kilpatrick, from the 13th District of Michigan, is the fifth woman elected to serve as chairperson of the Congressional Black Caucus (2007–2008). Prior to Kilpatrick's mother's election to Congress, she served in the Michigan State House for eighteen years. In 1978 when she was elected, Kilpatrick, a self-identified Democrat, was only eight years old; at twelve, his father was elected as a county commissioner, so the political ambience covered him like heavy dew. At age eight, he knew he wanted to be a state representative.

When my mother was elected to the Michigan State House of Representatives, I was eight years old and I went to the state capitol. It was the first time that I had been there and I was sitting on the house floor. I just thought that was the coolest thing, and the fact that my mother worked there was big. It was the initial thing that engaged me in politics. My mom worked at the state capitol, so I wanted to work at the state capitol. From that day, I determined that I would be a state representative, even before I knew what she did. I used to tell people that's what I am going to do. At eight years old, I told folks that I was going to work in the state house. I had tee shirts with the capitol on them, and I could just see myself sitting on the floor of the state house as a representative.

Although his parents, both teachers before entering politics, were divorced when he was ten years old, they remained a significant part of his and his siblings' life. They stressed the importance of education, spirituality, and political activism. Kilpatrick, a graduate of Florida A&M University with a degree in political science and a Juris Doctor from the Detroit College of Law, especially remembered that his father taught him about his history and heritage: "My father was a great student of history. I was heavily engaged in African and African American history from a very early age. I don't remember ever not knowing about the civil rights movement, or Egypt and the great kings of Africa." After the divorce of his parents, which deeply affected him, he became more independent, which was positive. On the negative side, his grades began to suffer around the sixth grade and Kilpatrick, who was accustomed to making As and Bs, was kicked out of school, probably for fighting. After he was thrown out of the Detroit Public Schools, from a portion of the seventh grade through the eighth grade, his mother forced him to go to Lansing Public Schools and permitted him to return to his neighborhood only on weekends.

His Lansing experience was diametrically opposed to his life in Detroit. It was the first time that he had not been politically involved. "I hated every minute of it, but looking back on it, I would say it was actually a good experience. That was the first time going to school with white kids and the school was about fifty/fifty black and white. I did not have anything political to do after school. It was a whole different setting for me. It wasn't a city, it was a small town. It made me love Detroit." In Lansing, Kilpatrick encountered his first racial experiences and one of them took place on his first day of class. "It was the first time I ever had a white male teacher. I remember very vividly that when I introduced myself in class, he asked, in front of everyone 'Was my father still in the picture?'" At that time Kilpatrick did not grasp its meaning. But upon relaying the story to his mother, she did. His visibly upset mother "jumped on

them for that." Kilpatrick indicated that he entered the Lansing School System
with the attitude that "no white person was going to say anything to me, they
had to be friendly or else." But they were not. So when he heard, for the first
time, the racial slur, "I don't like you, nigger," he exclaimed, "It blew me
away!" His time in Lansing, while alienating, had positive benefits. "It was a
positive experience for me because it was new and different. It taught me that
people live and go to school in different ways. There I was able to participate in
a neighborhood-school setting, something that I had not done since elementary
school. I did not have to come in the house when the street lights came on. You
could ride your bicycle freely in the neighborhood and you could attend school
in the neighborhood. And that was a different experience than anything that I
had ever done." In his youth, he could not value those experiences—he longed
for the comfort of his beloved city of Detroit. "There was a sense of self-determination with African Americans, especially since I grew up in an atmosphere
where African American people were running things. There were teachers,
lawyers, and doctors and they were smart. And my church taught us African
American studies. We weren't just slaves." In contradistinction, Lansing's
blacks didn't have that sense of self-determination. In fact, Kilpatrick observed
rampant apathy and disdain for the political process in their suburban communities since they lacked power to effect change. He further noted that the individualistic ethos of the suburban community undermined group solidarity. "I'm
here because I like my house and I want my kids to go to this school in this
neighborhood. People just learn to live in and accept that kind of environment.
The difference with me is that I learned from birth that everything touches the
body politic and I couldn't live in a community where I couldn't effect some
standards and I felt powerless. Most of our suburban communities around us are
white, male dominated, and I can't live in that kind of situation. I think it affects
a lot of African Americans that live there. They just don't participate." He
added, however, many middle-class African Americans do identify politically
more with issues in the urban core that surrounds them and would like to be politically connected, but they live outside the city. This demographic shift of the
African American middle class to suburbia has negatively impacted black politics, Kilpatrick speculates: "Now it seems as though it is different from the kind
of politics of the 1960s where everybody is spread out to their own existence, a
kind of individualistic island way of thinking, resulting in a whole lot of apathy
to participate in any kind of movement."

Kilpatrick's Perception of Generational Differences

While generational differences are evident in the larger population in the
post-civil rights era, this pattern also holds true for elected officials. It is Kil-

patrick's view that "when you talk about generational differences in terms of newly elected officials in the African American communities, it's such a mixed bag: you have Kwame Kilpatrick all the way to Cory Booker in Newark to Barack Obama in Chicago or Harold Ford in Tennessee. We are so different and we all come from different backgrounds." Despite their differences, they represent a bridge between generations. Kilpatrick sees himself as that bridge. "I see myself probably as the others see themselves, as a bridge between the older politics and the newer politics. But I think it is very geographically specific if you could be that bridge. Let me tell you what I mean by that. Nearly all older elected officials came out of some organizational politics. If they were Democrats, they came out of the union, they came out of some kind of church movement, and they came from some organizational body—NAACP or Urban League. If they were very big in some black organization or union organization, they were propelled forward. Well, that's just not true in the new generation of elected officials."

Kilpatrick believes,

Everybody got there a different way. Cory Booker, who was Ivy League educated, committed himself to being mayor of Newark. He had some friends in very high places, was well funded, lost one race, and came right back and won. Barack Obama was a local official who really lucked out and got into the national race when one of the frontrunners had a scandal and dropped out of the race, but he won when he gave that great speech. And now he's being talked about for president. But he really has no organizational background. Then there's Harold Ford and Jesse Jackson Jr., like me, are the second generation [of being politically active], but all of our parents were different. Jesse's father is well known for what he did, but Jesse is nothing like his father. He's economically focused and sees the new civil rights movement as being into the economy and who gets access to capital. Harold Ford is a lawyer like I am and his second-generation politics are different from mine in Detroit. He's from the South. He had to cross over and get white support from the hinterland.

Perhaps Kilpatrick sees himself as more analogous to a suspension bridge for his largely African American community in Detroit; that is, while responding to the needs of diverse constituents, he, too, must maintain a strong enough tie with core constituents to resist the bending and twisting of the truss.

I'm different. In Detroit, this is a very nationalist and revolutionary city. This is the home of the Shrine of the Black Madonna; the largest mosque of the Nation of Islam; and the largest branch of the NAACP in the country. It's a lot of nationalist and revolutionary folks here and then there's this strong black middle class that derived from the auto industry, teaching, and the post office, and there are more black architects and engineers here than any other city in America, which gets overlooked. It's probably the most expansive black community in the country. And at the same time, there is poverty. So you have to be a different kind of bridge to be able to work with the NAACP, the Shrine of the Black Madonna, and the Nation of Islam while building a bridge to the new economy, thinking for African American folks who believe that the next civil rights movement will be based on access to capital and entrepreneurship, venture capital, and the new industries diversifying our industrial base. I think I am that bridge for this community, where I think all of them can be bridges for their communities, but we all came at it a different way, which is something that didn't exist in our communities thirty years ago. I think that's why [the older generation of elected officials] is looked at as being so different, because everybody came out of a similar reality. Whether you were in New York or Detroit, or Chicago or Philadelphia, you were black and you were a Democrat and you got to it the same way. So I think that's the different thing today, is that all of us have come into these positions with various backgrounds, various levels of education, various ideologies or perspectives and we represent such a cross range of constituency.

While ideological differences have always been a historical reality in black politics, as politicians serve more diverse constituents in the post-civil rights era, unarguably, they become more accentuated. One distinction elected officials often confront is: How do they negotiate the thorny issue of race and racism? Are they likely to become more race neutral—that is, deemphasizing it, as they serve diverse constituents? Kilpatrick, who in 2000 was elected the youngest mayor in the history of Detroit, said of constituents: "They want Kwame Kilpatrick not to talk so much about black stuff, and they want Barack Obama to talk more about black stuff."

Trying to be a suspension bridge for a myriad of racial and ethnic communities can pose a dilemma, because constituents often respond like a beam bridge. The weight of public opinion and level of support, like the beam pushing straight down on the piers, sometimes causes black politicians to collapse. When I asked Kilpatrick about Harold Ford, the 2006 black senatorial candidate from Tennessee, and his campaign to appeal to white voters, he commented:

Yes, he was trying to cross over and he was doing a great job, but unfortunately he ran into those red-necked voters in Tennessee. But they made him black. At the end of the day, no matter how much he was trying to be just a good candidate for the senate, and color not being an issue, at the end of the day they made him a partying black guy. It's interesting. He was socially acceptable, but the best way to get him was to put him in a room with a white woman. That was terrible. It was like, you're light, but you are not white. And I know that he probably never expected anything like that. He probably thought all the race stuff had cleared up. But at some point it's going to come out. I thought his response to it was good, but he couldn't respond the way that he should because he had run a campaign about keeping race out it. So when the ad hit, he said, "Yes, they got me. I like women and I like football." So it was a good response and it got a laugh, but he couldn't argue that "we don't need this racism in Tennessee." Sometimes when you run so hard to not be impacted by racial issues, it is a very hard thing to be caught up in.

And I think with [Barack] Obama now, he's the darling of the United States but he's careful not to take any positions about race, which is interesting. . . . I really hope that Obama does okay, but it's a real trick bag when they build you up so much. I don't know where he can go. And I don't think that there's a ceiling, but I believe that at some point you are going to have to confront the issue of [race and racism] and how he comes out of it on the other side will be interesting.

Kilpatrick thinks that black politicians are more likely to deemphasize the role of race and ethnic politics than other ethnic groups.

Jewish politicians don't get into politics for themselves. They are going to be open and honest about their support of Israel in this country. An Arab would do the same thing, as would a Hispanic. I don't think white folks have much use for you if you can't impact change in your own community. As a Democratic leader in the state house, I was the first African American and the youngest to be in that position. There were thirteen black folks in the house. My colleagues tried to rope me into that position. I'm the same all the time. And they knew that I would watch their backs if they got me elected to that position. And I never tried to act white or be different. I think everybody across the board has respect for you when you just remain yourself. I think that the whole run to the middle in terms of race issues has affected our community, too. You can be a conservative Democrat, or you can be a moderate Republican. I don't have no beef with you. I don't have no beef with none of those folks. I think if it's an issue that concerns our community though, we're supposed to be in the same place—a kind of meeting of the minds or in the middle. And I just see that as a positive. I really, really do. If people could position themselves to be no color, in the final analysis they would make no gain for the community at all.

For many of his own constituents in Detroit, he said, "particularly the middle-class blacks, think that he is 'too black'" and the problem facing the black community is more economic than race. "Even though I think it's an economic argument also, folks here don't want me to be so 'black' (I'm putting that in quotation marks) in my perspective. But I think when you have an 80 percent African American community and African Americans don't have access to jobs, it is economic suicide. On the other side, I think a lot of people want Harold Ford to be more black as well as Barack Obama. So I think there's this constant push sometimes to bring everybody to a different perspective, instead of understanding the rainbow or the plethora of perspectives that are out there. We can all work together in lifting everybody up in our community, but we just come at it in different ways."

Kilpatrick understands that a racial and class divide exists within his city of Detroit, and the way that he comes at it is through creating more job opportunities. Here he offers this account of personal mobility of his family and other blacks who migrated from the South before deindustrialization occurred in the urban areas of the North.

> In Detroit you had people who were sharecroppers when they came here [from Alabama], and they got a job and earned an honest day's pay for an honest day's work. People, like my grandfather, came to work in the plants forty years ago and [were] able to move from the poor to the working class to the middle class in thirty-six years. He raised a congresswoman, lawyers, and teachers among his five children. So I think the common denominator is a job and access to money and it is the only way to change that divide.
>
> Seventy percent of the people in Detroit have their roots in Alabama, so they weren't bourgeoisie in Alabama. But they came here and they started working in the post office and the plants; they became teachers and elected officials, and all of a sudden, we had created this expanded middle class which then got these clubs—Jack and Jill, the Boule, the Masons, the Eastern Stars, Alpha Kappa Alpha, and Alpha Phi Alpha of which I am a member. The common thing that got these folks together, who were probably formerly very poor, was jobs. And I think the only way out of it to change this divide now is to get people working again.

Although the race and class divide intertwines, Kilpatrick thinks that poverty is the major issue facing America. "America can no longer afford poverty. Everybody needs to work." Not only is he concerned about the growing gap between the haves and the have-nots, he is also perturbed about the working poor and shrinking middle class. "The only way to sustain a city is a strong tax base, particularly a strong middle-class tax base. In America now, this shrinking middle class where you have this growing number of folks who don't have access to a quality job is a good way to benefit the global competition that is forcing more people out of work and into poverty. A lack of retraining programs and reentry programs in America is forcing people into poverty. Beyond Iraq and all the other rhetoric, the biggest issue facing America is the population of people that are living in poverty. So it is the [lack of] recognition of the working poor and people living in poverty that is eating us up from underneath. I don't believe that we will have a country in the next twenty years with that particular situation."

Kilpatrick wants to see poverty solved in his community with federal assistance. As cochair of the U.S. Conference of Mayors's Committee on Poverty, he, along with others, has coordinated a poverty task force to draft a policy for the 2007 majority Democratic Congress to help cities. At the local level, Kilpatrick stated,

> I'm pushing now for radical and revolutionary change to address emerging needs to determine where the jobs are. We also have a program here called Home Again. We brought the foundation community together and we are trying to align some federal dollars to help retrain people coming out of prisons. Education, reentry, and career technical training are the biggest things. We put our unions together, which have been an old boy network for a long time, because we are building so much here. We have about $20 billion in building. And then I have challenged a lot of rules to force headquarter businesses into forcing builders to hire eligible workers, because they struck down all of my race-based programs. I had all kinds of race-based stuff, but they took me to court and they declared it unconstitutional. They found old records of Mayor Young and then they said mine was all wrong. The state can pass the affirmative action ban, but I am going to keep doing what we have been doing—provide public employment and contracting to women and minority business. I assume that they will start something again next year, but I hope they get it kicked into federal court because I don't believe the state should be making decisions about affirmative action. So we're doing a lot of that stuff in our poverty initiative to move people from poverty to work.

Since class and mental health are related, he is working, at the state level, to help the city deal with this issue. "In Wayne County, about 70 percent of the mental health cases are in Detroit, so we are serving the population of the city that needs serving. The poverty situation in this city is unbearable," Kilpatrick stated.

Kilpatrick not only looks at the roles that the federal, state, and city governments must play in closing the class gap, he strongly believes that privileged African Americans have a responsibility in this effort. "It is incumbent upon the African American community to take care of our own. Our community will never be like the others until folks do what they should do—give back, organize themselves, and organize others like them. Philanthropy in our community comes predominantly from those outside the community. And I think until we figure that formula out, we will always be in the cyclical condition that we're in—death, poverty, crime, drugs, and a few people making it." Moreover, blacks must understand the urgency of the crisis and how their fate is integrally connected to the poor, such as the rollback of affirmative action measures impact the expansion of the black middle class.[17]

> Look at all the economic indicators, and all of the education gaps between us and whites. So when you look at the emerging pressure of the global marketplace, it

begs the question of where we fit in. I am concerned because I don't see the unity in our community that I think the times demand of us. I just see so much individualism and not a showing of independence and a showing of self-determination that we have to do something for ourselves. And I'm worried. I think about the future of our people here. Look at the number of people in prisons, the number of people graduating from college with degrees in higher education, look at the hopelessness of youth at such a young age. I'm a father, too, and I am concerned about what kind of future we are leaving for our children. This is something I think about every day. I can't go to a bright side. That's what I am sincerely worried about—the outlook. Comedian Chris Rock in one of his acts said first, there is a war between niggas and black folks and niggas will win it. And that's how I feel about that. And we got to figure out a way for black folks to start winning. Right now I feel that we really need some help from each other to turn this thing around.

For Kilpatrick, the class divide intersects with the growing generational divide. "I think it goes back to 'I got mine: you get yours' mentality." In this generational gap divide, many young people lack connection to an organization and if they are a part of one, many of the organizations are not socially active. "A lot of our new churches are not active organizations in the community or part of the community," acknowledged Kilpatrick. "The mega churches or the prosperity ministries or even if it is not a mega church, it is just a place you go to and then you go home. It does periphery stuff. It might have a food drive and that kind of stuff but it is not a part or a cornerstone of the community which it serves." For instance, some blacks believe their children will fare well in society and become productive members of it, but they have little concern about the child down the street or in the next block. But Kilpatrick says, "Well, that ain't necessarily true, because your kid got to marry somebody; he got to go to the prom with someone; he's got to walk past those kids and the pressure is so great." In reference to the generational divide, Kilpatrick commented to his mother that it was the fault of her generation.

It is your fault. You all taught us to go off to college and be educated. You all didn't teach us to take care of our community and about our responsibility to give back to the community. That was not part of our upbringing. Most of our parents—all of us thirty-somethings—told us to go to school, do our homework, get a degree, and do something great. That last part that we should bring something back to the community was not there. I think those growing up in the 1950s and 1960s, they got the responsibility part. You got to help the little brother do that. Go down the street and help those people cut grass. I think people got the community help thing together. You could not think about not voting in the 1960s. Now it is like—ain't nobody thinking about voting until election time. This community responsibility and civic responsibility happened a generation ago and we got to figure out a way to repair it. This whole individualism stuff, you get yours and I'll get mine, that stuff is killing us.

Conspiracy Theory: Myth or Reality?

Grappling with the urban ills is only one of the many concerns of big-city mayors. Like numerous black elected officials that I interviewed, Kilpatrick has also battled with the media for fair representation of his message and his image, which undermined the effectiveness of his leadership. When I posed the question to Kilpatrick about whether he thought an attempt to discredit black elected officials was a myth or a reality, in his own words, he told this story:

I definitely am spoken of differently from any other elected official around here. It has changed somewhat since the election [of 2005], since we beat them. But my first four years, it was a serious attempt to "niggerize" me. I came here a different way. The previous mayor was in the Boule, he was a part of all those social societies, he was a member of all the golf clubs, and he was in athletic clubs and the private clubs. I'm not in any of that and I don't have any interest in being in that. That's not what I do. I would rather come home at night and play with my kids. I don't do what has traditionally been done. So I think there are two problems with me—age and the fact that I wasn't a socially acceptable black person. That made me a real target. So a lot of people didn't know me. The community folks knew me, but not a lot of folks in the business community or the press. I really made a lot of inroads in the business community and we did quite well. But the press, from the time I came in office, they thought about me in a very negative fashion. They chose two white reporters to follow me. Their job was to find dirt on me. They had meetings behind closed doors. So it was a very horrible experience, my first four years. There is a neighboring county's chief executive who has a long tenure and a sketchy history on race relations, a white guy who kind of represents white people in this community, as opposed to me who represents black people in the community, made the papers together. He was caught driving drunk. It was a one-day story. They would speculate, I mean someone would say that the mayor was in a club drinking and that ran for two weeks.

When asked was there a basis for any of the accusations, Kilpatrick responded:

No basis at all. I've watched stories when my wife was in the bed about innuendos. One of the big ones was that I had a party here at the house with strippers. That started with an off-duty police officer. The attorney general launched a full investigation, talked to the neighbors who said there was no truth to it. [The attorney general] came back and said there was nothing to it, but [the media] couldn't let it go, because my reputation was that I was a party guy. Although I've built more houses than have ever been built, fixed more streets than have ever been fixed, got more new parks than ever in the city, opened up more restaurants—you name it. There was never a complaint about the job that we do, but it was all about, who is this guy and what can we do to tear him down. I talked to Marc Morial who was the [former] mayor of New Orleans and he told me it was coming. And he was right. It was every day. It has stopped now, but [it took place] for my first four years all the way through my reelection. This community kind of rebelled. In my reelection, I got about 70 percent of the black vote and my opponent got 92 percent of the white vote. So it was an interesting dynamic, even my reaction. But we won and now we have brought those two communities together, but they did something every day to try to present me in a negative way.

When asked in what ways he brought the community together, Kilpatrick remarked:

What I did is start what we call community conversations, which we have already had over fifty of them. I did them three nights a week. And I started during the election and I am still doing them now. I get a person who can get together twenty-five or thirty people in their home and I go into their living room and talk with them. I go into white homes, black homes, and Hispanic homes. What people do is call the office and ask for a conversation and I come over to their home and we have a conversation. I think what it did, it humanizes you. I did three last week. Even in a big city like Detroit, where people don't get to touch you, they only know what they see on the news, it is even more important for us to go into as many households and touch as many people as possible. So that's how we fought it. We fought it by people seeing the news stories and saying, "Well, I just talked to him the other night. I just don't get that." We fought it by hand-to-hand combat, we called it going out and engaging the community ourselves, having people ask the right questions and having them hear us talk about the issues, and I think that's what helped subside [the negative publicity] a little bit. The newspapers were all against me and for the first time in history, the television stations endorsed my opponent. It was a real wake-up call for them when I won. I had a real nice reception for the media, which surprised them. And I had a conversation with them which has worked so far. But I agree with the others, there is definitely a different way that the media covers African Americans. There's always the notion that there is some crooked something. They present it with that "gotcha mentality" which they really don't have.

Without question, his town-house meetings reshaped his message and image, admitted Kilpatrick. "That was the big thing that broke down this 'Legend of Kwame Kilpatrick.' I was kind of like the legend of me from the television. They made me a totally different person from what I really am." Kilpatrick believes this legend started from a 2003 hip-hop summit in Detroit sponsored by the NAACP to get young people to register to vote.

At that particular event, we had about fifteen thousand young people registered to vote on the spot and we had good speakers and we did a little concert for them. And at that event, Russell Simmons said, "We want to thank Kwame Kilpatrick who is a hip-hop mayor." The next day, they put in the paper that I'm the new hip-hop mayor, and how I should be ashamed to be called that because hip hop degrades women and from that point on is when they really started to go straight negative. They wanted to make me the worst guy ever and the hip-hop mayor thing became a recurring thing in a lot of the articles that were being written. And so when I would be asked about it, I would say, "Thanks to Russell." He thought it was complimentary and that was cool. I guess I grew up in the hip-hop era, but I don't want to be confined by anything. So that's cool. I got respect for a lot of the articles but that's not really who I am. But it was what it was, and that's when it took off in a negative way. It bothered me from the perspective of how it was being used against me.

To counteract the negative image, he continued to engage the community by scheduling numerous debates with his opponent during his reelection for his second term and by interacting with the grassroots, in arenas where his opponent and others dared to tread.

We got the people that nobody else could touch. The folks that operate out of their cell phones. They don't have a home phone. You can't poll them. We worked the beauty shops, the barber shops, the churches, the clubs, black bars in the city, and we had the most extraordinary grassroots efforts and we still engage in efforts with them. I stayed very close to the beauty and barber shops because we thought we had to change the conversation in Detroit, and there's no better place to do that than in churches, beauty and barber shops. And we changed the conversation about whatever was happening on TV. I invited all the beauticians and barbers to my home. We had three hundred people in my house who were beauticians and barbers and we had a conversation about the city of Detroit and about the things that they heard in the press. And I think it helped greatly to change the conversation. Somebody getting a haircut might say, "Man, I don't like that Kilpatrick." And the barber would respond, "I was just at his house." We changed all that. Also, I went to the cab drivers at their association meeting and we sat together for three hours and had one of those conversations I told you about. And that changed the perspective of a lot of people getting a cab. I went to the bus drivers and had a conversation with the bus drivers. We had about 150 bus drivers and I sat with them about three hours and talked about their issues. The conversation in the city started to change because people talked to me. I began to have a conversation with people who liked me or supported me, and they had a conversation with me. That changed the conversation. We were looking at the polls and the polls showed that my opponent was going to win. It was different because the people that we talked to and engaged every day were polling the most likely voters and they knew that we were making an impact on the unlikely voters, people that they never expected to see at the polls. We had young voters, but we wanted senior citizens, too. I won the senior citizen demographic. We won the 18–35 demographic and we got more people to turn out in that demographic, but we raised that from 4 percent, which is traditional in the city of Detroit in the 18–35 demographic, to 35 percent.

During Kilpatrick's first four years in office, the gust of negative publicity would sometimes bend his spirit, but like a strong oak tree in restless and unrelenting winds, he never broke. So how did he manage to negotiate his personal trials?

It was tough from a personal level. The strength of my relationship with my wife helped a lot. It was real life versus political life. My ten-year-old twins and my four-year-old don't care anything about that. All they want to do is wrestle, and go about their work and school. They could care less about what is going on. And that's real life. When you walk in it is "Daddy, look what I did in school." "Daddy, can you come play basketball with us?" "Daddy, we want you to go here or there or can you come to my game." It is always an escape from political life. I have a very strong family thing and that is an escape, I have a strong wife who handles this stuff pretty well most of the time, and then right in the middle of it is church. For eleven days, I fasted and had prayer. Personally that helped me a lot.

When Kwame Kilpatrick was asked, what would you consider your greatest accomplishment as the mayor of Detroit, he answered by saying it was the blackout of 2003.

I think that my major accomplishment was the [blackout]—you know we had a blackout, the largest North American blackout that ever happened in 2003. All the lights went out in the afternoon. Nobody had any lights throughout the city. We organized a coordination of our emergency response, and I am so proud of the people of this city. That was the first time we talked about defense. That was real successful. It was 90 degrees outside, but we got our senior citizens out of the high rises, we got everybody water, and you know CNN was reporting there was pandemonium and exploding riots. And really, nothing happened. We were walking the streets with our brothers and sisters who were caring for our community. Now I think it was one of the most fiercely moving things that I have ever gone through, but also my greatest accomplishment.

Kilpatrick, now in his second term as mayor, will no doubt have many more accomplishments. The gusty winds had ceased and a calm breeze wafted over Detroit City Hall when I interviewed him in November 2006. If Kilpatrick continues to ascend the political ladder, will he remain the suspension bridge for diverse African American communities? Will his guiding principle, he says of "helping my race," be compromised if he ever runs for political office in more racially and ethnically diverse milieus? For the young mayor who pronounced, "I don't hate nobody but I love black folks and collectively we can move it all and accomplish what we try," his legacy is still blowing in the wind.

From the standpoint of the older politicians that I interviewed, they believe that younger elected officials more than the ones of their generation are more self-serving careerists. While Kilpatrick's political perspective appears more closely aligned in a myriad of ways with the old guard who came out of the civil rights era, one can only wonder whether his orientation is typical of his cohort. As black elected officials serve more diverse constituents and as the fissures along class, generation, ideology, and partisan lines within African American communities grow wider, will the needs of black constituents be compromised, especially the poor? If self and family before community become the paradigmatic mantra for a new generation, then the hard-won political battles remain continuously in jeopardy, despite the fact that over 9,500 black elected officials represent the federal, state, regional, county, municipal, judicial, law enforcement, and education levels.

These gains have come at a heavy price and are the results of the long struggle of blacks in this country, which culminated in the Voting Rights Act of 1965. Blacks have viewed the right to hold office as an important means to gain a foothold toward freedom and justice in the United States and as a way to improve their economic and social conditions. Plainly, the black struggle in this country remains as an unfinished symphony. Will the new generations of black elected officials be the drummers for the community or for self? And will the black community hold their elected officials accountable?

7

Black Artists: The Soul of Black Communities

The artist was chosen as the embodiment of the soul of the black community, which in one sense represents a shared ethnic awareness and pride. But in another sense, I am referring to the essence of a community of agents' implicit and explicit ontological assumptions of reality, principles of life, feelings, actions, and moral and spiritual groundings that are reproduced by artists. Black artistic creators, as noted by David F. Dorsey in "The Dual Aesthetics of Black American Artists," are likely to derive their inspiration and passion from the struggle of blacks for cultural, socioeconomic, and political power. As he intimates, "The persistence, strength, and independence of the African cultural tradition in America is nowhere more evident than in art, especially music, dance, and oral expression. Therefore the black artist in these fields is likely to be blacker than his audience."[1] Is Dorsey's assertion applicable to the visual artist? John Biggers, visual artist of the pre-civil rights era, believed it to be true. Biggers saw this persistence, strength, and independence of the African cultural tradition in African American artists among various generations in the African Legacy, a nationally traveling exhibition in the 1990s. "In this African Legacy, the trained and untrained artist who had been on the same road came to ascendancy. It appeared that the power of the African consciousness has never weakened. Both trained and untrained African American artists in African Legacy had profited from a value relationship rather than analysis and perspective."

The retention of Africanisms is not surprising to Dorsey. "Artistic creativity cannot flourish in a closed soul. In choice of content or emphasis at the very least, the multifarious poignancy and the artistic complexity of the black culture in America will demand expression in its heirs." On the other hand, however, he points out, "Equally the ubiquity, frequency, and dominance of Western artistic materials (acrylic paint; saxophones; that sculptor of sentences, the typewriter) and arbiters (the museums, the record company, *Downbeat*'s critics) will lighten the blackest artist."[2] If Dorsey's declaration of the duality of artistic spirit has merit, it may be a crucial gauge in assessing generational changes among black visual artists in a market-driven economy. While the power of the African consciousness is strongly embedded in Biggers's art, are there generational differences between the pre- and post-civil rights visual artists in their ethnic consciousness? Are there generational differences between the pre- and post-civil rights visual artists in their attitudes toward success? "The way I look at life comes out in my painting—what we think, live for, and die for," said Biggers. "If you paint for yourself and clarify your thoughts of your deepest feelings, you are not trapped by success. Art is its own reward: do not expect to be paid for it!" In quoting James Baldwin, he stated, "'You can be a great success, but never be a great artist. You can be a great artist and never have success.' It is marvelous when the two can come together. I feel especially grateful to do things with the approval from society about what I am doing. I enjoy monetary rewards. But I would paint if I never sold a picture. This process is sacred to me."

If differences do exist among artists, might these changes be the weathervane for generational value shift among black professionals employed in the diversity of occupations in the post-civil rights era? Let us turn our attention to the artistic arena for directions of the winds.

SOCIAL STRUGGLE AND PERSONAL IDENTITY

"The struggle of the artist in the Western world has meant the struggle of personal sacrifice. Nobody caught more hardship than Vincent van Gogh. No one contributed to the field more than he. Every artist has van Gogh's struggle and being black adds another dimension to that struggle within that struggle," claimed John Biggers, a visual artist.

To imagine the solitary creative process of a black artist in juxtaposition to the throng of people surrounding a black politician is to capture the invisibility of artists in the black community. Not only is the visual artist often invisible, but one's product and creation is largely devalued. Whereas the presence of black politicians is seen as central to blacks' collective welfare, visual artists are not. For the artist to remain largely invisible and devalued by the larger society and by the black community is to negate the transformative power of visual art in the struggle for social equality and economic opportunities and in healing the psychic and social wounds of a community. bell hooks, in *Art on My Mind*, speaks to this reality.

Indeed, with respect to black political life, in black liberation struggles—whether early protests against white supremacy and racism during slavery and Reconstruction, during the civil rights movement, or during the more recent black power movements—the production of art and the creation of a politics of the visual that would not only affirm artists but also see the development of an aesthetics of viewing as central to claiming subjectivity have been consistently devalued. Taking our cues from mainstream white culture, black folks have tended to see art as completely unimportant in the struggle for survival. Art as propaganda was and is acceptable, but not art that was concerned with any old subject, content, or form. And black folks who thought there could be some art for art's sake for black people, well, they were seen as being out of the loop, apolitical. Hence, black leaders have rarely included in their visions of black liberation the necessity to affirm in a sustained manner creative expression and freedom in the visual arts.[3]

David Dorsey has speculated that black artists oftentimes are "blacker" than their audience. Hence, they may be in the vanguard of political leaders who often express the values, wishes, and aspirations of the community. For example, during the black cultural movement of the late 1960s and 1970s, some visual artists clearly viewed art as having a significant role in the self-definition and self-determination of African Americans in the struggle for political and social liberation. Sharon Patton noted that during this time, "There was a call for a revolutionary art. The dictum 'art for art's sake' was repudiated. Art should reflect cultural values and 'must expose the enemy, praise the people and support the revolution.'"[4] For such black artists' groups as AfriCobra, the purpose of their art was to reclaim African culture for political and cultural reasons and to establish a relationship between artists and the African American community. Thus, they were interested in making art relevant for the black masses that appealed more to the senses than to the intellect. Consequently, art was more representational than abstract, resulting in a raging debate about culture, race, and community. bell hooks, cultural critic and writer, noted that, "As black artists have broken free from imperialists' white supremacists notions of the way art should look and function in society, they have approached representation as a location for contestation."[5]

Black artists who adopted a nonrepresentational or abstract style during the late 1960s and 1970s, except that which emulated African design, were interrogated about their identity and their commitment to the community, since such art was labeled as white mainstream and therefore irrelevant to the black struggle. "How black are you," became the rallying cry!

Claudia Widdiss: Art for All Humanity

Claudia Widdiss, born in 1950 in Harlem, New York, to a seamstress mother and a singing waiter father, has intimate familiarity with that era. This professor of art in sculpture at Eastern Connecticut State University grew up in Harlem in the 1960s.

> For someone who grew up in the 1960s, the questions I raised are: Am I going to be a black artist or just an artist? What will be the content of my art? Will I be a platform for the people, my race? Am I going to go for art for art's sake— enjoying mainstream America? A lot of black artists find themselves in this predicament, which comes out of this double-consciousness. I am one of many black artists who have this search for identity in our work. What am I going to say? How am I going to talk about this American experience? Every artist has to talk about some experience that is reflected in his art in some way. For the black American, this double-consciousness comes out vividly. You can see it when you look at black art. One can visualize this deep internal conflict.

Clearly, these black artists' groups of the 1960s and 1970s raised the level of awareness and appreciation for black art and black aesthetic in the African American community. bell hooks reminds us that, "Representation is a crucial location of struggle for any exploited and oppressed people asserting subjectivity and decolonization of the mind."[6] However, for some black artists, the limited perspective of what constituted black art was too confining to express the depth and universality of the human experience and the multiple pertinent social categories such as race, class, and gender that an individual or group might occupy within a society.

Widdiss thought she had to solve this problem of being a black female artist. "I thought at one point I had to solve this dilemma. I had to come up with this answer, and everything would be clear, and I would be the artist that the black community wanted. I felt that would be the thing to do; but now I don't think I can solve this dilemma. I go through periods where the dilemma of the black-white conflict and the male-female conflict comes out distinctly in my work. At other times, I need to balance the pain of that reality. I have to deal with the universal themes of the human condition, because if you cut me, my blood is red like everybody else's. I am a human being first." At various points in her life as an artist, she has focused on different themes. In her universal search, she may focus on "just the energy of how a flower grows; just the movement of the sky; just a feeling—nothing concrete—where you say this is a man or a woman. I have a need to deal with feelings and often you can't tell what a feeling is." Her panoptic feelings include her childhood memories of her seamstress mother making patterned curtains to cover the police gates on the windows of their two-and-half-room gray-stone apartment in Harlem, as depicted in her *Healing Curtains* series. One of her aluminum sculptures is hanging in the J. Eugene Smith Library at Eastern Connecticut State University. "The police bars on every window made awful shadows from what little sun could come in," recalled Widdiss. Her sanguine mother, Dorothy Widdiss, created curtains with a spirited Afrocentric pattern to cover the bars, which she realized were there to protect her "against the rage of a very frustrated community, but which had also come to symbolize the hostility of society at large." But Widdiss stated, "Those windows really made me feel like a prisoner just as the bars that started spreading across New York stores and windows that serve to remind me of the boundaries that I could not cross." In focusing on those elements of her basic humanity, she hopes that the transformative feeling of her *Healing Curtains* from bars to healing, as well as other pieces, is communicated to a diverse audience. "I am black and female, and I hope that all that will be reflected in my statement. I think that's all I can do, and I want to represent the whole planet, not just blacks. I am part of the world."

The feelings manifested in her art encapsulate the complexity of her lived experiences of coming of age in Harlem in the midst of the politically turbulent black nationalist movement, and being a witness to the destructive forces of the streets—teenage pregnancy, drugs, and death—that claimed the psychic and physical lives of her fifteen- and seventeen-year-old-friends. To escape the mean streets and find peace with her spirit, art became her balm in Gilead and her saving grace. It was from her talented artistic older sister who never made peace with her own spirit that Widdiss developed her love for art. "The first time a hammer and chisel was in my hand, I was sixteen and a student in the Harlem Youth Opportunities Unlimited–Associated Community Teams (HARYOU-ACT). The idea of discovering a unique shape, hidden inside a square block of stone was fascinating to me. I wanted to learn everything I could about carving. For the next four years, I studied stone and wood carving, along with clay modeling and drawing. My carvings during this period were figurative, but the forms were gradually becoming simplified."

Although her white teachers encouraged her artistic talents, Widdiss was especially influenced by the black artists working in the community arts programs in 1960s with whom she could readily identify. She spent her waking hours studying and making art at the Art Student League in New York, a private white academy, and at the National Academy of Fine Arts. At the Art Student League, she won the Chaloner Prize Grant to study in Europe. On the day Widdiss, who is fair skinned, received the scholarship, one official exclaimed: "But you have white blood in you, don't you?"

All the euphoria, all the art for art's sake left me like someone had slapped me in the face, because I had been thinking art was colorless. It ended up that I was still just the black wonder child. I felt that whatever talent I had was attributed to my white blood, because she didn't say congratulations or anything, but only that I had white blood. I was hurt by what the woman had to say. I remembered that the president of the academy had written a letter of recommendation and ended it by saying, "She is a wonderful black girl." I asked myself, "Why did he say that?" Once in Europe, I wondered whether I had gotten the scholarship because I was a good artist or because I was a wonderful black girl. I felt all of that was absurd. And I was angry. It was a real turning point in my life, where I had been passive, and really wanted to enter a white world to escape from my blackness by leaving Harlem every day and going into the white world. At this point, just before going to Europe, I got into my black bag. I taught at Pratt Institute, teaching young blacks between the ages of seventeen and nineteen to draw. I also went up to Spanish Harlem and worked with the grassroots program trying to do something there. I felt very strongly at this point that I had to do something for the black community, because black people were looking at me as black and not as an artist, so I was confused. I left for Europe and read as many things as I could about blacks. It allowed me to concentrate on perfecting my art, and it eliminated me from being so obsessed with anger. Perhaps if I had stayed in America, the perfection of my art might have taken a backseat to my involvement in the community.

There in England, she worked as an apprentice to sculptor Denis Mitchell, who had assisted Barbara Hepworth for many years. Mitchell generously shared his wealth and knowledge about sculpture, and while working for him, she learned how to use a variety of tools for carving and metal work. During this time, in a private studio, she continued her work, which had become simple carved abstractions. When her scholarship was renewed, she moved to Carrara, Italy, and rented a studio in a shop with marble artists. From these excellent craftsmen, she learned how to use pneumatic tools, as well as developed more skills in stone carving. After returning to the United States, she continued as a working artist and filling odd jobs for survival. Eventually, she enrolled in college where she received her BFA in sculpture from Rhode Island College and her MFA from Southern Illinois University at Carbondale. Since 1993 Widdiss has been teaching at Eastern Connecticut State University and making art. Married to artist Arnold Prince, she has exhibited extensively and her work figures in a number of permanent collections such as the Omni International Hotel, Spelman College in Atlanta, and at the J. Eugene Smith Library at Eastern Connecticut State University.

Between 1978 and 1983, Widdiss made a series of woodcut prints, and her work was labeled as feminist art or white art, usually by black men. She defied those labels others attached to her.

I think that with the conflict of living in America as a black person, you cannot avoid the external environment and the events that are occurring around you. I can't pretend that I don't see them. And those things trigger internal themes in me to spur me to create. Some things are personal, but I tried to merge my personal conflict and to try to express it as a microcosm of my black brothers and sisters. Other things are expressed in a more universal feeling. Or it can be expressed using African themes. I think I have been less successful in some of my prints. People will see them and say, "I know what that means, I felt that too." And so I know my feelings are very real, so long as they exist in other people that tell me there are some serious problems out there for black women, especially. Some say I'm a feminist, and that I hate men; some see my work and say that I make white art. I get all kinds of things. In terms of hating men, this is more likely to come from black men.

The issue of sexism was a dominant theme in her print series—the issue of impressionable black women. "And also in certain pieces, the issue of just racism comes across," she said. Widdiss no longer wrestles with her youthful dilemmas of being black enough, for she has come to terms with her blackness and her femaleness and wants her art to connect to all of humanity, particularly after the 9/11 tragedy of 2001. She works in various media, and her art is influenced by many cultures and time periods, including African, Native American, and Haitian cultures. "I feel that even those works of mine that express the physical aspects of an Afrocentric message have a universal meaning," she noted.

Too often in the black community, art has been viewed in a binary oppositional way, as representational or nonrepresentational, Eurocentric or Afrocentric, positive or negative. hooks articulates this concern.

In the past, particularly in segregated schools settings, the attitude toward art was that it had a primary value only when it documented the world as is. Hence the heavy-handed emphasis on portraiture in black life that continues to the present day, especially evident if we look at the type of art that trickles down to the masses of black folks. Rooted in the African American historical relation to the visual is a resistance to the idea of art as a space of defamiliarization. Coming to art in search of only exact renderings of reality, many black folks have left art dissatisfied. However, as a process, defamiliarization takes us away from the real only to bring us back to it in a new way. . . . There must be a revolution in the way we see, the way we look.[7]

For Widdiss, "every artist has to talk about some experiences that are reflected in his or her work," so it is central to her that we rethink the way we see and look at art. "I want to feel like when I die that I have been a useful person and I left behind something—that I did something to make the human condition better in some way. My philosophy is regardless of what is happening in my life, the enormous struggle it takes to be an artist—black and female—I don't want to lose sight of that goal. I want to leave something behind that is good." To incorporate new ways of thinking and seeing, hooks suggests that "such a revolution would necessarily begin with diverse programs of critical education that would stimulate collective awareness that the creation and public sharing of art is essential to any practice of freedom. If black folks are collectively to affirm our subjectivity in resistance, as we struggle against forces of domination and move toward the invention of the decolonized self, we must set our imaginations free."[8]

ARTISTS IN FOCUS

Artists, particularly marginal ones, perhaps more than any other professionals require greater passion and sacrifice because the creative process and the product may not be valued by the larger society, by the black community, or by those elites who control the cultural production of art—art historians, museum curators, art galleries, art critics, art collectors, and patrons of the art. These elites influence the standards by which art is defined and judged, what artist or art work is accepted or represented in museums and galleries, or collected and patronized. So this reality reminds us that art is integrally interconnected to politics. Although artistic freedom is an ideal notion, artists do not create in a vacuum. Within this democratic, capitalistic society, the artist is constrained by pivotal social forces of classism, racism, and sexism, as well as other pertinent essentialisms. This is translated to mean that they have to adhere to the Western white male middle-class model to be accepted into the mainstream. If an artist is accepted in the mainstream, he or she must balance artistic freedom with the commodification of his or her product. While Claudia Widdiss can appreciate monetary rewards, she has chosen artistic freedom over the commodification of her works of art. "As an artist, my idea of success is to continue to be a prolific artist, in spite of the odds, to find a way to create no matter how very little money, materials, and personal tension. You know, it is nice to have a little money, but when all is said and done, it is the work that history is going to be concerned with. Many artists work in poverty, others have worked in affluence, but my whole idea of success is creativity. Being creative is being professional." Although, she pointed out, "I work very hard. But I do not get adequate respect no matter what I do, there is always the question mark, 'Is it enough?' 'Will I be accepted now?' 'Will the doors be finally opened?'"

Widdiss, sculptor, printmaker, and painter, is sandwiched between John Biggers, muralist, painter, and graphic artist, and Steve Prince, printmaker. As in the larger society, the styles and forms of black art, such as graphic landscape painting, biblical painting, social realism, abstract expressionism, black aesthetic, or postmodernism, have flourished and declined during various eras, as represented by these three artists. While black aesthetics was an influential movement in the late 1960s and 1970s when Widdiss was studying to become an artist, in Biggers's earlier years as an artist in the 1940s and before the civil rights movement, black aesthetics of social protest were vehemently repudiated by the black community and by white cultural critics. In the 1980s and 1990s, when Prince was training for his profession, the controversial debates over black art versus mainstream art had subsided. While some artists continue to view "art as an aesthetic and technical enterprise," numerous others in the postmodern era are "searching for ways to express their individual lives and genealogy of different cultures in order to enlarge the viewer's understanding of black people and what constitutes black art in the United States."[9] While Widiss was perhaps influenced to a greater extent by such sculptors as Henry Moore, Isamu Noguchi Kouros, David Smith, and Barbara Hepworth, who had a common artistic background in cubism, futurism, constructivism, Dadaism, and surrealism, Biggers was more inspired by social realism of the 1930s and 1940s and although Prince came of age in the postmodern era, he is more influenced by social realism and black aesthetics.

As artists/critical teachers, similarities and differences exist among them. Each artist felt a similar commitment to the artistic calling and the willingness to make sacrifice to transform society through art. bell hooks says, "Art constitutes one of the rare locations, where acts of transcendence can take place and have a wide-ranging transformative impact."[10] Unlike Widiss, whose formative years of art training were grounded in the Eurocentric tradition of creating art for art's sake, Biggers, who was influenced by his Jewish professor, an Austrian expatriate fleeing the Nazis, never had any desire or inner conflict about whether to create art for art's sake. He viewed art as a transformative mechanism and social protest. Prince, who came under the influence of his mentor, John Scott, art professor at Xavier University in New Orleans and McArthur Fellow, is very much in the tradition of John Biggers and views himself as atypical of his generation. Each artist came of age during a different time that significantly impacted his or her body of works. Biggers's formative years were during the Great Depression in the rural South, Widiss grew up in the urban North during the civil rights and black power movements, and Prince came of age in the post-civil rights era, an era of electronic communication and computer technology and globalization of economies and the McDonaldization of cultures.

While Biggers's formative years were in totally segregated settings, Widiss and Prince had more interracial contact in theirs. Prince, who lived and attended school in predominately white environs, had even more contact in his early years than Widdiss who attended a black Lutheran school through the seventh grade before entering predominantly white institutions. Their intergenerational era shaped the way they experienced racism. For Biggers, it was more overt and circumscribed in his life than Prince who only recognized the subtle manifestations later in his development. Each artist's talent was nurtured within the family. While Biggers and Prince were influenced by an older artistic brother, Widdiss's artistic talent was inspired by her older sister. Biggers accidentally came to the profession when he came under the tutelage of his college mentor, in contrast to Widdiss and Prince who undertook art as a chosen profession earlier in their development. Interestingly, sexism and hypocrisy in religion became the catalyst that helped to raise the three artists' level of consciousness of sexual inequality, particularly Biggers's and Prince's, and transformed their relationship with the church. On the one hand, Biggers and Widdiss embraced their spirituality, but they rejected formal religious affiliation. On the other hand, Prince replaced his Catholicism with Pentecostalism.

These comparisons cannot begin to explain the breadth of these artists, because regardless of social background they have all felt the sting of how race has affected the way their work is perceived by those who control the cultural production of visual artwork. While Widdiss's life has been highlighted, the focus now turns to John Biggers, born in 1924, and Steve Prince, born in 1968; they are forty-four years apart. As each tells his story, the reader can see differences and similarities emerging between the two generations.

John Biggers: An Artist for All Times

The life path of John Biggers, internationally acclaimed painter, sculptor, teacher, and philosopher, would carry him far from the dusty roads of Gastonia, North Carolina, near Crowders Mountain where he was born April 13, 1924, and grew up as the seventh child of seven children during the Great Depression. It was a time when migrants and hoboes walked the rails, remembered Biggers. "Once a weather-beaten Indian man came to our house during the Depression and he begged for bread. My mother prepared him a meal and gave him some of my father's clothes. I was about four or five when he called me aside and told my parents, 'This boy is a seventh child of a twin.' My father was a twin. He said that I was supposed to do something that had meaning to humanity." And for Biggers, art was that contribution to humanity.

Art, which was always respected in his home, was Biggers's earliest authentic experience in creativity. Beginning as a preschooler, he and an older brother, from whom he learned to draw, would recreate annually, as a spring festival, the whole city of Gastonia out of the clay under their house. "We carved animals, cars, wagons, and we made water—creeks and branches. We had pigeons, rabbits, popcorn fields, and family life. My brother copied pictures from the Bible while I watched and reproduced them as a small child. A part of our growing up was not only making animals, but also learning to draw. It was a part of growing up like playing baseball, basketball, and football." His grasp of sculpture and architecture was impregnated and sensitized during his innocence of youth.

Biggers's artistic imagination was also nourished by his parents. As a creative storyteller of folklore, history, and mythology, his father, a minister with whom Biggers spent much time, was an avid reader who enjoyed translating from a Latin Bible. "When he translated the Bible, it was like the Lord speaking himself. As I sat around and listened to the older men who were also ministers, it later influenced my paintings of the elders philosophizing about daily occurrences." His father was also a teacher who instructed his pupils in a one-room schoolhouse. Here, as his father went from one class to the next, Biggers, who spent some of his time being educated by him, learned to read early, and in this milieu he developed a love for history and literature that dealt with the human condition. Through these media, he obtained ideas about his art. From his father, who also worked in the coal mines of West Virginia during the summer to supplement his salary, Biggers learned to be a craftsman. Before the Depression, Biggers's father was also a shoemaker and carpenter who owned a small shop. As a young boy, Biggers recalled that his father would come home from school and work in the shoe shop until eight o'clock in the evening. At the sound of his footsteps, with the heavy aromatic scent of tobacco and apple covering him, the children rushed to hug their father, to pull his hair and ear, and to have him empty his pockets for candy and peanuts. These were vivid memories that captured the imagination of Biggers's family life. When Biggers was twelve his father died, but he left a major impact on him. His strong work ethic, integrity, and generosity were the chief influences. "As a minister, my papa did not accept a salary and this impressed me. He felt no person should be paid to preach because you are dealing with a soul and the spirit." He also admired his father's can-do spirit; although he had only one leg, he used it creatively to play ball and as a lesson to remind his children "there was no such word as 'can't' and one should never use it."

Biggers remembered that his father was also a visionary mystic who could look into the future and predict events of death, illness, and so on, after looking into the red coals of fire and after drinking from a cup. Biggers told this story about his father, whose ancestral background was a mixture of African, Caucasian, and Indian: "My mother was a laundry woman and we were crossing the street when we were hit by a car. My mother's knees were injured and I received only minor scratches. My father came to the segregated wing of the white hospital because he saw it in the fireplace—a young boy and a woman hit by an automobile—and that could have been my mother and me. So he came."

Though his father had a major influence on Biggers's life, his mother had an even greater one. After his father's death, his mother, a housewife who occasionally cooked for white folks, had to go to work full time as a laundry woman. Educated by white New England teachers in a private academy, Cora Biggers, his authentically and morally strict mother who did not imbibe alcohol or smoke, was uncompromising in her belief system; and for Biggers, she would become the lasting inspiration for his art.

> I was the last child and I helped my mother wash the clothes in the pot. I remember that she was not ashamed to do that work. Honesty had a great meaning in her life. In this sweaty type of dirty labor in which you are handling the dirty, nasty clothes of other people—we are really handling others' waste—and you turned those dirty things into bright clothing, which have been renewed. You hang them on the line and they sparkle and smell good. I learned something early about a process and a cycle in life. When you scrub things, how wonderful it can be. I understand from my mother what baptism meant. Their souls are being transformed. Using the analogy of washing clothes, she related to her children this life's process. That is what I try to get across in all my creative work, this transcendence. This is so basic it can't be missed. We are transforming the dank and dark into the light.

From his mother, he gleaned further insights about the renewal and recycling process of quilting, whose beautiful mosaic patterns were created from the family's "worn-out clothes." "Times were hard so you could not waste scrap materials used for quilting, so you had to cut with precision. We would take an old dress or pair of pants and reassemble them and make a new product from many piles of old clothes. Again, it was a renewal." Biggers realized that as he grew older. "My work was based more and more on the structure we used to build quilts and the transforming of dirty things into clean things and renewing things. This is like the cycle of nature, decaying and creating."

Even in the midst of the Great Depression, his mother also taught him to see beauty in the drudgery. Biggers remembered that, "In the darkest moment, when the barrels were empty, she always saw beauty in something. Even when she had her hands in boiling water, my mother could still look up and see the beautiful ice crystals forming on the trees, instead of getting lost in the drudgery. She always told us to look people straight in the face and stand straight. If you have beliefs and ideas, you had to live by them. The African proverb says, 'As long as a dead person is remembered, the person is still living.' This applies to those one loves and remembers daily." His mother's reaction to life's adversities typified his community. "The Depression brought out the best in my community. People emphasized getting along and they were forgiving and optimistic. They were true Christians, and that shaped my values. Faith was what held them together, despite the hypocrisy of the ministers. So my art tries to capture the will, spirit, and optimism of the people."

Educational Influences

After grade school, Biggers left Gastonia to attend boarding school. There he absorbed ideas about ecology, how to build order in the environment, and as a work-study student, he experienced the value of a strong work ethic. But, as in his earlier encounters with hypocrisy with ministers, Biggers was again presented with life's contradictions, which offered insights into gender inequality and the human condition. When working his nightly shifts on campus as a student fireman, he would often observe sexual misconduct between the men faculty and the young girls. He was perturbed and felt it was unfair that some teachers sexually exploited the girls, while at the same time maintaining a school policy of separation between the sexes. Later, when some teachers lied about his having sexual conduct with a girl, he was almost expelled from school. After his uncle interceded with the principal, who was also an honest missionary, on Biggers's behalf, he was not sent home. "I was affected by these incidents—the hypocrisy of seeing the sexual immorality of some teachers with one another and with the students and then lying on me. I knew that something was evil and diseased in society. This made me sensitive to the plight of my sisters and women I've dated. I wanted to protect them." Ironically, in 1991 the alumni of the school invited him to present a sermon on the grounds of the church where the now-defunct Lincoln Academy was located. Nearly sixty years after his sermon, which dealt with slides of his work, Biggers said, "A man I had known who was on the staff of Lincoln Academy came up to me and said, 'I asked for your forgiveness, because I knocked you into the ground.' 'What are you talking about?' He said, 'I slayed you. I want you to forgive me.' He dropped his head and walked away." Similarly, in 1990 Biggers was amazed when he encountered the teacher who prevaricated about him at a meeting of the Links, an exclusive black women's civic and social organization. After praising his contributions, she remarked, "If there was anything I've ever said against you when you were a student, I am sorry."

Seemingly, his schooling became a training ground not only for understanding gender inequality but also race and class. Attending his black segregated public school, he experienced racism beyond the school's walls and internalized racism within it.

Light-skinned students sat on the front row, brown-skinned in the middle, and black-skinned students sat in the back. From the first grade, I felt something was wrong. I had friends who were black and those who were as white as the white kids. I could never get over the teacher, whom I truly respected, practicing this. A young lady with blue eyes, brown straight hair, and fair skin came from a big family, and she was dumb, but yet she was protected by the teachers and promoted and passed along with As and Bs. They crippled her. The race and class problem was very strong, and had a major impact in turning me away from religion. When people say you must be pure in heart and treat everybody right, I observed too much hypocrisy. I realized early that color and class didn't make a difference to me. Even though my father was a minister and teacher, I very easily identified with the common people. I felt they were getting it from both ends, black and white.

Biggers gleaned relevant lessons from these experiences: "I learned early that you have to make decisions. You cannot run around on the horns of dilemmas. And once you make it, you have to use all your intelligence to fight whatever that battle is. I was always fighting for whom I thought was the underdog and who was being taken advantage of." These lessons helped to prepare him for life.

The Hampton Experience and the Influence of Viktor Lowenfeld

After Biggers graduated from Lincoln Academy, he entered Hampton Institute in 1942 as a trade student in plumbing. Enlarging his understanding of the environment, he took courses in drafting, and he also studied under Joseph Gilead, a master builder and potter. Desiring to further understand his milieu, he decided to take a course in drawing from Viktor Lowenfeld, a Jewish immigrant who had come from Austria during the Hitler era. He had heard about Hampton Institute and its art expressions and wanted to be there to work with young people. Biggers said of Lowenfeld,

Viktor Lowenfeld was a genius in understanding the educational process and creative expression of youths. When I heard Lowenfeld speak about the possibilities of art, there were no limitations. We knew of the physical limitations of segregation. But Lowenfeld said we could not be limited by anybody. The meaning of art is expression, but it is deep inside of you—your most secret things. You can laugh with anybody, but you can't cry with anybody. This is what the canvas becomes for an artist—your dearest friend and your most trusted friend. I never heard anybody speak this way. I thought art was illustration. I did not know that it dealt with the soul as such. This intrigued me to know that I could control something and no one really had anything to do with it unless I let them. Art became something I could grasp and plumbing became immediately boring to me. Art allowed me to be a normal human being without all kinds of doors and locks that hemmed you in and I got myself into art.

Lowenfeld had such a major impact on Biggers that he worked all day on his art. Often he would miss a class in mathematics or English or he would work through lunch and dinner. Lowenfeld would ask, "Have you had anything to eat today?" His teacher would take him home for lunch or dinner.

Lowenfeld had gotten a letter from the State Department and his temperament and expressions had changed. He was like a person in a coma and I noticed tears were running down his face. He said, "I received a letter from the State Department," and he said the letter informed him of names who had been burned in Hitler's gas chamber. And he looked at me and said, "They burned these children and old people simply because they are Jews. They segregate you, they discriminate against you, but they are not killing you this way. Don't you see why you must understand the world you live in and with your art you can say something about it?" That statement lived with me daily. I shall never forget it. This is when prejudice took on another depth. I realized there was another dimension to prejudice and the human society is very complex. It affected me and it was a great decision for me. I was committed to painting not just what we call pretty pictures, but to deal with a revelation of the human condition.

From Lowenfeld, Biggers and other students learned about the German culture. "Viktor Lowenfeld could arouse your interests in identifying with other people's problems and projects and you really got excited. He had a world of positiveness as he had tragedy and there was a wonderful wholeness we experienced with Viktor." So when Lowenfeld left Hampton Institute for Pennsylvania State University, Biggers followed his mentor and teacher, despite losing two years toward his college degree and thirty hours of credits.

In 1946 Biggers graduated with bachelor's and master's degrees in education from Pennsylvania State University and later he earned his doctorate in education from there. At the university, Biggers was challenged in a more rigorous academic environment. Unlike his mentor Lowenfeld, other professors did not encourage him.

The people told me that I would never be an artist and to drop it. I had no sensitivity. I had no aesthetics. I was wasting my time. At the same time they were saying that, we had already exhibited at the New York Modern Museum of Art. The reason why they said this was because I did not approach art in the usual manner. I only drew black things and they did not see anything or any concept that was not European art. It was a nonacademic approach to art, as well as racism was at issue. Lowenfeld's philosophy gave the assurance to go forward. I had almost twelve years of art before Pennsylvania State. I did not need to argue with the teachers. I just walked out of their classroom. Teachers were telling me I couldn't paint, but my paintings were on exhibit at their school. There are as many approaches to art as people—from realism to abstractionism. Afrocentric fads would come and go, but Viktor never changed.

At Pennsylvania State University, when Biggers participated in a political rally led by Jews, Lowenfeld told him to express his politics through his art. Although he did not understand the significance of Lowenfeld's position at the time, he later realized Lowenfeld was attempting to convey ways to speak truth to power. "I hope as I get older, I get more subtle—before I would ram my fist in your face. There is a young person's art and there is art of an old person. My values are still very much the same, there is, however, a greater depth to life. One must deal with the human condition and the racial condition is just one dimension. Can I, as a black American with a certain kind of history, portray that life and reach a German or Japanese, no matter what one's background? Can't I have an effect on anyone anywhere, whether my characters are black or not?" Throughout Biggers's artistic career, Viktor Lowenfeld's philosophy guided his stroke of the hand on canvas.

Speaking Truth to Power through Art

Unlike many artists who moved to New York and Europe, Biggers remained close to his Southern roots, always remembering the dusty, muddy roads he had traveled near Crowders Mountain and always wanting to keep close to his background. When he went to Greenwich Village, he found that he didn't have anything in common with the people there. So his feeling was that if he had anything to say on canvas, it would have to be said in the South where black people's roots really are. "I was always moved by jazz and Negro spirituals. I paint by it—*Wings Over Jordan*, the blues singers from the 1930s, and old guitar players, like Josh White and Lead Belly. I still receive this folk joy."

After Biggers left Pennsylvania State University, he and Hazel, his wife and longtime partner, moved to Texas where he accepted a position at Texas Southern University. There he established the art department in 1949 and remained its head for thirty-five years until his retirement. At Texas Southern University, he experienced the dank and darkness and the renewal and transcendence in his life and the re-creation of his experiences in his art. As Biggers mentioned earlier, every artist has van Gogh's struggle and being black is another dimension to the struggle within that struggle. His struggle to create meaningful art at Texas Southern University was no exception. In his own words, he told stories of his trials and triumphs not only at Texas Southern University but throughout his life.

When the New York Museum of Modern Art exhibited works of Hampton students in 1946, I had several pieces, the most outstanding of which was *Dying Soldier*. I painted my thoughts as a soldier dies on a battlefield. In those memories were the lynchings, raping of young girls, elderly people scrubbing floors and sweeping streets. Here is where people were dying for democracy on the battlefields of Europe. Here is when I got into my inner thoughts about the sacrifices I would make, if I had to die. When this painting was critiqued by a critic at the New York Museum of Modern Art, he said this was not art, it was some propaganda of an art teacher whose influence was like a jackhammer, making kids paint things that had nothing to do with art.

For Biggers, this appraisal had a sense of déjà vu.

This was the same criticism that teachers gave at Penn. But Viktor told me, "You must do art for yourself and you must love it." In my expression, I felt an inner joy when I tried to paint some of the things we felt when we were washing clothes [in Gastonia], when we had to buy coals to put in those stoves. I wasn't interested in still life. I didn't want to paint an apple. I wanted to eat an apple. I didn't want to paint a flower. I was interested in expressing what life was to me and what our struggles were. In those things, I also drew pictures of my love life at Hampton, and my relationship with the boys and girls at Hampton. It was not only about hunger, pain, and exploitation, but also about beautiful things.

"Critics in the 1930s and 1940s thought black art was voodoo," claimed Biggers. Consequently, as a teacher and as an artist, like Viktor Lowenfeld, he wanted to help students at Texas Southern University, and all of humanity, to understand the meaning of the African ancestral art. But in his lifetime, Biggers had seen "absolute hostility towards black expression." In the 1930s and 1940s, Hampton Institute was no exception. So much hostility existed on Hampton Institute's campus in Virginia. "They hated the art department. There was a great movement to destroy art. I had two murals destroyed—one in the gym, and I left works in the boathouse and it was torn down. You have to accept your work being destroyed, just as a parent loses a child or you lose a limb. Anytime you paint on public buildings, you have to know there is the potential of their being destroyed. There is no security and safety. Therefore, you must do the things that you truly love to do. Art is its own reward. Do not expect to be paid for it." So Biggers was not deterred by the opposition to his art, for he understood that "This is the way life functions," the intertwining of negative and positive forces in the renewal process. Nearly fifty years later at Hampton University this transformational advancement of the visual arts began, when Biggers unveiled a pair of murals—*House of the Turtle* and *Tree House*—commissioned by William R. Harvey, president of Hampton University, for the foyer of the William R. and Norma B. Harvey Library. "William

R. Harvey has made Hampton University one of the great museums in America with its African American collection, and we should congratulate him," claimed Biggers.

The Hampton murals were not his only loss. "In Texas Southern University, there were many people opposed to black art like they were at Hampton Institute. The most meaningful mural I've painted was cut to pieces in Texas. I am sure it was done by people who never appreciated the art program at Texas Southern University, even though it brought national recognition to the university." While destructive life forces in Texas were a part of his artistic endeavors, creative life forces were in balance. While the Pennsylvania Art Academy refused to exhibit the works of his students or other exhibits in New York, Pennsylvania, Washington, D.C., and Boston turned down his exhibits, their works were accepted in Texas. In 1951 he exhibited his first works in Texas and won the show. Few places existed then for young artists to exhibit, except the Woodruff Hale's Show at Atlanta University in Georgia. "This created excitement every spring when the exhibit occurred and prizes were given. We had patrons of the arts from Texas that supported our department. They brought us kilns and supplied us with materials, even when the state did not. Our students exhibited in every citywide and statewide exhibit from the 1950s to now. From Texas, we went to top studios in New York. We didn't get paid for painting murals, only the materials were bought for us. But this experience prepared us for how to paint murals. It is one of the most marvelous chapters in my life to have gone to Texas and worked there."

Biggers related another experience of life's creative synergy that took place in East Texas.

P. Y. Gray, a Negro educator, who retired back in the 1950s contacted me to paint a mural on the history of black education in East Texas. The mural showed regal scenes and ministers collecting nickels and dimes to build the first school, a one-room school. P. Y. Gray expanded the school to three or four rooms. We painted the expansion. This mural was housed in the high school there and a few years later integration came and the black principal felt he had to take the mural down. The majority of the schoolboard was white, as well as the students, so I know the dilemma he was in as an administrator. The mural was taken down and put in a woodshed and remained there for seventeen years until Olive Jensen Theisen, who is white, came to East Texas to a community college and started an art program. Some black students told her they knew where a mural was and she went to the woodshed and found it. As soon as she saw it, she said, "This is the work of John Biggers." Her husband, John [Theisen], a furniture maker for the public school and a leader, went out among his people and said, "Let us get this mural restored. It is our culture and let us put it back in the school." People listened and damn if they didn't do it. They put the mural in the new school, which is now mixed and has a white principal. We went for the unveiling and we had people from every segment of East Texas and it was truly integrated. We had to tell the story about the mural and we brought in P. Y. Gray's son to do it. He had left East Texas and had gone to Los Angeles and had retired because he couldn't get a job in East Texas. When he told the story of the hardships, the people wept and it was gratifying. The white superintendents and the black and white preachers all embraced this mural in East Texas, the most backward part of Texas. It is one of the finest things that ever happened to me in art. The community changed and came together around my art. If art does that, it has meaning. In many places that mural would have been destroyed. John built the frame and the support system. The day he finished, he dropped dead. Because of this, I gave three prints to schools in that part of East Texas in honor of John Theisen's name.

Biggers also gave the community college where Olive Jensen Theisen works a complete set of all the prints done in the name of her husband to start a John Theisen Gallery, which he was the first to exhibit. Olive Theisen put together a collection of all the works that Biggers had done in the publication, *The Murals of John Thomas Biggers.* "Out of East Texas experience, the most backward comes to light," remarked Biggers.

Paris, a small town, which is also in East Texas, commissioned him to paint a mural; and from supportive East Texas patrons of the arts, he received his first major commission to do a mural and sculpture in downtown Houston Music Hall. These same patrons wanted to buy the *Ananse: The Web of Life*, a collection of works that records his discoveries in Africa, and to give them to the people of Texas.

In 1957 John Biggers traveled to Ghana with a grant provided by UNESCO. Later he visited Nigeria and other African countries in search of an understanding of his African heritage. The individuals who controlled his wealthy patron's foundation refused to purchase the body of works. "They were not going to invest in a nigger. Back in the 1980s in Texas, the city council voted against having the art faculty at Texas Southern commissioned to do an art work. They didn't want no nigger art. These groups of women who wanted to have the work commissioned never stopped. In the 1980s, it was accepted and acknowledged.

In concluding this interview in the mid-1990s, Biggers reminded us that, "In this strange world we live in, positive things happen—no matter if the negative has been overpowering. Thank God, I didn't die before I retired. The problems in the university can kill you if you take them too seriously. The sole contradiction of Texas Southern University is my students are on the arts commission of the state."

Before Biggers's death in 2001, he received a myriad of accolades and commissions, so he was a "great success and a great artist." "It is marvelous

when the two can come together. Certainly my being the artist in residence at
Hampton and Hampton buying my pictures for their collection and giving me
the commission to paint the mural is one of the highest values to me. I feel
especially grateful to do things with approval from society and people enjoy
what I'm doing. I enjoy monetary rewards. But I would paint if I never sold
a picture. This process is sacred to me." The murals—*Tree House* and *House
of the Turtle*—that he created at Hampton University, along with his mural at
Winston-Salem College in North Carolina, were his last, and they summed up
his philosophy of life and speak to the rampant rapaciousness of corporate
capitalism in deforestation and his concern for maintaining a natural harmony
with the environment.

> The mural I did at Hampton is a combination of a lifetime of subjects, and also
> because I painted my first mural at Hampton in 1942. The murals I composed
> when I first painted are composed like my last one. I did not realize this until
> I was almost finished. I kept feeling what I was doing I had done before. The
> subject was not the same, but how it was done. I have painted the female fig-
> ure—the black woman—during my whole career. Mythologically, the first
> concept of mother is the tree, and the second concept of mother is the great
> serpent in the tree. Mother is the woman, the tree and the serpent and all kinds
> of religion grew out of this view. The very last mural I painted at Hampton
> University is the great tree mother. I've attempted to humanize the tree as the
> mother embracing the whole family of man. As times proceed upward, they
> become the stars, the heaven. But all that is the tree and it is an important point
> about the evolution of my work. And because of this, I studied trees in Africa
> and sometimes I draw trees, but they have never taken over the whole canvas.
> When we think in terms of sensitivity of vegetation of preparing a place for
> man and when we see people destroying the forest to make toothpicks and toi-
> let paper, it really means people murder their mothers just for nothing and it's
> wholesale murder that goes on just for economics. Trees that take thousands
> of years to grow, we cut them down and think nothing about it. This is the
> most ravishing aspect of a capitalistic society. I think it is completely out of
> control because without vegetation, there is no oxygen. We depend upon the
> oxygen to live. I feel the tree, in its creating a place for animals to live, is our
> power. The tree might be more important than me. It only prepared a place
> where we could come up on this earth. We are wiping out the tree for some
> commercial purpose. The tree is so magnificent, so heroic, that we cannot hear
> it cry. We commit genocide upon it. Now we know that the tree cries and re-
> acts like animals, but just at a lower decibel. I think artists have known this for
> sometime. Trees are becoming important to me and I will use them in my
> work. The palm tree, vineyard, sycamore, and fig trees are truly our parents. I
> believe a fine should be put on people who cut down a tree. I think we should
> take a census of trees and if we do that, we'll have more respect for trees. I re-
> ally believe that.

When Biggers was born, the life chances for African Americans were severely constrained in the rural South. Hence, when Biggers had the opportunity to study at Hampton University, he initially chose plumbing as a profession for making a living and not until by happenstance when he met his mentor that he thought of art as a profession. In contrast, Steve Prince, who was born after the civil rights movement, had the option to decide whether he wanted to become an illustrator or artist in a diverse setting. Despite their vast time differences, their art is steeped in social realism and social protests used to transform society and to open dialogue for bringing people together around issues of social inequality and social injustice. While highlighting pain and despair, their work has a transcendent quality.

Steve Prince: Speaking Truth to Power

> I believe that I have gifts, and I can't be selfish with them. I share them and I don't share them with arrogance, but with love. I have been given certain gifts, and how can I give them to someone who can take the same gifts and take their ideas, add to them, and pass it on. So that's a teacher's responsibility . . . I go to people with love, with genuine care, to share, wanting to teach, instruct, and of course, it is steeped in morals, ethics, and values, and those kinds of things are very integral in how my work is formulated and in what I do as a person. So I do not take teaching lightly. But I see it as a calling. I was called to teach and to share.

Through his art, Steve Prince was called to teach and share. As a visual artist, spirituality forms the taproot of Steve Prince's existential being, his life, his work, and his art. Born and reared in the Crescent City, he received the Bachelor of Fine Arts from Xavier University in New Orleans in 1991, and his Masters of Fine Arts in printmaking and sculpture at Michigan State University in 1995. Prince has shown nationally in numerous groups, solo, and in juried exhibitions, and he is the recipient of a bevy of awards. He has created several private and public commissions for national and international patrons, and he conducts workshops across the nation, where he teaches his craft to people of various ages. Prince asserts, "My sensitivity to all people is due to my upbringing and experiences. What I believe is scripturally taught, that is, we are all human beings and that we are alive and have souls, and we live and we die. With that in mind, my whole thrust is, I don't care who you are, I am going to teach you, or share with you, as best there is, the truth, as it has been revealed to me."

Familial Influences

Perhaps when Prince's grade school teacher admonished him for drawing, he was endeavoring even in his youthful innocence to teach and speak truth to power. "My teachers would call home and tell my parents, 'Steve is always drawing. And maybe you need to get him into an art class.' I had to be in the third or fourth grade, and it got to its heaviest when I got to the sixth grade. I drew constantly. That's all I wanted to do. And I felt sometimes that I was born in the wrong era, because I knew if I were born during the time of Michelangelo, my parents would have dropped me off as an apprentice." But, Prince said, "My parents did not have a whole lot of money to put me in an art class, so they kept me supplied with paper, pencils, and those kinds of things. My mom and my dad were always encouraging me to be creative, not by just saying, 'Steve, be creative,' but by never discouraging it. And I would draw all the time, even after I got in trouble in school for drawing too much." An older brother, nine years his senior, was the catalyst that cultivated his love for creating. "As a little brother looking up to a big brother, I just admired everything he did. I idolized everything he did. I loved his drawings and I would copy off of them. I would say that the love for creating was cultivated with me looking at my brother." Prince's imagination was unlimited in how he used his creativity. "I drew on anything I had—tape, wood, boxes, anything. I would beg my parents for Star Wars toys, and they said we are not buying all that junk for you. So I copied the Star War toys and made them out of cardboard. And the kids wanted my toys more than theirs because my toys had more gadgets on them. So, if I didn't have it, I made it."

What were those earliest and strongest influences that shaped the context and content of Prince's need to speak the truth through his art? Plainly for Prince, his father, a chemical salesman, and his mother, an insurance woman, instilled in him and his three older siblings, the importance of spirituality and the value of education, strict discipline, and a strong work ethic. "My parents were definitely strict, and I thought I had too many barriers on me. I wanted to have more freedom and that was in high school. I had a curfew on me hard. When twelve o'clock hit, I was supposed to be in that door, and I wasn't going to get back out again. I followed the rules. I broke them every now and then, but on the whole, I was a good son, but just as any teen, sometimes I challenged them." To instill the work ethic, his parents supported his "little weekend and summer grass cutting business as a kid."

Religious Influences

In the devoutly Catholic Prince family life, religion was its centerpiece. So unarguably, his religious faith and training became the underpinning of his spiritual and religious foundation, and salient themes in his life and his art. Here, Prince tells the story of its influence.

When I was in the fourth or fifth grade, I was very mischievous and constantly causing problems in class. I was the class clown, and I was always disruptive. I would constantly be sent to detention for this and all the other things I was getting into. And by going to church, I began to feel guilty about what I was doing. But I could not stop what I was doing, so it was just this battle going on inside me. It was like I had an angel on one side and the devil on the other and I was just fighting this battle. I would pray and ask God to help me to break this pattern that I was in. And when I was in the sixth grade, a priest came to our classroom and he spoke to us about becoming an altar boy. I was sitting there thinking, "Altar boy! That's what I want to be." I thought that was a means by which I could get closer to God and to the church, and He could begin to help me change my ways. So I ran home to my parents, "Mom, a priest came to our class looking for an altar boy and I want to be an altar boy." And she said, "Okay."

Since it was customary for Prince to become quickly jaded about new ventures and relinquish them, he had to reassure his mother of his stickability if accepted as an altar boy. Until the eighth grade, Prince served as an altar boy, and it changed his life. "That began to shape my life because now I am in this public eye spot of the church and being bad was in contradiction to that. So I had this moral barometer that the church began to enact upon me. And I had this in my head. 'Okay, I can't act up anymore because I'm an altar boy and I am supposed to be setting an example.'" As an altar boy, he became very involved with the visual aspect of the Catholic Church, particularly its symbols.

I used to be enthralled with the church just because of the sacred spirit and the design—the high ceilings in our Catholic Church, the stained-glass windows, the Stations of the Cross, which is the fourteen steps of Christ's march to Calvary, the statues of Mary and Joseph, and Jesus, even the crucifix upon the altar of Christ, the smell of incense, the pews, the holy water, the urn in which the wine was in, the wafers, the host, the confessional—"Bless me Father for I have sinned"—all of these symbols. The hymnals, the songs, the big pipe organ in the back of the church—all these things are just etched in my memory, and today, I just think about the smell and I can remember what they looked like. And so, all these things began to feed me and my visual vocabulary. Later I began to think about the purpose of the stained-glass windows, with so much art, which of course is a reference to God and giving the greatest things—gold and pearls and jewels—which are supposed to represent that. But other things that stood out for me was all the jewels, the colors, patterns, and stories attached and associated with them really began to impact me.

On the one hand, Prince was drawn to the church because it was confirming; on the other hand, he began to distance himself from the church because of its contradictions. "One of the main contradictions that pushed me away from it was the lack of female involvement in the church." His feminine consciousness developed early as a result of being around his mother and sisters. Since his older brother, whom he looked up to, did not want to be bothered with him, he gravitated toward the women in the family. In the kitchen where his mother, sisters, and other women in the neighborhood gathered, he comfortably entered their circle with small talk and with his sideshow antics and mimicries. Though he entered the circle as the sideshow, he did not participate in substantive discourse about sexism in the church, but he quietly listened. On one such occasion, he heard how upset one of his sisters, who is five years older, was when she was not permitted to become an altar girl because it was only for boys. "I remember my mom stating that was in the church. So the questions began to formulate and I was beginning to see the contradictions that were in the scripture. And when I finished high school and went on to Xavier, I still had a strong belief that there is a God. That never left me, but I got very disillusioned by the church. I concluded that I did not really have to go to a space to worship God. I could worship God whenever I wanted to. And so, I didn't feel that the church space was that important." He began to question his relationship with the church, often wondering, "Why do I have to go to church to the priest to confess my sins? Why couldn't I go directly to God to confess my sins? Why does the priest have to be the mediator? And I decided I didn't need a mediator, if I wanted to speak to God, I could go directly to Him. Then the scriptures began to reveal to me that Christ becomes that mediator. So the priest is just a vehicle on this earth that God may use to spread his word. That's when I began to formulate a lot of ideas right there and they are reflected in my art."

Educational Influences

Prince grew up not only attending the Catholic Church, he was also educated in Catholic schools from kindergarten through college. During his junior and senior year in high school, Prince studied art history under the tutelage of Margeret Bettale. "She drove so much art history into me that it made my head spin. I learned a lot about world arts through the training that she gave me. I remember just looking at slide after slide and having to know about the period and know about the artist. I didn't appreciate it until I got to college."

Whereas Bettale positively affirmed Prince, in this same Catholic, coed high school, another teacher did not. However, for Prince, it was an aperture to reflect about the priest's ideas of women's role in the church.

> This teacher reflected many of the ideas that the priest had expressed that women should not have a major role in the church and worship. Everyday at the beginning of class, he would have a student to read the scripture in front of the class. But he never asked any female students. He would always ask male stu-

dents to read the Bible out loud. And one day, a female student challenged him and asked, "Why don't you ever ask any female students to come up here and read the scripture?" And he went on to explain that men were the proper ones to do this and used the Apostles. And I had a problem with that. I did not know how to articulate it, but I knew that something was wrong with that.

Later when Prince drew his version of Michelangelo's *Madonna and Child*, which was exhibited at his school, the picture ran afoul of the teacher.

I made a copy of [*Madonna and Child*] in pencil. It was a painting, but I drew it in pencil. I copied everything. I took my time with it and it was one of the strongest drawings. It was like my little badge of pride every day. I would go by and look at it and I felt so good that it was there. And one day, I came to school and I looked on the wall and the only thing left was the tape, and I really thought someone stole my artwork. I ran to the office and said, "What happened to my artwork out in the hallway?" And the reply was, "I don't know." So I went running down to my art room to Mrs. Bettale. And I said, "Mrs. Bettale, somebody stole my artwork. It is off the wall." She said, "No, that's not what happened. I have it." "What happened? Did it get damaged or something?" She said, "No, it didn't get damaged. The civics teacher said that it was inappropriate to have an image of nudity on the wall." I said, "What image of nudity? It is Jesus, the baby." But he had said it was inappropriate, so we had to take it down. I was just confused, and I said, "What is wrong with it? It's just a child." Then I began to understand the issues some people can have about the human body. For years I went on this thing of showing the human body and taking the clothes off of it. I said, "We got to get away from this stuff of constantly seeing the body as this thing that we got to cover up all the time." Then I began to understand the politics associated with that and the things around the body, especially the female body. And even throughout history, we hear about covering up the body with fig leaves, because there were shifts within the church. And I just had concluded that when God created us, he made us like we are. He didn't make us with clothes on—just straight naked. Therefore, I will return that way right back to him. So that was another key element that began to form my ideas about my art.

Influence of John Scott

From his college basketball coach, Prince learned that John Scott was an incredible artist. John Scott also happened to be the godfather of the coach's son. When Prince received a basketball scholarship offer to Xavier University in New Orleans, his college coach arranged a tour of the campus, which included the art department. Prince was so inspired by the enthusiasm of the art students that he knew he wanted to attend Xavier University. There he came under the influence of John Scott, his mentor. He described his initial encounter with him and the impact he had on his life and his art.

I will never forget our first meeting, the student-professor meeting, and he was just sitting back and he was doodling. It looked like he was not even engaged in the meeting. As a young college student at another transitional point in my life, I was just looking around at the professors and I couldn't keep my eyes off of him. And he was just sitting around with his legs crossed over and had this book in his lap doodling. Then finally, it was his turn to speak. And there was a presence about him as he spoke to us and he had us on the edge of our seats as he spoke. And I think the greatest experience I had there was a humbling experience to the point that when I started taking classes under him, I realized how talented he was, not only as an educator, but as an artist. I immediately started gravitating toward him. I was so humbled by him to a point that I was silenced by him. The only thing there was left to do was to go to him and just learn. If he and I were in a room together, I could hardly speak. He would speak and I would feel that I was saying something stupid. I just wanted to be around him. Every time I came to him, it was out of complete hunger. I wanted to learn. Teach me. Then that respect grew beyond that. It grew to where I sat and watched his mannerisms. I started to build a relationship with his kids, some of whom went to Xavier with me. I'd built a relationship with them, especially one of his daughters. We became friends and that gave me an entrée even to John Scott's home. I used to go to his house and hang out there. So now we see him as a teacher; now we see him as an artist; now I began to see him as a family man, as a father—all these facets of him. I sometimes would go hang out over there late at night, and he would be working in his studio on campus. All of the students were gone, but because I stayed on campus, I would go to the art department any time I wanted to. I would go over there at twelve o'clock or one o'clock in the morning. And he would be there working. He would be painting on his sculptures and I would be sitting around there watching him. I would also ask him a question every once in a while, but I had to muster up the nerve to ask a question. I had to think it out before asking it, and he gave me an answer. And many times we would be sitting in total silence. He would be working and I would be watching. And so Scott became to me a father figure, an artist; he became a teacher to me and I would say I wanted to be a professor just like him.

After college, Prince studied art at Michigan State University. "The reason I went to Michigan was because it was John Scott's alma mater. And when I said I wanted to follow in his footsteps, I meant I wanted to follow everything. So he was integral in my getting into Michigan State, and one of the things that he really wanted me to do was finish Michigan State University and return to Xavier and take his place. That's what he would always tell me. He would say, 'I want you to take my place at Xavier.' And I had plans on doing that but, of course, life changes and you make different plans, so I didn't get a chance to go back there."

Over the course of his graduate studies, Prince finally opened up with his mentor. "I finally broke my silence and began to talk to him. And when I began to talk I couldn't stop because I had built up all this stuff over my four years at Xavier and it just poured out. And so I would call him up and talk to him on the phone. I would ask him different questions. I would trade different processes with him over the phone and tell him about projects I was doing in class, and he would tell me about different projects he was working on and different commissions that he got, and I would share with him the same things. So over the past fifteen years, we traded back and forth." Scott left Prince two aphorisms that guided his life: "Remember, your imagination is your only limitation." And when he shared his processes and techniques with Prince, he would say, "Just pass it on."

Prince's Art: Race, Racism, and Black Aesthetics

Race and racism are central themes in Prince's art. "Throughout my life, I have not had a whole lot of instances where I had racism come at me. I had a few things that were subtle, which I pick up a lot in my artwork in terms of seeing some of the things and observing some of the effects of racism and some of the effects of the long-reaching arms of racism and how it has permeated itself inside of our culture. A lot of my work and a lot of my observations come of seeing that." Although Prince grew up in a predominately white neighborhood, he said that he never felt the sting of racism or at least, he did not recognize it. When his parents said he could not sleep over at his white peers, he did not understand that they were trying to protect him from racism; nor did he grasp until later that the white parents would let their children play with him, but they would limit their children's time. Inside the walls of his home, racial talk shaped the contours of his parents' lives and permeated his psyche. "In New Orleans, I grew up with fear of the police, because there were many instances where young black men were taken off by the police and brutalized. And we heard different stories that were happening, so it was like an interior code between us. It's like a black code. You say, 'Don't do this and don't do that,' and if the police say something to you, don't look at him in the eyes. We were taught certain things about how to interact with the police. Be sure you reply, 'Yes, sir' and 'No, sir.'"

Prince's father told one racial story that is indelibly etched in his memory. Before Prince's father became a chemical salesman, he worked in a New Orleans country club, and while on duty working behind the bar this incident occurred.

> He was a mixologist. So he was behind the bar and his boss told him that this was a big party and he couldn't leave from behind that bar. If you leave from behind this bar, you're going to be fired. My father knew he needed that job, knew he needed to provide for his family, and knew that if he got blackballed, he wouldn't find another job. So he stayed behind that bar. He stayed behind the

bar for so long that he actually had to go to the bathroom. So he had to urinate in a cup. Some of the things that he has embedded in him are deep-seated. As a kid, I couldn't understand why he had this feeling toward white people. I was in school at the time, and I didn't sense this level of hatred. That's not to say it wasn't there. A lot of it has to do with my own naiveness. My own youth didn't allow me to see a lot of things and also my personality—I'm kind of happy-go-lucky. And I probably had things coming at me and didn't even know it was there. It wasn't until I got older and more mature that I began to look back and see things. I suddenly made connections with the kids that I used to play with in the community. I did not notice it then, but their parents monitored the amount of time that I had with them. They would let me play with them for a little bit and then cut it off. My parents were constantly trying to point this out to me but I was like, "They are my friends." I had to be ten or eleven years old at the time. I remember different instances that when I reflect back, I see what my parents saw a little clearer. I was going to school with all these white kids and I was friends with them, but the friendship never carried over outside of school. I wasn't in their homes. That relationship pretty much stopped there in school. We had a relationship and then we just kind of went away and then we came back to school and we were friends.

Like black artists throughout history, as an adult, racism, though more subtle, has blocked his footpath. "I found that in terms of this whole art journey that I have been on, it is very tough to get my work out there and respected. When I was in graduate school, I kept hearing that my work was like illustration, that it wasn't fine art." His graduate professors were basically saying that his work was not critical, that it was about making pretty pictures and to put it in the realm of illustration to knock it down, to place it in a hierarchy, as lower or lesser than fine art. "I would challenge it. I would ask them to define for me, what is illustration and what is fine art? And no one could ever give me a concrete explanation as to what that meant. I was making stuff that was recognizable and all my other peers were making stuff that was abstract and all these hierarchical forms. I was doing the same things, but I was doing it and encapsulating them into stories." Earlier, when Prince was considering Temple University for his advanced studies, he asked one of the professors in the art program to critique his work. He said, "I saw your work when you sent your application in and we thought your work was pretty much illustration. You may want to look into going into another kind of medium."

> I wanted to go into printmaking, and my understanding of printmaking as a medium is very much steeped in social realism. And even going back in time, we think about a lot of political cartoonists in the 1700s and 1800s, and think about all the wood engravings and wooden etchings and all the different processes they were using to make comments about the government, and about the different ways that the poor were being held down and the rich were getting

richer. I wanted to find myself in that line. I wanted to get in that line as the voice of protest to go against these things that are holding us back. I wanted my stuff to speak about race and racism in its overtness and covertness in terms of society, and its domino effects, and its effects on how it is tearing down family structure. I wanted to speak to it and unearth it—pull back the veil and reveal it and to speak about it in open forum.

Prince has had an opportunity to pull back the veil and to reveal not only the depth and impact of racism, but how it is so closely interwoven with classism and sexism. After graduate school, when Prince and his wife, Valerie, who was completing her Ph.D. in English, and their two young children moved to Maryland to accept teaching positions in high school, they became youth directors in their newly chosen Pentecostal Church in Washington, D.C. This experience was pivotal in deepening the meaning of these essentialities and his analysis of society, which is reflected in his art.

> In that depressed area of Washington, D.C., everywhere you saw drugs, prostitutes, and anything you can come up with in your mind. It was happening there. We were so into the streets. We would go into the streets and pull the youth in the church. We pulled so many youth in the church that they started pulling their parents, because with children going to church it affected their parents and they started to bring them in. We did that for four years and it really began to shape and to change me. We didn't have any money because we were fresh out of graduate school and we did what I did as a child. I just made something from nothing. So that's the same attitude I began to display. I said, "We got to begin to use the creative process as an alternative to violence. How can we utilize our gifts to combat what's going on in our community?"

Combating the crisis facing urban youth became more urgent for Prince who was still teaching in Maryland and working in the streets of Washington, D.C., when his father, a very strong-willed, masculine persona, had a near death experience in New Orleans. It was another pivotal moment for Prince and his art when he entered the hospital room of his deathly sick father.

> I remember we went to intensive care to see my dad and I walked into his room and he was so swollen and disfigured from the surgery that he had, the only way I was able to recognize him was when I saw the mole structure on his chest. I said, "There he is right there." I knew my father, I knew his chest. Seeing him like this was just wrenching because he was always a pillar in the household and now he was all laid out helpless. It really hurt deeply. We could only see him for thirty minutes, and then we had to wait for two hours to go back and see him again in intensive care. The second or third time I went by myself and there was a priest walking around the room praying over different people in the room. And I asked him if he would come over with me and pray over my father. So he and

I reached and held hands across the bed, and I put my hand on my dad and he put his hand on my dad and I began to pray over my dad. And it was then I got a revelation within my heart that he was going to be all right. And the other revelation I got was not to weep over his flesh. But to pray for his soul—that his soul would have entry into heaven.

This first-time, near-death experience of a close one, along with working with urban youth, is reflected in his art.

A lot of my work is based on scenes that are affecting our youth and the importance of our young in terms of them passing on traditions, and not only with their passing on traditions, but with them carrying the torch in time, going forward, and [understanding] how important they are in terms of the foundation of our nation and to our world. I am thinking from a spiritual standpoint about souls—that although there is this idea that souls can be lost or souls can be won—I believe that for those youth that we worked with out there as youth directors. And also my father when he was so close to death, was he right with God? I don't know that. Only he knows that, and only God knows that. I prayed over my father, asking that if he was not right with God, then keep him here until he is. That was the prayer that I put out for him. . . . I got greater understanding through my father about life and death in that moment, and then about the effects of the things about which we, as parents, as mothers and fathers within a community, can have upon a child, and how those effects replicate themselves and how you end up getting these concepts of curses.

His father's illness and his work with youth changed him. "I know I don't have time to play. Life is too short. And if life is too short to play then you have a sense of urgency about what you are trying to say. You're not going to pull any punches when you say it. Even some of the pictures I make, I look at them and say, I stand behind it. I am not saying anything that is not the truth. So if it is not the truth, please tell me and correct me, then I will modify it. If I am saying what's the truth, then let's talk about it." As Prince began to marinate and reformulate ideas about the meaning of life and death and about race and racism in America and the interconnection with class and gender, the new paradigmatic shift filtered into his work and, for him, it was a pivotal moment. However, Prince is keenly aware that presently "race and issues of race representations" are not a part of the politically correct discourse of our colorblind society of the post-civil rights era. Nevertheless, he is interested in changing the milieu through his art and his talks about the issue. Although Prince has many opportunities to give talks and to enter juried exhibits and win, as with many black artists, his art is not being collected by major museums, an important venue for deconstructing white supremacy and the myth of the declining significance of race and racism.

I was speaking at the Chrysler Museum [Norfolk, Virginia] and before I began to speak, the major curator was talking about the black art collection that they had garnered for years in Chrysler's collection and they were now looking for up-and-coming young artists. I almost raised my hand and asked, "Why am I not in this collection? I live right here in the Hampton Roads. I have some level of potency and I'm winning awards in this area. I've shown in pretty much every one of the shows and I have worked with most of the people involved, so seriously, why am I not being shown?" I think they tried to push me into a box to say that I am only speaking about the African American experience. I may be speaking about the African American experience or speaking from that standpoint, but I really mean all of life's experiences. . . . When I speak about the *Brown v. Board of Education*, I am not speaking about the black kids and the Little Rock nine entering the school in Little Rock, Arkansas, I am not talking about that. What happened to those people who were standing outside hollering and threatening and yelling, "Nigger, go away." Where are they now? Where are the other people you see in those photographs where black bodies are being lynched and they are having a good time like they're at a picnic? Hundreds of thousands of people were out there witnessing the dismemberment of black bodies across the South. Where are they now? How did they integrate into society? What was the shift, and what was the shift that occurred to say this black person is a man, or this black person is a woman? And that's the kind of stuff I challenge people on. What do you carry inside your heart and what do you harbor inside your household or your little enclave that still exists that carries or perpetuates a lot of the ignorance that was reported back in that time period? Did it all of a sudden disappear when Martin Luther King said, "I have a dream?" Where is the shift? I don't believe that shift is happening. I just think that political correctness allowed people to think, "We don't have to say it, just don't do it." It's more or less not to say it overtly, but it is an action or lack of action.

Being politically correct is not Prince's Achilles' heel.

Artists create out of what they experience and I think some of their strongest works come from that. It comes out of what you experience, what you understand, and what you know. That needs to be respected. It is that experience and the person creating out of truth as they best know it. Creating out of all your experiences is not being respected in the black artists. If van Gogh can make the *Potato Eater*, I can relate to it. I see that as a group of people sitting down at a table that don't have a lot of means. So eating potatoes every day because the crop wasn't good that year means they were making ends meet like any other family you might see in America. It is just a representation of the truth or the understanding of the environment which you grew up in. He's creating Dutch landscape and I am creating American landscape. That's the thing, we got that word that keeps separating us—African American concept and they keep us bracketed in there. It places us over here somewhere.

Pigeonholing and bracketing black artists' works can be severely limiting. Prince says, "It is even problematic that I am going to the Chrysler Museum and the group that I am involved with is called 'Friends of African American Art.' That term categorizes the art; it should be termed 'Friends of the Arts.'" Of course he understands that it is a double-edged sword. "That's a limited kind of way in which I portray that because there has been such lack of support for African American art and artists of color represented in museums, we need to have friends of African American art so we can get a stronger representation of African American art in there. But it is still like it's pushing us down in a corner." This limitation impacts how the patrons and curators of museums see a work by a black artist portraying the black experience. Prince cites this example of a work by Benny Andrews and how the curator interpreted his art piece to the supporters of the black artists.

> I can't remember the title of the art, but a woman was sitting inside of a Victorian-style home and she was sitting in a chair in this room and she is the only one there. And she had in her a lap a sewing loom, or it might have been a tray. And there was a conversation with the group who was trying to interpret this piece. The voice who was looking at this piece interpreted it as this black woman who was a servant in this house. The curator is actually saying this to the group, "I am really puzzled by this. I don't know what it is." And he basically said, "Well, this woman is probably a servant and she is taking a rest." And then I said, "That's very limiting. Why can't she be the owner? Why can't that just be her style—just a middle-class woman relaxing in her living room?"

> Whenever the black body is portrayed in certain spaces, the view is limited—it is limited to a slave's narrative. Why can't the narrative transcend the slave vision? It is always attached to that. We carried on this ball and chain. This historical facet, of course, is a part of us and we should not forget that. We should constantly talk about that and we should still feel the effects, but by the same token the gaze on the black body is still feeling the effects of that, over and over again.

Prince is all too familiar with having his artwork confined by racial stereotypes or limited to only the black experience, so his role as a critical teacher is to deconstruct old assumptions for his audience. "People look at my work and they are limited by that, but when I begin to talk about it, I began to open them up to another layer. And they say, 'Oh, my gosh, how would I ever know that if you weren't there to tell me about it!'" On one occasion, when he presented a workshop in New Hampshire, he remembered that one man commented to him, "That's interesting. I'm not familiar with that story that's associated with African American history." An Asian woman in the audience raised her hand in rebuttal, "No, sir! That's just not African American, that's American history." Prince concurred with the woman and added, "There is a problem with the way people view [black] art, which is filtered right through the educational system."

Prince created a piece of art about the Little Rock Nine. He wanted people to see it as an American experience, and not solely as the black experience. This is how he described that piece.

> It's a horizontally dominated piece and it shows the nine youths walking alone, but I did it in a way that the figures are forced into a confined space and compressed in there and in the background. I show white people jeering and cursing at them and telling them to go away, go back to the jungle—all this stuff being spewed at them. And then I show the national guardsmen flanking them from the front and the back. I constructed the piece in such a way that it looks like a train. It looks like the bodies are moving. I wanted to evoke this idea of the inevitability of integration in America. We cannot continue to live that lie, "All men are created equal." You talk freedom and yet you have people subjugated and separated. I believe that that had to be torn down and it was just a matter of time. I also used Paul in the Bible, and I go specifically to Ephesians where he talks about putting on the whole armor of God—his putting on the helmet of God and his double-edged sword and girding your body up and getting ready for battle in a spiritual context and that's one of the ideas that I am trying to invoke. I believe that some spiritual battles have been waged within America, within the world for that fact, and that that is what I was trying to invoke within the piece. But I also felt there was a spiritual protectiveness that was girded about these bodies to protect them as they entered into the school. That's all going on in the image. Some people will look at it and call it just black history. But don't put that word in front of it. It is not just black history. It is American history.

The duality of the human condition, whether it is race, class, gender, or religion intertwined, is always embodied in his art. His piece *Stillborn* deals with a pregnant mother. "She probably has twins in there," said Prince.

> The mother and father are husband and wife, but there is no dissolve between the two, and so the left arm becomes the mother's and the right arm becomes the father's. And on her belly is this giant crystal ball to show you all the things that are going on in the community, and there are some really serious things going on in her belly. And *Stillborn* in one instance is a child being dead at birth. And in the background I use a flock of birds and it looks like a series of triangles that are dissected right triangles. That's what they are and it creates a pattern that is called a flock of birds quilt pattern. These have been used by abolitionists to help slaves escape. Of course that is being contested right now. But I think it is a profound concept that quilts can be utilized to help them navigate and negotiate spaces. This is the background of the piece, so, when people look at the piece, they immediately think of death, but whenever I talk about it I say that in spite of all that is going on, in spite of all the pain that this child might be born

into, they are still born. I changed the concept. It is still born instead of stillborn. So those kinds of pieces may look negative, but then you flip the words and it becomes a positive. It's transcendent.

In another piece, *In the Line of Fire*, Prince portrays the transcendent quality of urban education in America.

> In one instance, you might think *In the Line of Fire* is about gunshot. But in another sense, if you think from a spiritual standpoint, the fire is in line with the whole spirit-power. That's what I'm trying to show in the piece. There is a target on one of the kids' dress that gets nullified by the other person that is standing in front of it. And it is protective. So it is like this ultra protectiveness is going on. It is like pieces that walk down this path, which is a checkerboard and which indicates crossroads which we embrace daily. We all embrace crossroads. I have seventeen middle and high school students coming into the school. And then I show you how they come in with their bodies, they come in with their culture, they come in with their spiritual beliefs, they come in with a history, they come in with a song upon their lips, they come in with great leaders that will come into this educational system and go out as leaders in the world.

How does Prince maintain his integrity and his soul in a materialistic market-driven economy?

> When I was in undergraduate school I was thinking about being a commercial artist and I was going to do things like design billboards and banners, basically the whole marketing realm. But I quickly turned away from that because I've always wanted to just make art and make things about what I felt and what I saw and experienced. It is tough to stick to that, especially when you are trying to get your work out there and trying to garner the funds to make a living, to survive, to support a family, and those kinds of things. And I've had twinges within me to pursue a different path and to do different work and stop the work that I am doing, because I've felt that a lot of it just goes unseen. And people say how great and wonderful it is, but they are not buying it. "Oh, your work is great, it's wonderful, I love what you're saying and you move me." So I end up getting a bunch of cheerleaders, but I don't have anyone who is actually buying the team. I get a few here and there but I'm not getting the kind of support that I would love to have to be able to continue to do my work. But that's not going to stop me. I'm committed to it. I am not doing it for praise. I would love to have folks be supportive. A lot of people would support me but they are afraid of the statements I make. "I can't put this on my wall." "This is a powerful piece, but I could never put this on my wall." There are other people who buy my works and they may say, "I got to have so and so." Because they understand what I'm trying to do and I am not afraid of issues.

In Prince's observation, the artworks that receive the most acclaim are usually more abstract and less politically charged or benign than those within the confines of what is considered African Americanesque. The works that are "not really heavily controversial and the ones that tend to almost reify a lot of negative stereotypes seem to be the ones that I have seen get a lot of play. Individuals who also make a lot of abstract and sculpture pieces might get some play as they tend to be benign in terms of their very beautiful constructive form." He observed this pattern of response of collectors with his own mentor, John Scott. Scott's earlier artworks were more politically charged; however, as Prince noted, "The point at which he received his greatest following was when he switched to more abstract form. The acceptance of him as an artist grew exponentially because now it is beautiful form. It is not about the statement he may be making, although he is still making some of the same statements." A similar pattern is evident in John Biggers's later works. "I am not knocking Biggers's work and I respect it to the fullest, but his strongest following came when he got deeper with his more spiritual, *The House of the Turtle*. John Biggers became highly symbolic and most people could not read the symbolism and, therefore, it was more the patterns and the abstraction and geometry of his pieces that became more appealing, more dominating and they couldn't see the stuff—the stuff with the pots and the urns and the mothers and the washboards. He never got rid of it, but the person with the trained eye knew it and saw it. He got to the point where he just got so layered in so many symbols that he had symbols on top of symbols and that was because he was so knowledgeable." However, for those who control the production of art, Prince sees it as unfortunate that the cultural critics fail to understand the various layered meanings of black aesthetics, so it truncates racial and cultural understanding and healing. "We live in a society that wants to surround ourselves by images that make us feel comfortable or we appear to be comfortable. But I think that is so damaging societally when you are not talking or not communicating."

Unlike many of his young artists, he is following in the tradition and the footsteps of artists like John Scott, his mentor, and John Biggers. Like his mentors, Prince is "always about trying to move on and find joy inside of the pain."

My vocabulary is getting deeper and deeper. That is just because I'm getting older and reading more and experiencing more things. I'm making new connections daily, and so my vocabulary gets bigger in terms of how you see life. It's about how can I look at a leaf a different way? How can I look at a leaf and look at it beyond a leaf? I cannot look at a leaf or a tree and not think of all the great labor that is associated with the wood. That same wood that can make paper, that same wood that made a ship, that same wood that made a plank, that wood that has so many multiple meanings and so many multiple planes, and so many multiple constructions, that same wood in and of itself is a place where somebody was lynched, somebody was dismembered. All those things are just imbued with so much history. And when I walk around, I sometimes think about where I am and who traversed this land before me. And the foundations that were laid and I am walking in those same footsteps with the same responsibility. These people risked their lives, gave their lives, for these ideas and I say what can I do in my time? What can I do in my generation? Can I do the same thing? Can I act with the same amount of bravery that those people did? Can I go with the same level of fearlessness that they did, or will I fold with the pressure? I think about the world around me and I think about all the labor, all the pain, all the being ostracized and I think of my father urinating in the cup. Everything comes back to my mind like a flood.

In the words of John Scott, Prince knows that he must "Just pass it on." One such opportunity came after Hurricane Katrina when he invited thirty-five New Orleans artists who suffered the ravages of the hurricane to exhibit in a show that he created, titled *Art for Adults: Reflections from Katrina*. The proceeds were given to the artists to assist them in continuing their work. Interestingly, Prince, who is from New Orleans, was there exhibiting his work *In My Father's House* during Hurricane Katrina.

Although two generations separated Prince and Biggers, each felt a strong commitment to use his art not only to transform the African American community but all of humanity. Likewise, Widdiss has begun to see her art, especially her *Healing Curtains* as a change agent for global healing. However, she is concerned that too many young artists have become trapped by monetary success. "The means of success in America is generally equated to monetary success. Success in art is now valued in the same light in terms of how much, how many, what important collections, how many catalogs? People who are studying art in undergraduate and graduate school, before they have studied enough or done enough soul searching and creativity, they are plotting strategies for marketing and political connection to monetary success and high visibility. They are coming out with producing a formula for a defined market. That is across the board, whether black or white."

If younger artists are losing their souls, what are the implications for community, culture, and consciousness? Will there be enough young Steve Princes of the black community to continue raising the level of consciousness in the black community and the larger society about the unfinished agenda of racial, class, and gender oppression?

8

Chaos or Community:
Facing the Twenty-First Century

The introductory vignettes about a cup of sugar are a metaphor for changing black communities. At the turn of the twentieth century in America, the black community's sugar bin was nearly empty. The race was largely poor and uneducated and lived in the rural, segregated South in a period depicted by Rayford Logan as the nadir. Yet culturally, we were more communal and our collective consciousness was more elevated, so we felt a greater sense of duty to dip into that bin and share a cup of sugar with neighbors. At the turn of the twenty-first century, the sugar bin is at least half full. We are wealthier, better educated, more urban and diverse regionally and ethnically, as well as more integrated into the mainstream of white America. But despite our overall improved socioeconomic condition, we are more individualistic and less willing to share a cup of sugar. In essence the caring and sharing black community of the pre-1960s, with its collective ethic of service in ideology and praxis, declined in the post-1960s. In this work I ask: What cultural and structural changes account for this shift in community, culture, and consciousness from a collective ethos to an individual ethos? How have these changes affected the service orientation of the black community in general and the dominant black professions of the pre-1960s in particular? Are there generational differences in service orientation? What factors might facilitate or mitigate a collective ethos?

To answer these questions, I looked at chief cultural and structural transformations and events that impacted the value shift of blacks' collective ethos and service orientation: the alterations in the economic sectors; the milestones of World War I, World War II, and the civil rights movement; and the transition of three major cultural phases—the postfigurative phase, which I equate with the World War I generation; the cofigurative phase, the generation of World War II; and the prefigurative phase, the civil rights generation.

These alterations and events helped to shape the sense of community, culture, and consciousness of those who were born or who grew up during certain time periods. In the lived experiences of three generations of black professionals in three different eras, we can discern the value shift from the "We" model in the pre-1960s to the "I" model in the post-1960s. In the World War I generation, the "We" model prevailed. The ideology of service and uplift of the black community was the dominant collective ethos and was consistent with social action. The black middle class spearheaded most uplift, reform, and liberation movements, hence the rationale for my focus. In the World War II generation, particularly the cohort who came of age during the civil rights era, the "I" model and the "We" model were in conflict. The ideology of service and uplift of the black community was in flux and was evidenced in its credo and praxis. In the civil rights generation, the "I" model dominates. The ideology of service and uplift of the black community is now being replaced by an individual ethos of self-fulfillment, which is exhibited in attitude, belief system, and behavior. Two significant factors influencing a service orientation for individuals in the civil rights generation are the extent of contact with black networks and knowledge of black history.

These generational changes are illuminated in the dominant pre-1960s professions of blacks: education, medicine, ministry, and business. Prior to integration in the 1960s, these occupations were service oriented. In the profession of education, those of the World War I generation, like Yvonne Walker-Taylor, felt it was their duty to train students in the racial responsibility of uplifting the black community. In the civil rights generation, the emphasis shifted to developing one's own career, as exemplified by Keith Walton. A salient intervening variable that consistently affects the "I" model is the racial milieu of the undergraduate educational experience. Those trained at traditionally black undergraduate institutions have a greater sense of community, culture, and racial consciousness than those trained at traditionally white institutions. This finding is not surprising, since the historical mission of HBCUs is to instill a collective, uplift orientation into their students. Furthermore, those with a stronger collective consciousness are perhaps more likely to select HBCUs.

In the profession of the ministry, the World War I generation was directed toward collective liberation and empowerment. Joseph Lowery used his ministry as a mechanism to fight race and class injustices. The civil rights generation is more concerned with personal power and self-aggrandizement. Recall that Jesse Battle indicated that, while his father thought it was shameful to think of ministry and money in the same sentence, money was his primary concern. Likewise, medicine has shifted from being patient-centered to being profit-centered. Craig Appleton admitted that his motive for entering the specialty of radiology was for money and more predictable hours. Clearly, the tendency to be involved as a leader and change agent in black communities, such as Clinton Warner, has diminished. Similarly, in business, the ethic of communal empowerment, whether through capitalism or economic cooperatives, has been eroded by the dominant desire for personal acquisition. This is exemplified by Victor Ellington, who was born into the civil rights generation and does not wish to have any linkages with black communities. He contrasts sharply with James Paschal, who was born into the World War I generation and who was instrumental in providing support to the civil rights movement.

Although the first edition of the book discussed only the dominant occupations of blacks in the pre-1960s, this updated work supports the idea that this generational pattern continues to prevail as blacks have entered new occupations and social spaces in government and in private for-profit, not-for-profit, and self-employed venues as accountants, administrators, artists/performers, brokers/financial analysts, corporate executives, journalists, lawyers, mayors, scientists and engineers, and computer scientists and analysts in the 1960s. With fresh memories of the civil rights struggles, many of the first wave of the integrated generation were more likely to be imbued with the ideals of collective racial service and uplift in their new professions. George Davis and Glegg Watson, in *Black Life in Corporate America*, suggest that blacks entering corporate America in the 1960s were more likely to be race ambassadors with a strong social consciousness. A significant number of these trailblazers who penetrated the corporate culture had a liberal arts background. One pre-1960s corporate couple they interviewed stated: "We went to college at a time when business was looked down on. Anyone could turn fifty cents into a dollar. . . . But what do you do with that dollar? Do you help or hurt someone? We were social worker types conditioned by our parents to racial service and responsibility and not to get out there and do everything we could to make a dollar."[1] As the second generation became more assimilated into the dominant cultural values of individualism, the collective ethos of service and racial uplift was supplanted.

What are the implications of a waning collective ethic for black communities in the twenty-first century? As we settle into the global village, with more diverse black communities in the millennium, we can speculate about a number of challenges. First, the color line was more subtle and covert at the end of the twentieth century than at the beginning. It is reasonable, then, to postulate that post-1960s generations are less likely to identify or acknowledge the impact of racism. Thus they are more likely to be deracialized and to experience greater psychic discontinuity and less racial consciousness than previous generations.

Second, since blacks are in diverse milieus, formal mechanisms for passing on race lessons and the legacy of ancestors' strengths in overcoming odds are less operative than in the pre-1960s. Louise Patterson and William Holmes Borders, whom we met earlier, were midnight stars of the World War I generation who embodied our racial persecution and our glory. With towering strength, they overcame odds and pointed the way to service and uplift of the black community, setting a course for the next generation to follow. But now, even while urban schools are again becoming segregated, white teachers are predominant, so black youth will not likely be taught a revolutionary pedagogy and legacy to "lift others as we climb." With the decline of blacks entering the higher education academy to teach, a "whitening" of faculty is also an emerging pattern at HBCUs, where service orientation has been a heritage.

Third, since the divide-and-conquer tactic has been a strategy of the oppressor to control the oppressed, it is likely to exacerbate. In the World War I generation, it was colorism. In the World War II generation, it was education and color. In the civil rights generation, it is the politics of class, ethnicity, age, gender, and sexual orientation. In essence, the pre-1960s black communities were more homogeneous in marriage and familial structure, religious orientation, educational level, economic status, political orientation, ethnic makeup, and gender orientation than those of the post-1960s. Accordingly, we have a greater chance of being sundered and manipulated by hegemonic political forces along these lines outside and within black communities, subverting our strength and energy to organize for collective action and empowerment.

With the eroding of economic, political, and civil rights at the end of the twentieth century, we need collective strength to defeat this new nadir in the twenty-first century. There is a great need to utilize formal mechanisms in our communities and develop other mechanisms to address these issues, and to educate blacks about how the color line is the enemy that binds all of us and about its linkage to the question of gender, class, ethnicity, age, sexual orientation, or the differently abled. Yet, such a movement toward community, culture, and consciousness becomes a challenge with greater diversity in a rapidly changing postmodern society. Clearly, the emerging communities of the civil rights generation are different from those of the past and unfamiliar to the elders who are experiencing these rapid changes. They lament, in the words of Margaret Mead, "No other generation will experience what we have experienced. In this sense we must recognize that we have no descendants, as our children have no forebears."[2] The elders cannot experience what their children are experiencing. So how do we link elders with youth to articulate the collective identity narrative, which includes our glories and persecutions and which allows for the circulation of the cultural trait of collective empowerment and service? We cannot continue to move forward in the twenty-first century with an individualistic ethic, and yet we cannot return to the past, because the youth have never experienced what their elders have.

Is there a way out of this quagmire? Is there a way to synthesize or reconceptualize this dialectical tension between the "I" model of youth and the "We" model of elders? Amitai Etzioni, a sociologist, suggests a way out.[3] He proposes that the "I" and "We" model should replace the limitation of the "Me First" model in the social sciences. The ontology of "I" and "We" emerges from the neoclassical Western model of being, where the concept of I, emphasizing individual tendencies, is synthesized with We, underscoring concern for others. If we reconceptualize the dialectical angst in a more holistic way, perhaps we can move sure-footed in this millennium. Martin Luther King, Jr., in *Where Do We Go from Here: Chaos or Community?*, points us in this direction by reminding us that "'I' cannot reach fulfillment without 'thou.' The self cannot be self without other selves. Self-concern without other-concern is like a tributary that has no outward flow to the ocean. Stagnant, still, and stale, it lacks both life and freshness."[4] This model of being sees the interdependence of individuals and the community. Stephanie Coontz, in her book *The Way We Never Were*, reminds us that Americans are so imbued with the myth of self-reliance and individualism that they underestimate the reality of their interdependence and the tradition of dependence on others, beginning with the colonists.[5] The ideology of individualism and self-reliance is often used to justify inequality in the social order. It assumes people pull themselves up by their own bootstraps. For young blacks to embrace such a notion is to adopt a false consciousness, which is antithetical to their racial group's interest. Though this interdependence of self and group is disavowed in the folklore of American culture, it is the basis of the African-centered model, where the "I" is in essence an extended self. The African-centered "We" orientation stresses "unity through ideology" in juxtaposition to the neoclassical idea of "unity through common goals or specific aim."[6]

Ideally, a movement toward community, culture, and consciousness would extol an ideology of service to others and would embrace and build caring black communities that would confront existential issues of discrimination, poverty, peace and justice, profit, greed, and human misery. It would incorporate multiple definitions of identity, inclusive of ethnicity, class, gender and sexual orientation, age, or any affected groups. Our common group identity becomes a process in a continual state of construction. Our particular identity (gender, class, ethnicity) and our common group identity (race) interact and shape each other in a constant process of change.

To build caring communities, it is crucial to understand our racial history as it connects with these other social identities. Race, language, and culture are sufficient to sustain group cohesion. "Such cohesion appears to depend upon a group constantly living and re-living a dialectical relationship between its past and present, with a projection for certain values for the future."[7] Our common group identity in the form of a racial narrative can tell the story of one or several particular identities. It can be an "utterance" that is meant for oneself and for the group. Anthropologist J. L. Amselle defines the identity in Africa as "the utterance of differences considered as a system of relations; based on oppositions it creates, however, a ground for negotiation, for establishing balances of power, because such an utterance is made possible by forgetting about the conditions in which society and polity have actually been produced."[8] Cemented by a common racial narrative of victimization and veneration and a past cultural orientation built on ideas of relations, we can then look to the future to build caring black communities. In this "system of relations, negotiation, [and] establishing balances" in the culture of the civil rights generation, to paraphrase Margaret Mead, the young must ask the questions, but the elders must work on the answers with them to teach and embrace service to others.[9]

In asking questions and seeking answers, we must look beyond borders of race, culture, class, and gender to embrace all humanity. We must celebrate individuals, like philosopher Tom Regan, who are toiling in the vineyards to expand our moral sensibilities and to build caring communities. "I write of a new generation, the Thee Generation," declared Regan.

> It is a generation of service: of giving not taking, of commitment to principles not material possessions, of communal compassion not conspicuous consumption. If the defining question of the present generation is, What can I get for me?, the central question of this new generation is, What can I do for thee? . . . Only by acting for the other does one come to know one's self, not in isolation from the ties that bind each to all but in affirmation of them.[10]

Notes

Introduction

1. Margaret Mead, *Culture and Commitment* (New York: Columbia University Press, 1978).

2. Mead, *Culture and Commitment* (1978), 25–26.

3. Personal conversation with Charles F. Simmons, July 1994.

4. Kevin K. Gaines, *Uplifting the Race: Black Leadership, Politics, and Culture in the Twentieth Century* (Chapel Hill: University of North Carolina Press, 1996).

5. Robert Hill, *The Strengths of Black Families* (New York: Emerson Hall, 1972). For a discussion of retentions of African cultural values and practices, such as communalism, extended family, and spirituality, see Andrew Billingsley, *Climbing Jacob's Ladder* (New York: Simon & Schuster, 1992); Niara Sudarkasa, "African and Afro-American Family Structure," *Black Scholar* 11, no. 8 (1980): 37–60; Dimitri Shimkin, Edith M. Shimkin, and Dennis A. Frake, eds., *The Extended Family in Black Societies* (The Hague: Mouton Publishing, 1978); James N. Kerri, "Understanding the African Family: Persistence, Continuity, and Change," *Western Journal of Black Studies* 3, no. 1 (1979): 14–17; Wade Nobles, "African Root and American Fruit: The Black Family," *Journal of Social and Behavioral Sciences* 20, no. 2 (1974): 52–63; "Africanity: Its Role in Black Families," *The Black Scholar* 9, no. 2 (1974): 10–17.

6. Billingsley, *Climbing Jacob's Ladder*, 36.

7. U.S. Department of Commerce, Bureau of the Census, *Statistical Abstract of the United States* (U.S. Government Printing Office, 1997), 63.

8. Gaines, *Uplifting the Race.*

9. Benjamin P. Bowser, "Generational Effects: The Impact of Culture, Economy and Community across the Generations," in *Black Adult Development and Aging*, ed. Reginald L. Jones (Berkeley, CA: Cobb & Henry, 1989).

10. Aldon Morris, *The Origins of the Civil Rights Movement: Black Communities Organizing for Change* (New York: Free Press, 1984).

241

11. Todd Gitlin, *The Sixties: Years of Hope, Days of Rage* (New York: Bantam Books, 1993), xiv.

12. Bowser, "Generational Effects," 5.

13. Robert N. Bellah, Richard Madsen, William M. Sullivan, Ann Swidler, and Steven M. Tipton, *Habits of the Heart: Individualism and Commitment in American Life* (Berkeley: University of California Press, 1985).

14. Daniel Yankelovich, *New Rules: Searching for Self-Fulfillment in a World Turned Upside Down* (New York: Random House, 1981). See also Christopher Lasch, *The Culture of Narcissism* (New York: Norton, 1979). For traditional values of Euro-American culture, see Robin M. Williams, Jr., *American Society: A Sociological Interpretation*, 3rd ed. (New York: Knopf, 1970); Robert N. Bellah et al., eds., *Individualism and Commitment in American Life* (New York: Harper & Row, 1987); Andrew Jamison and Ron Eyerman, *Seeds of the Sixties* (Berkeley: University of California Press, 1994).

15. Lasch, *The Culture of Narcissism*.

16. Alexander W. Astin, William S. Korn, and Ellyne R. Berz, *The American Freshman: National Norms for Fall 1990* (Los Angeles: Cooperative Institutional Research Program, American Council on Education, 1990).

17. Daniel Bell, *The Cultural Contradictions of Capitalism* (New York: Basic Books, 1976); Robert Bellah et al., *Habits of the Heart* (Berkeley: University of California Press, 1985); Amitai Etzioni, *An Immodest Agenda: Rebuilding America before the Twenty-First Century* (New York: McGraw-Hill, 1982).

18. "Faking the Grade," *ABC Primetime Live*, Transcript 374, November 3, 1994.

19. Paul Rogat Loeb, *Generation at the Crossroads* (New Brunswick, NJ: Rutgers University Press, 1994), 55.

20. Greg J. Duncan, Timothy M. Smeeding, and Willard Rodgers, "The Incredible Shrinking Middle Class," *American Demographics* 14, no. 5 (1992): 34–38.

21. Ibid.

22. Martin Kilson, "The Black Bourgeoisie Revisited: From E. Franklin Frazier to the Present," *Dissent* 30, no. 1 (Winter 1983): 92.

23. *Statistical Abstract of the United States* 1997, 63.

24. M. Belinda Tucker and Claudia Mitchell-Kernan, eds., *The Decline in Marriage among African Americans* (New York: Russell Sage Foundation, 1995).

25. Mead, *Culture and Commitment*, 49.

26. Robert A. Nisbet, *The Sociological Tradition* (New York: Basic Books, 1966), 47–48.

27. Billingsley, *Climbing Jacob's Ladder*, 71–73.

28. For African survivals in black Americans, see: Linda James Myers, *Understanding an Afrocentric World View: Introduction to an Optimal Psychology* (Dubuque, IA: Kendall/Hunt, 1993); Wade W. Noble, "African Philosophy: Foundations for Black Psychology," in *Black Psychology*, ed. Reginald Jones (Berkeley, CA: Cobb & Henry, 1991); Molefi Kete Asante, *The Afrocentric Idea* (Philadelphia: Temple University Press, 1987); Molefi Kete Asante and Abu S. Abarry, eds., *African Intellectual Heritage: A Book of Sources* (Philadelphia: Temple University Press, 1996); Melville J. Herskovits, *The Myth of the Negro Past* (Boston: Beacon Press, 1958);

John Mbiti, *African Religions and Philosophy* (New York: Praeger, 1969); Niara Sudarkasa, "An Exposition on the Value Premises Underlying Family Studies," *Journal of the National Medical Association* 67, no. 3 (1975): 235–39; Carter G. Woodson, *The African Background Outlined* (Washington, DC: Association for the Study of Negro Life and History, 1936).

29. James P. Pitts, "The Study of Pace Consciousness: Comments on New Directions," *American Journal of Sociology* 80, no. 3 (1974): 672. See also Thomas A. Parham, "Nigrescence: The Transformation of Black Consciousness across the Life Cycle," in *Black Adult Development and Aging*, ed. Reginald L. Jones (Berkeley, CA: Cobb & Henry, 1989).

30. For an insightful discussion on political consciousness and collective action, see Aldon Morris and Carol Mueller, "Political Consciousness and Collective Action," in *The Frontiers of Social Movement Theory*, eds. Aldon Morris and Carol Mueller (New Haven, CT: Yale University Press, 1990).

31. Michael Omi and Howard Winant, *Racial Formation in the United States* (New York and London: Routledge, 1986). These authors support the thesis that racism is mutable and has been so historically in this country. See also Lois Benjamin, *The Black Elite: Facing the Color Line in the Twilight of the Twentieth Century* (Chicago: Nelson-Hall, 1991).

32. For a discussion of the permanence of racism in the United States, see Derrick Bell, *Faces at the Bottom of the Well* (New York: Basic Books, 1992).

33. William J. Wilson, *The Declining Significance of Race* (Chicago: University of Chicago Press, 1978).

34. Janet E. Helms, *Black and White Racial Identity* (New York: Praeger, 1993), 7. Helms notes, "Racial consciousness refers to the awareness that [socialization due to] racial-group membership can influence one's intrapsychic dynamics as well as interpersonal relationships. . . . Racial identity pertains to the quality of the awareness of the various forms in which awareness can occur, that is, identity resolution."

Chapter 1

1. Peter M. Bergman and Mort N. Bergman, *The Chronological History of the Negro in America* (New York: New American Library, 1969), 327.

2. David McBride and Monroe H. Little, "The Afro-American Elite, 1930–1940: A Historical and Statistical Profile," *Phylon* 42, no. 2 (1981):105–19.

3. Daniel M. Johnson and Rex R. Campbell, *Black Migration in America: A Social Demographic History* (Durham, NC: Duke University Press, 1981), 65.

4. E. Franklin Frazier, *The Negro in the United States* (New York: Macmillan, 1957), 689.

5. For an in-depth profile of Louise Thompson Patterson's formative years, see Lois Benjamin, *The Black Elite: Facing the Color Line in the Twilight of the Twentieth Century* (Chicago: Nelson-Hall, 1991). She can be found under her assumed name, Lula Brown.

6. Bart Landry, *The New Black Middle Class* (Berkeley: University of California, 1987), 21.

7. For a discussion of passing in the pre-1960s, see St. Clair Drake and Horace Cayton, *Black Metropolis*, vol. 1 (New York: Harper & Row, 1962), 163–71.

8. Mary Frances Berry and John W. Blassingame, *The Long Memory: The Black Experience in America* (New York: Oxford University Press, 1982).

9. Bergman and Bergman, *The Chronological History of the Negro in America*, 428.

10. Berry and Blassingame, *Long Memory*, 278.

11. Richard B. Sherman, "The Teachings at Hampton Institute: Social Equality, Racial Integrity and the Virginia Public Assemblage Act of 1926," *Virginian Magazine of History and Biography* 95, no. 3 (1987): 279.

12. Frazier, *The Negro in the United States*, 603. Though Brown claimed the guest was General Smuts from South Africa, other sources cite Sir Gordon Guggisberg, governor of the Gold Coast. See Edward K. Graham, "The Hampton Institute Strike of 1927: A Case in Student Protest," *American Scholar* 38, no. 4 (1969): 673.

13. "The Hampton Strike," *Crisis* 34 (December 1927): 345–46.

14. Louise Thompson, "With Langston Hughes in USSR," *Freedom Ways* (Spring 1968): 154.

15. Bergman and Bergman, *The Chronological History of the Negro in America*, 466.

16. Bergman and Bergman, 457.

17. Bergman and Bergman, 453.

18. Bergman and Bergman, 455.

19. William Holmes Borders, *Forty-fifth Pastoral Anniversary, 1937–1982* (Atlanta: Josten's American Yearbook Company, 1982), 27.

20. Borders, 18.

21. Borders, 137.

22. Borders, 279.

Chapter 2

1. Mary Frances Berry and John Blassingame, *The Long Memory: The Black Experience in America* (New York: Oxford University Press, 1982), 276.

2. Yolanda T. Moses, "Black Women in Academe: Issues and Strategies," *Project on the Status and Education of Women* (Washington, DC: Association of American Colleges, 1989), 17.

3. Martha E. Dawson, *Hampton University: A National Treasure* (Silver Spring, MD: Beckham House, 1994).

4. Reginald Wilson, "A Good Thing a Bell Curve Didn't Block the GI Bill," *Black Issues in Higher Education* 11, no. 24 (1995): 42–43.

5. Charles Whitaker, "Is There a Conspiracy to Take Over Black Colleges?" *Ebony* (October 1986), 83–84.

6. Jimmie Briggs and Lori S. Robinson, "Black Colleges Under Fire," *Emerge* (September 1993): 27.

7. Richard Majors et al., "Cool Pose: A Symbolic Mechanism for Masculine Role Enactment and Coping by Black Males," in *The American Black Male*, eds. Richard G. Majors and Jacob U. Gordon (Chicago: Nelson-Hall, 1994).

8. Ernie Suggs, "Searching for the Best: New Leaders of HBCUs Have a Broad Vision of the Future," *Black Issues in Higher Education* 14, no. 3 (1997): 27.

9. Hugh R. Fordyce, *1993 Statistical Report* (New York: United Negro College Fund, 1993), 17.

10. Fordyce, 17. See also Ayana Davis and Melody Locke, "Black Teacher Percentages Low at HBCUs," *Hampton Script* (Virginia), October 19, 1993.

11. For a discussion of the black identity development model, see William E. Cross, Jr., *Shades of Black: Diversity in African-American Identity* (Philadelphia: Temple University, 1991), 189–223.

12. Cross, 201–2.

13. Kenneth W. Jackson, "Black Faculty in Academia," in *The Racial Crisis in American Higher Education*, eds. Philip G. Altbach and Kofi Lomotey (Albany: The State University of New York Press, 1991), 136–37.

14. Cornel West, "The Dilemma of the Black Intellectual," *Journal of Blacks in Higher Education*, no. 2 (Winter 1993–1994): 60.

15. B. Denise Hawkins, "Scholarly Path to Change," *Black Issues in Higher Education* 14, no. 14 (1995): 25–26.

16. Cross, *Shades of Black*, 190.

17. For a discussion of the demographic changes, see Joseph T. Durham, "The 'Whitening' of HBCUs," *University Faculty Voice* 2, no. 8 (1998).

18. Arthur Levine, "How the Academic Profession Is Changing," *Daedalus* 126, no. 4 (1997). See the entire volume for insights into the changing profession. See also William G. Bowen and Derek Bok, *The Shape of the River* (Princeton, NJ: Princeton University Press, 1998) for the long-term implications of considering race in college and university admissions.

19. See Christopher J. Lucas, *Crisis in the Academy: Rethinking Higher Education in America* (New York: St. Martin's Press, 1996); Robert L. Lenington, *Managing Higher Education as a Business*, American Council on Education (Phoenix, AZ: Oryx Press, 1996).

Chapter 3

1. Peter M. Bergman, *The Chronological History of the Negro in America* (New York: New American Library, 1969).

2. Wyatt Tee Walker, *The Soul of Black Worship: A Trilogy Preaching, Praying, and Singing* (New York: Martin Luther King Fellows Press, 1984), 6–7.

3. Mary Frances Berry and John W. Blassingame, *The Long Memory: The Black Experience in America* (New York: Oxford University Press, 1982).

4. James D. Tyms, *The Black Church as Nurturing Community* (St. Louis, MO: Hodale Press, 1995), 68.

5. Michael Battle, "A Call to a National Dialogue: The Challenge of a Black Theology to the African American Church," in *A Call to a National Dialogue and Reflection on What Does It Mean to Be Black and Christian?* eds. Forest E. Harris and Donna E. Allen (Nashville, TN: Kelly Smith Institute, 1992).

6. Max Weber, *The Sociology of Religion* (Boston: Beacon Press, 1963).

7. William C. Turner, foreword to *Sacred Symphony: The Chanted Sermon of the Black Preacher*, by Jon Michael Spencer (New York: Greenwood Press, 1988), x–xi. See also Robert Joseph Taylor, Linda M. Chatters, and Jeff Levin, *Religion in the Lives of African Americans: Social, Psychological, and Health Perspectives* (Thousand Oaks, CA: Sage Publications, 2004).

8. E. Franklin Frazier, *The Negro in the United States* (New York: Macmillan, 1964), 57.

9. Personal interview with Michael Battle, then chaplain of Hampton University and director of its Ministers' Conference and Choir Directors-Organists Guild, July 1994. Any reference to Michael Battle is based on this conversation, unless otherwise specified.

10. Tyms, *The Black Church as Nurturing Community*, 68.

11. James H. Cone, *A Theology of Liberation* (Philadelphia and New York: Lippincott, 1970).

12. Cain Hope Felder, *Troubling Biblical Waters* (Maryknoll, NY: Orbis Books, 1989), 137; see also Mary Sawyer, *Black Ecumenism: Implementing the Demands of Justice* (Valley Forge, PA: Trinity Press International, 1994).

13. Lisa Daniels, "The Chosen Few," *Daily Press* (Newport News, VA), June 13, 1993, G1.

14. See Andrew Billingsley, *Mighty Like a River: The Black Church and Social Reform* (New York: Oxford University Press, 1999), 199, 204–5.

15. Billingsley, xxiv.

Chapter 4

1. Encyclopedia Britannica, "Hippocratic Oath: Traditional Text," www.brainy encyclopedia.com/encyclopedia/hi/hippocratic_oath.html (retrieved June 26, 2007).

2. Robert D. Orr and Norman Pang, "The Use of the Hippocratic Oath: A Review of 20th Century Practice and a Content Analysis of Oaths Administered in Schools in the U.S. and Canada in 1993," www.sequel.net/~twilight.

3. Barry M. Manuel, "A Hippocratic Oath: A Contemporary Version," *New England Journal of Medicine* 318, no. 8 (1988): 521–22.

4. Carter G. Woodson, *The Negro Professional Man in the Community* (Washington, DC: Association for the Study of Negro Life and History, 1934). See Thomas J. Ward, Jr., *Black Physicians in the Jim Crow South* (Fayetteville: University of Arkansas Press, 2003); Ridlon Florence, *A Black Physician's Struggle for Civil Rights: Edward C. Mazique, M.D.* (Albuquerque: University of New Mexico Press, 2005); Gilbert R. Mason, with James Patterson, *Beaches, Blood, and Ballot: A Black Doctor's Civil Rights Struggle* (Jackson: University Press of Mississippi, 2000).

5. Jessie Carney Smith and Robert L. Johns, eds., *Statistical Record of Black America* (Detroit, MI: Gale Research, 1995), 684.

6. William James, "The Black Experience in Medical Education: 1840 to 1980," *Report of EDRS* (1984), 3. See James Summerville, *Educating Black Doc-*

tors: A History of Meharry Medical College (University: University of Alabama, Press, 1983).

7. W. Michael Byrd and Linda A. Clayton, "An American Health Dilemma: A History of Blacks in the Health System," *Journal of the National Medical Association* 84, no. 2 (1992): 191–92.

8. W. Michael Byrd et al., "African-American Physicians' Views on Health Reform: Results of a Survey," *Journal of the National Medical Association* 86, no. 3 (1994): 191–99. See also Tony Brown, "Investigating the Links Between Race, Stress, and Health," *Black Americans Newsletter* 4, no. 1 (1996); Currents of Health Policy: Impacts on Black Americans (Parts 1 and 2), *Milbank Quarterly* 65, Supplement 2 (1987).

9. Frederick W. McKinney, "The Economic Survival of Black Physicians: Swimming in the Turbulent Waters," *Review of Black Political Economy* 15, no. 1 (1987): 55.

10. W. Michael Byrd and Linda A. Clayton, "An American Health Dilemma: A History of Blacks in the Health System," *Journal of the National Medical Association* 84, no. 2 (1992): 189–200.

11. James, "The Black Experience in Medical Education, 1840 to 1980," 5.

12. Darlene Clark Hine, "Co-laborers in the Work of the Lord: Nineteenth Century Black Women Physicians," in *The Racial Economy of Science: Toward a Democratic Future*, ed. Sandra Harding (Bloomfield and Indianapolis: Indiana University Press, 1993), 210–27.

13. See Marcia Bayne-Smith, ed., *Race, Gender, and Health* (Thousand Oaks, CA: Sage Publications, 1996); Diane L. Adams, ed., *Health Issues for Women of Color: A Cultural Diversity Perspective* (Thousand Oaks, CA: Sage Publications, 1995); Evelyn C. White, *The Black Women's Health Book: Speaking for Ourselves* (Seattle, WA: Seal Press, 1990).

14. Woodson, *The Negro Professional*, 104.

15. James, "The Black Experience in Medical Education," 3.

16. James, 4.

17. *The American Education Data Book*, vol. 1, *Higher and Adult Education* (Fairfax, VA: Frederick D. Patterson Research Institute/United Negro College Fund, 1997), 106.

18. Aubrey W. Bonnett and Frank L. Douglas, "Black Medical Schools," *Social Policy* 14, no. 4 (1983): 24.

19. Kevin A. Schulman et al., "The Effect of Race and Sex on Physicians' Recommendations for Cardiac Catheterization," *New England Journal of Medicine* 340, no. 8 (1999), 618–26; Wilburn H. Weddington et al., "Quality of Care and Black American Patients," *Journal of the National Medical Association* 84, no. 7 (1992): 569–75; Sandra L. Gadson, "Third World Health Status of Black American Males," *Journal of the National Medical Association* 98, no. 4 (April 2006), 488–91.

20. For a discussion of issues affecting women of color in particular, see Marian Gray Secundy, "Ethical Issues in Research," in *Women Issues for Women of Color*, ed. Diane L. Adams (Thousand Oaks, CA: Sage Publications, 1995), 228–38.

21. Bonnett and Douglas, "Black Medical Students in White Medical Schools," 23.

22. Harold E. Cheatham and James B. Stewart, *Black Families: Interdisciplinary Perspectives* (New Brunswick, NJ: Transaction, 1990), 56.

23. Warren J. Ferguson, "The Physician's Responsibility to Medically Underserved Poor People," *It Just Ain't Fair: The Ethics of Health Care for African Americans*, eds. Annette Dula and Sara Goering (Westport, CT: Praeger, 1994), 128–29.

24. George Ritzer, *The McDonaldization of Society* (Thousand Oaks, CA: Pine Forge Press, 1993), 9–10.

Chapter 5

1. John Hope, "The Meaning of Business," in *The Negro in Business*, ed. W. E. B. Du Bois (New York: AMS Press, 1971), 57.

2. Hope, 60.

3. Paul Lindsay Johnson, "The Black Entrepreneur," *Crisis* 92, no. 4 (1985): 150.

4. A. Wade Smith and Joan V. Moore, "East-West Differences in Black Economic Development," *Journal of Black Studies* 16, no. 2 (1985): 131–54.

5. Smith and Moore, 145.

6. John Sibley Butler, *Entrepreneurship and Self-Help among Black Americans: A Reconsideration of Race and Economics* (Albany: State University of New York Press, 1991), 74.

7. Peter M. Bergman and Mort N. Bergman, *The Chronological History of the Negro in America* (New York: New American Library, 1968), 329.

8. Du Bois, *The Negro in Business*, 8.

9. Roy F. Lee, *The Setting for Black Business Development: A Study in Sociology and Political Economy* (Ithaca: New York State School of Industrial and Labor Relations, 1973), 105.

10. Gail H. Towns, "A Piece of History: Clark Atlanta University Buys Historic Paschal's Hotel-Restaurant," *Black Issues in Higher Education* 13, no. 4 (1996): 52.

11. Lee, *The Setting for Black Business Development*, 145.

12. United States Commission on Minority Business Development, *Final Report* (1992).

13. Melvin Oliver and Thomas Shapiro, *Black Wealth, White Wealth: A New Perspective on Racial Inequality* (New York: Routledge, 1995); Thomas M. Shapiro, *The Hidden Cost of Being African American: How Wealth Perpetuates Inequality* (New York: Oxford University Press, 2004).

14. Paula Mergenhagen, "Black-Owned Businesses," *American Demographics* 18, no. 6 (1996): 24, 26; "Survey of Business Owners-Black-Owned Firms: 2002," *Black Summary of Findings, Table F* (U.S. Census Bureau) www.census.gov/csd/sbo/black-summaryoffindings.htm (accessed August 25, 2006).

15. Frank McCoy, "Will Clinton's Plan Work for Us?" *Black Enterprise* (June 1993), 218.

16. United States Commission on Minority Business Development, *Final Report* (1992), 99.

17. Smith and Moore, "East-West Differences," 139. For a discussion of black entrepreneurs in the post-civil rights era, see Michael D. Woodard, *Black Entrepreneurs in America: Stories of Struggle and Successes* (New Brunswick, NJ: Rutgers University Press, 1997).

18. From the Associated Press and reported in "Report: Minority Business Owners More Tech-Savvy," *Daily Press* (Newport News, VA), May 11, 1998, A3.

19. National Foundation for Women Business Owners News, "Minority Women–Owned Firms Thriving," *Burton Women's Business* 2, no. 1 (1998): 6.

Chapter 6

1. Audrey Edwards and Craig Polite, *Children of the Dream: Psychology of Black Success* (New York: Doubleday, 1992), 5.

2. David A. Bositis, *Diverging Generations: The Transformation of African American Policy Views* (Washington, DC: Joint Center for Political and Economic Studies, 2001), 46.

3. John Zaller, *The Nature and Origins of Mass Opinion* (New York: Cambridge University Press, 1992).

4. David Bositis, *Changing of the Guard: Generational Differences Among Black Elected Officials* (Washington, DC: Joint Center for Political and Economic Studies, 2001), 12.

5. *Voting Rights Act: Renew, Restore,* www.votingrights.org (accessed January 20, 2007).

6. Bositis, *Changing of the Guard: Generational Differences,* 4–19.

7. David A. Bositis, "Political Report: Black Elected Officials: 1994–1997," *Focus Magazine,* Joint Center for Political and Economic Studies (September 1998).

8. David A. Bositis, *Black Elected Officials: A Statistical Summary* (Washington, DC: Joint Center for Political and Economic Studies, 2003).

9. Martin Kilson, "American Politics 2002: Maturation Phase," *State of Black America 2002* (New York: National Urban League, 2002). See also Ronald W. Walters, *Black Presidential Politics in America: A Strategic Approach* (Albany: State University of New York, 1998); Ronald W. Walters and Robert C. Smith, *African American Leadership* (Albany: State University of New York, 1999); Marcus D. Pohlmann, *African American Political Thought* (New York: Routledge, 2003).

10. Bositis, *Changing of the Guard: Generational Differences,* 14.

11. Seth Goddard, "Keeping the Faith: Civil Rights and the Baby Boom." An interview with Congressman John Lewis, exclusive to *Life* magazine, www.life.com/Life/boomers/lewis.html.

12. Frank McCoy, "Can the Black Caucus Be Bipartisan?" *Black Enterprise* 24, no. 6 (January 1994): 22.

13. Bositis, *Changing of the Guard: Generational Differences.*

14. Bositis, 9.

15. Jeffrey Kraus, "Generational Conflict in Urban Politics: The 2002 Newark Mayoral Election," *Forum* 2, no. 3 (2004): 1–15. See also Juan Williams, *Enough:*

The Phony Leaders, Dead-End Movements, and Culture of Failure—and What Can We Do About It (New York: Crown Publishers, 2006).

16. Askia Muhammad, "To Be Young, Republican and Black," *Washington Informer* 32, no. 45 (August 8, 1996): 14.

17. Benjamin P. Bowser, *The Black Middle Class: Social Mobility and Vulnerability* (Boulder: Lynne Rienner Publishers, 2007).

Chapter 7

1. David F. Dorsey, "The Dual Aesthetics of Black American Artists," in *Beyond Black or White: An Alternate America*, eds. Vernon J. Dixon and Badi G. Foster (Boston: Little, Brown & Company, 1971), 70.

2. Dorsey 75.

3. bell hooks, *Art on My Mind: Visual Politics* (New York: New Press, 1995), 3.

4. Sharon F. Patton, *African-American Art* (New York: Oxford University Press, 1998).

5. hooks, *Art on My Mind*, 5.

6. hooks, 37.

7. hooks, 4.

8. hooks, 4.

9. Patton, *African-American Art*, 235.

10. hooks, *Art on My Mind*, 8.

Chapter 8

1. George Davis and Glegg Watson, *Black Life in Corporate America: Swimming in the Mainstream* (Garden City, NY: Anchor Press/Doubleday, 1985), 21.

2. Margaret Mead, *Culture and Commitment* (New York: Columbia University, 1978), 61.

3. Amitai Etzioni, "The 'Me First' Model in the Social Sciences Is Too Narrow," *Chronicle of Higher Education*, February 1, 1989, A44.

4. Martin Luther King, Jr., *Where Do We Go from Here: Chaos or Community?* (Boston: Beacon Press, 1968), 180.

5. Stephanie Coontz, *The Way We Never Were: American Families and the Nostalgia Trap* (New York: Basic Books, 1992).

6. Linda James Myers, *Understanding an Afrocentric World View: Introduction to an Optimal Psychology* (Dubuque, IA: Kendall/Hunt, 1993), 98.

7. Rutledge M. Dennis, "Du Bois and the Role of the Educated Elite," *Journal of Negro Education* 46, no. 4 (1977): 401.

8. Denis-Constant Martin, "The Choices of Identity," *Social Identities: Journal for the Study of Race, Nation and Culture* 1, no. 1 (1995): 8.

9. Mead, *Culture and Commitment*, 74.

10. Tom Regan, *The Thee Generation: Reflections on the Coming Revolution* (Philadelphia: Temple University Press, 1991), 3.

Index

8(a) Program, 132, 142
13th District of Michigan, 184

ACTION, 180
Adeyiga, Olanrewa, 128
affirmative action, 70, 72, 83, 124, 155, 190
African American studies, 186
African Legacy, 199
African Methodist Episcopal Church, 41–42, 93, 97
AfriCobra, 201
Afrocentric perspective, 67
Afrocentrism, 68, 91
Ahoskie, North Carolina, 149
Akpan, Kufra (pseudonym) 55–59, 71
Akron, University of, 143
Alfred Street Baptist Church (Alexandria, VA), 76
Allen, Lisa (pseudonym), 40, 64
Allen, Senator George, 172–73
Alpha Phi Alpha Outstanding Leadership Award, 82
American Baptist Theological Seminary, 178
American College of Occupational and Environmental Medicine (ACOEM), 114, 116

American College of Surgeons, 109
American Conservative Union, 181
American Medical Association (AMA), 102, 104–6
American Society for Information Service, 143
Americans for Democratic Action (ADA), 181
Amselle, J. L., 240
Ananse: The Web of Life (Biggers), 217
Anderson, Marion, 62
Andrews, Benny, 230
Angelou, Maya, 16
Anglican Church, 85
antiwar movement, 6
Appleton, Craig (pseudonym), 103–4, 127–28, 237
Aptheker, Herbert, 30
Arafat, Yasser, 84
Armed Forces Institute of Pathology, 116
Art for Adults: Reflections from Katrina, 234
Art On My Mind (hooks), 201
Art Student League, 203
Association of Black Sociologists (ABA), 61

Association of Medical Colleges, 109;
33 percent of approved schools
closed to Blacks, 109
Atlanta Board of Education, 106
Atlanta Citizen of the Year, 33
Atlanta City Council, 180
Atlanta Committee for the Olympic
Games, 134
Atlanta Constitution, 29
Atlanta, Georgia, 20, 29, 31, 33, 102,
106, 108, 110, 131, 134, 136, 186,
204
Atlanta University, 39–40, 216
Attucks, Crispus, 32
"Aunt Jemima," 68

back to Africa movement, 25
Baldwin, James, 200
Baltimore, Maryland, 116
Baptist, 115
Battle, Jesse, 78–79, 236
Battle, Michael, 80, 90
Bell, Daniel, 7
Bell, Derrick, 7
Bellah, Robert N., 7
"Beloved Community," 179
Berry, Mary Frances, and James
Blassingame, 22, 39, 75
Bethune, Mary McLeod, 27–28
Bettale, Margaret, 222–23
Beyond the Man, 32
BFA (Bachelor of Fine Arts), 204, 219
Big Rock Jail (Borders), 31
Biggers, Cora, 210
Biggers, John, 199–200, 206, 219,
233–34
Bill Cosby Show, 70
Billingsley, Andrew, 11, 97
Birmingham, Alabama, 29, 159
Black Achievement Award, 82
black artists, 199–201, 206, 226; blacks
see art as unimportant for survival,
201; interconnected to politics, 206;
often devalued, 200; politics of the
visual world not affirmed, 201;

racism blocked footpath of, 226;
require greater passion and sacrifice,
206; soul of black community, 199;
struggle of personal sacrifice for, 200
"Black Bourgeoisie Revisited, The"
(Kilson), 8
*Black Church As Nurturing Community,
The* (Tyms), 75
black clergy, 75–78, 94–97; benefits to
black men of being, 75; chief
communicator of nurturing
community, 76; comparison of young
and older clergy, 77, 94–97;
distinction between priest and
prophet, 76; formal education
changing the worldview of, 78; most
revered in black community, 75;
predomination of, 75; proclaimed
gospel of liberation, human dignity,
justice, 76; role of, 75
Black Codes, 15
black community, 2–4, 7–8, 10, 56,
61–62, 65, 102, 104, 115, 117, 124,
132, 137, 153, 155, 163, 200, 206,
234–35, 237; black physicians as
intelligent and resources for the, 102;
black physicians could only serve
black patients in the, 102; black
sociologists as change agents in the,
61; caring and sharing attitudes of,
56; dearth of role models in, 65;
economic changes, 7–8; economic
development of, 132; high esteem
assigned to, 104; implications for a
waning collective ethic in the, 237;
paucity of doctors alters medical
services in, 104; pre- and post-1960s
differences in the, 235; segregated,
62; services in, 104; shifts in, 2, 3,
88; social upbringing in the, 115;
soul of, 4; working class in, 65
Black Enterprise's 100 Top Companies,
139, 141, 143, 147; ascent, descent,
and renewal of, 132; black
entrepreneurs, 131–33; continual

obstacles of, 132; development
behind segregated walls, 133
Black Issues in Higher Education, 54,
136
Black Life in Corporate America (Davis
and Watson), 237
black middle class, 18
black ministers, 76, 80, 95–96;
Christians, 76; Nation of Islam's, 76;
pre-1960s, 80, 95–96; post-1960s,
80, 95–96; value shifts among three
generations of, 80
black nationalist movement, 89–91
black physicians, 102–5; board
certification required to practice, 103;
civil rights generation physicians high
income specialties, 103; encounter
professional and income inequalities,
105; greater specialization in 1960s,
103; intimately familiar with patients,
102; missionaries of good health in
the black community, 102
black politicians, 155
black power movement, 53, 66, 90, 121,
126, 207, 207
black studies, 64, 67–68, 71
Black Wealth, White Wealth, (Oliver and
Shapiro), 146
blackout of 2003, 196
Blassingame, John, 22, 39, 75
"Bloody Sunday," 179
Blueprint for My Girls (Shiraz), 153
Blueprint for My Girls Network, 153
BMW (British Motor Works), 146
Board of Consumer Cooperative, 31
Bonnet, Aubrey, 115, 118
Bontemps, Arna, 26
Booker, Cory, 174
Borders, Juel Pate, 110–13, 123
Borders, Julia Pate, 25
Borders, William Holmes, 12–16, 29,
25–27, 30–32, 110, 238
Boston, Massachusetts, 16, 150
Boston University, 41–42, 94
Bowser, Benjamin, 6

Brandeis University, 178
Brewton, Alabama, 47–50
Brooklyn, New York, 124
Brown, Charlotte Hawkins, 28
Brown, Clarence E., 79
Brown v. Board of Education, 229
Buffalo, New York, 79
Burroughs, Nannie, 28
Bush, President George H. W., 131–32,
143–44
Bush, President George W., 176

California, Berkeley, University of, 18;
Red Summer (1919) at, 18
Canaan Baptist Church (Harlem), 98
Canada, 101
Canon Corporation, 168
Capitol Hill, 177
Carnegie Corporation for the
Advancement of Teaching, 104
Carpenter, Vincent, 148–50
Carrara (Italy), 204
Carter administration, 140
Carter, President Jimmy, 136, 168, 180
Carver, George Washington, 108
Cascade United Methodist Church
(Atlanta), 82
Catholic Church, 221–22; lack of
feminine involvement, 221
Catholics, 220
Central Michigan University, 143
Central State University, 143
Chaloner Prize Grant, 203
Chapman, General Samuel, 22
Chattanooga, Tennessee, 28
Chesapeake Financial Services, 149
Chesapeake, Virginia, 149
Chicago Ecumenical Institute, 82
Chicago, Illinois, 15–18, 29–30, 110,
124, 186–87
Chinnery, Lind, 103, 125–29
Christian religion, 81–82
Christianity, 87
Chrysler Museum (Norfolk, VA),
229–30

Church of God, 115
Church of God in Christ, 97
Cincinnati, Ohio, 116
Cincinnati, University of, 116
City Council of Portsmouth, 174
Civil Rights Act of 1954, 61
Civil Rights Congress (CRC), 30
civil rights era, 106, 150, 196, 236
civil rights generation, 3, 6, 8–10, 16,
    36, 54, 62, 71–72, 94, 96, 106,
    124–25, 132, 236–38; broad
    economic market, 8; differences
    between the generations of World
    Wars I and II, 9, 96; education more
    specialized, 10; effects of
    transformation on most privileged
    blacks, 9; increated professional
    mobility, 10; value shifts most
    discernable in, 9
civil rights movement, 6, 16, 46, 49, 52,
    59, 61, 80–81, 83–84, 86, 89, 90–91,
    95–99, 115, 119, 121, 126–27, 132,
    135–36, 155, 157, 166, 172, 177–78,
    182, 184–85, 201, 207, 217, 219,
    235, 237
Clark-Atlanta University, 137, 178
class divide, 189–91
Cleveland, Ohio, 65
Clinton, President Bill, 16
Coaching Group, The, 147
cofigurative phase, 2, 3, 236
color line, the, 4, 25, 36–37, 41–42, 48,
    106, 111, 120, 163, 237–38
colorism, 238
Columbia/HCA, 128
Columbia University, 21, 178
Columbia University Teachers' College,
    72
Combs, "P. Diddy," 153
Commission on Minority Development,
    144
Communist and Socialist movements, 26
Communist Party, 26, 28–29
community (*see also* black community),
    2, 4, 6, 10, 11, 13, 48, 241

community conversations, 193
Community Development Corporation,
    138
Compromise of 1877, 15
Congregational Education Society, 27
Congress, 177, 180
Congressional Black Caucas (CBC),
    181, 183–84
Connerly, Ward, 180
consciousness, 2, 6, 11, 13, 239;
    community to culture to
    consciousness, 11; defined, 11
contemporary advocates for health care
    justice, 105
contemporary parody of Hippocratic
    oath, 101
Continuous Beam Accelerator Facility
    (CEBAF), 168
Coontz, Stephanie, 239
Council of African Affairs, 30
countercultural movement, 6
Crescent City (New Orleans), 219
Crisis, 24, 28
Cross, William E., 69
Crowders Mountain, 208, 214
culture, 2, 6, 10, 11, 13, 239;
    communalism for blacks' survival,
    11; defined, 10; social heritage of a
    people, 11
"culture of narcissism," 7

Daily Press (Newport News), 23–24
Dallas, Texas, 19
Damons, Dash, 153
Davis, General Jefferson, 34
David, George, 237
Dayton, Ohio, 96
Dean Witter, 148
Def Jam Records, 153
deindustrialization, 189
Democratic Leadership Council, 183
Democratic Majority Congress, 190
Democratic Party, 28
Democrats, 135, 139, 156, 172, 180,
    184

Department of Corrections, 120
Depression, The (*see also* The Great
  Depression), 107, 133, 158–59
desegregation, 10, 13
*Desperate People Pray Desperate
  Prayers* (Lightner-Fuller), 98
Detroit City Hall, 204
Detroit College of Law, 185
Detroit, Michigan, 182–83, 184, 187,
  189–90
Detroit Public Schools, 185
Dett, Nathaniel, 108
Dobbs House, 136
Dobbs, Mattiwilda, 31
Dorsey, David F., 199, 201
Douglas, Aaron, 26
Douglas, Frank, 115, 118
Douglass, Frederick, 108, 145
Downbeat magazine, 200
Drake, St. Claire, 19
Dreisden, Theodore, 29
Drum Major for Justice Award (SCLC),
  45
"Dual Aesthetics of Black American
  Artists, The" (Dorsey), 199
DuBois, W. E. B., 15, 16, 19, 20, 24, 28,
  30–331, 37, 39, 40, 61, 68, 108
Duke University, 90, 178
Dun and Bradstreet Corporation, 151
Durham, North Carolina, 132
Durkee, J. Stanley, 22
Dutch Reformed Church of America, 48
Dyer Anti-Lynching Law (1925), 22

East Texas, 216–17
Eastern Connecticut State University,
  202, 204
Ebony magazine, 33, 82
Edmund Pettus Bridge, 179
education and color, 238
Edwards, Audrey, 155
Elders, Surgeon General Joyce, 105
Ellington, Victor, 150, 237
Ellison, Ralph, 26
Emancipation, 39, 132

Emancipation Proclamation, 20
Emory University School of Theology,
  82
Enron, 7
Enyche Clothing, 153
Episcopal denomination, 86
Etzione Amitai, 7
Evanston Consumer Cooperative, 27
Evansville, Illinois, 16, 21, 24, 31
expressive individualism, 7

Fannie Lou Hamer Award, 30
Farrakhan, Louis, 76
FBI (Federal Bureau of Investigation),
  30, 169
Field Foundation, 179
Fifth District of Georgia, 177
Fisher, Rudolph, 26
Fisk University, 22, 106, 178
Flexner, Abraham, 104
Flexner Report of 1910, 104
Florida A&M University, 185
Follow Me (Borders), 31
Ford, Harold, Jr., 183, 186–89
Ford, James W., 27–29
Fortune 500, 100
Franklin, Mayor Shirley, 181–82
Franks, Gary, 181
Frazier, E. Franklin, 31, 61
"Friends of African American Art," 230
Frost, Robert, 16

Garrett County, Kentucky, 142
Garrett Theological Seminary, 21
Garvey, Marcus, 25
Gaston, A. G., 164–65
Gastonia, North Carolina, 208, 211, 215
GED (General Educational
  Development), 149
gender discrimination, 45, 111–12
gender line, 4, 45
General Motors Corporation, 114, 116,
  139
Generations at the Crossroads (Loeb), 7
Georgetown University, 178

George Washington University, 125

Georgia National Guard, 33

Ghana (West Africa), 217

GI Bill of Rights, 5, 47, 57

Gilead, Joseph, 212

Gitlin, Todd, 6

God, 78–82, 90, 92–94, 96, 123, 145, 161, 221–22, 228, 231

God is Real (Borders), 31

God's work, 112

Goddard, Seth, 180

"Go down Moses, Way down in Egypt Land and Tell Old Pharoah, Let My People Go" (Borders), 35

Golden Plate Award of the Academy of Excellence, 138

"Gospel of Gender Equality," 93

Gray, P. Y., 216–17

Great Depression, The, 21, 173, 207–11

Great Migration, The, 5, 16, 18, 65, 189; blacks' migration to urban North and South during, 5

Greenwich Village, 214

Gregg, James E., 22–24

Hale, Frank, Jr., 61–64, 69, 71

Hall, Jim, 75, 85–88, 96

(Hall), Pauline, 88

Hammond Theological Seminary, 78

Hampton Institute (now Hampton University), 22–23, 40, 164–65, 212–13, 215

Hampton Roads Minority Business Development Center, 150

Hampton strike, the, 23–24

Hampton University, 22, 46, 50, 80, 152, 172, 215–16, 218–19

Hampton University Ministers' Conference, 81, 94

Hampton, Virginia, 103

Harlem, New York, 202–3

Harlem Renaissance, 19, 25–26

Harper, William, 102, 104, 106, 108, 113

Hartford, Connecticut, 21

Harvard University, 49, 172, 176

Harvey, Norma, 49

Harvey, William R., 46–51, 55, 71, 73, 215–16

HARYOU-ACT (Harlem Youth Program in arts and culture), 203

Hatcher, Maria (pseudonym), 1, 2, 5

Hawkins, Denise, 62

Hawkins, Frances, 1, 2, 5, 9, 40

Hayes, Roland, 31, 62

Head Start, 98

Healing Curtains Series, 203, 234

Hegel, G. W. F., 36

He Is Only a Throne Away, 45

Hepworth, Barbara, 204, 207

Herring, Cedric, 61

Herskovits, Melville J., 31

Hillsborough County, Florida, 148

hip-hop mayor, 194

Hippocratic oath, 101

Historically Black Colleges and Universities (HBCUs), 41–43, 46, 49, 51, 55, 59–60, 62, 72, 236, 238

Hitler, 32

Hitlerism of Georgia, 33

HMOs (health maintenance organization), 103–4, 128

holistic approach to health, 105

Holley, James W, III, 172–77, 181

hooks, bell, 201–2, 205, 307

Hoover, J. Edgar, 170

Hope, John, 21, 31, 131–32

Hopper, Frank A., 33

House of the Turtle (Biggers), 215, 233

Houston Music Hall, 217

How I Got Over, 84

Howard University, 22, 76, 121, 178

Howard University Medical School, 104, 113, 118, 127–28

Howard University School of Dentistry, 174

Hughes, Langston, 26–27

Huntsville, Alabama, 82

Hurricane Katrina, 234

Hurston, Zora Neale, 26–27

"I Am Somebody" (Borders), 31
IBM (International Business Machines), 139
"I" Model, 236, 239
Indianapolis, Indiana, 16
In My Father's House (Prince), 234
integrated generation, 155, 237; equal employment opportunities, 155; networking, 155; sense of entitlement, 155; set-asides, 155
International Labor Defense (ILD) 28, 30; arm of communist party, 28
International Workers Order (IWO), 29
In the Line of Fire (Prince), 232
IRS (Internal Revenue Service), 146
issues of desegregation, 55; brain drain, 55; fiscal problems, 55; underenrollment, 55

Jackson, General Stonewall, 34
Jackson, Jesse, 100
Jackson, Jesse, Jr., 187
Jackson, Maynard, 136, 181
Jackson, Sandra (pseudonym), 2, 58–60, 71–72
James, Sharpe, 183
Jefferson Laboratory, 168
Jesse Menifield Rattley Center, 172
J. Eugene Smith Library, 204
Jewish politicians, 189
Jim Crow, 37, 48, 163, 173, 177
Jim Crow laws, 33
John F. Kennedy Profile in Courage Award, 177
John Lewis Scholarship Fund, 178
John Theisen Gallery, 217
Johnson, Charles, 31, 61
Johnson, James Weldon, 39
Johnson, President Lyndon B., 105
Joint Center for Political and Economic Studies, 155–57, 167, 172, 181, 182
Joint Chiefs of Staff, 166–67
Jones, Leslie Renai Stiff, 113
Jones Valley Finance Company, 164

Judeo-Christian ethics, 4
Juris Doctor, 185

Kansas City, Missouri, 62
Kansas, University of, 42
Kennedy, President John F, 16, 89, 182; New Frontier, 16
Kennedy, Robert, 6
Kentucky State College, 142
Kilpatrick, Congresswoman Carolyn Cheeks, 184
Kilpatrick, Mayor Kwame, 157, 173, 182–196
Kilson, Martin, 8
King, Martin Luther, Jr., 6, 76, 81–83, 89, 135, 166, 179–80, 183, 229, 239
Knoxville College, 82
Kouros, Isamu Noguchi, 207
Ku Klux Klan, 83

Landry, Burt, 18
Langley Air Force Base, 165
Lanham Act, 47
Lanham, Maryland, 142
Lansing Public Schools, 185
Lansing School System, 185
Lasch, Christopher, 7
Lead Belly, 214
Lee, General Robert E., 34
Lee, Roy F., 138
"Legend of Kwame Kilpatrick," 194
Levine, Arthur, 72
Lewis, John, 177–81
Lexington, North Carolina, 95
liberal arts education versus industrial education, 40
"Liberation Lifestyle," 84–85
liberation pedagogy, 57
Lift Every Voice and Sing, (Johnson), 39
Lightner-Fuller, Ann, 93–96
Liles, Kevin, 153
Lincoln Academy, 211–12
Lincoln, C. Eric, 100
Links, the, 211
Little Rock Nine, 229, 231

Locke, Alain, 24, 26
Loeb, Paul Rogat, 7
Logan, Rayford, 15, 235
Long Memory (Berry and Blasingame), 22, 75
Los Angeles, California, 18–19
Loveland, Ohio, 142–43
Lowenfeld, Viktor, 212–15
Lowery, Joseph, 81–86, 92, 135, 236

Macon, Georgia, 15, 20–21
Macon Telegraph (Georgia), 20
Mad Rhythms, 151–52
Madonna and Child (Michelangelo), 223
Making Sense of the Sixties (PBS Documentary, 1991), 6
Malcolm X, 6, 76
Man of the Year, 33
March on Washington, 1963, 177
Marshall, Thurgood, 33
Martin Luther King, Jr. Historical Preservation District, 106
Martin Luther King, Jr. Non-Violent Peace Prize, 178
Marxism, 36
Marxist studies, 30
Maryland Black Businesses for Bush, 143
Maryland Blacks for Bush/Quayle Committee, 143
Maryland Bush for President Finance Committee, 144
Maryland Bush/Quayle Committee, 144
Mason, Charlotte Vandervere Quick, 26–27
Mason, Rufus Osgood, 26
Massenburg Bill, 23–24
Maxima Corporation, 136, 141, 143
Mays, Benjamin, 108
McCarthyism period, 30
McDonaldlization of cultures, 207
McDonaldlization of Society, The (Ritzer), 128
McDonald's, 128

McDuffie County, Georgia, 134
MCI, 7
McKenzie, Fayette, 22
Mead, Margaret, 2–3, 6, 10, 238, 240
Medicaid, 97, 102, 105, 114, 117, 122
Medical College of Pennsylvania, 110–11
Medical model, 105
Medicare, 102, 105, 114, 117, 122
"Me-first" attitude, 127
"Me-first" model, 71, 247
megachurch, 99
megacorporation, 98
"Me" generation, 7; ethic of self-fulfillment, 7; labeled culture of narcissism, 7; promotes winning at all costs, 7
Meharry Medical College, 102–4, 106, 108, 113, 116, 118, 125–26
Memphis, Tennessee, 136
Menifield, Alonzo, 154
Menifield, Altona, 154, 160
Men Must Live As Brothers (Borders), 31
Meschrabpom Film Studio, 27
MFA (Master of Fine Arts), 204, 219
Miami, Florida, 86
Michelangelo, 220, 223
Michigan Occupational and Environmental Medicine Association, 116
Michigan State House of Representatives, 190, 192
Michigan State University, 224
Michigan, University of, 116
Mighty Like a River (Billingsley), 97
Miller, Colbert (pseudonym), 120–23
Miller, Crystal, 71
Miller, Kelly, 22
Million Man March, 97
Minority Business Development, 131–32
Minority Enterprise Small Business Investment Company, 138
Mississippi Freedom Summer, 179

MIT (Massachusetts Institute of
  Technology), 162
Mitchell, Denis, 204
Mobile, Alabama, 83
Montana, University of, 88
Montgomery (Alabama) boycott, 6
Monticello, Mississippi, 96
Moore, Henry, 207
Moore, Jean V., 132, 148
Morehouse College, 20, 31, 40, 56, 108,
  131, 178
Morehouse Medical College, 104
Morial, Marc, 193
Morris, Aldon, 6
Moses, Yolanda, 42
Muhammad, Askia, 183
Mule Bones (Hughes), 26
Murals of John Thomas Biggers, The,
  217
"Mystic Trumpeter," 81

NAACP Spingarn Medal, 178
nadir period, the, 15; Black Codes
  reenacted in, 15; Civil Rights Act
  repealed during, 15; race was poor
  and uneducated in, 15
Nashville, Tennessee, 88, 186
Nation of Islam, 187
National Academy of Fine Arts, 203
National Action Network, 77
National Association for the
  Advancement of Colored People
  (NAACP), 26, 28, 33, 109, 123,
  186–87
National Baptist Convention, 97
National Center for Health Statistics, 4
National Council for LaRaza Capital
  Award, 178
National Defense Committee, 30
National Education Association Martin
  Luther King, Jr. Memorial Award,
  178
National Foundation for Women
  Business Owners, 151
National Lawyers Association, 30

National League of Cities, 159, 168
National Medical Association (NMA),
  102, 105, 117
National Negro Business League, 133
National Origins Quota Act (1924), 5,
  18
National Trust for Historic Preservation,
  Preservation Hero Award, 178
Nationalists Movement, 133
"Negro and Communism, The"
  (DuBois), 28
Newark, New Jersey, 186
New Black Middle Class, The (Landry),
  18
New England Journal of Medicine, The,
  117
New Frontier, 16
"New Jack," The, 125, 127
New Negro Movement, 19
New Orleans, Louisiana, 19, 29, 207,
  225, 234
Newport News City Council, 167
Newport News City Hall, 172
Newport News, Virginia, 159, 166–69
New School for Social Work, 26
New Testament, 81, 85
New World experiences of blacks, 11
New York Museum of Modern Art, 215
New York, New York, 16, 26–27, 30,
  94, 124, 187, 203
Nisbet, Robert A., 10
Nixon administration, 34
Nixon, President Richard, 138
Norfolk State University, 3
Norfolk, Virginia, 229
Northwestern University, 21
Notre Dame, University of, 66

Oakwood College, 63
Obama, Barack, 183, 186–189
Office of Minority Enterprise, 138
Ohio State University, 57, 61, 63–64
"Old Glory," 32
Old Testament, 80–81, 86
Oliver, Melvin, 146

One Hundred Black Americans for Bush Committee, 143
Origins of the Civil Rights Movement, The (Morris), 6
Orr, Robert, and Robert Pang, 101
Ortega, Daniel, 84
OSU Black Cultural Center, 64
Owens, Hugo, 172
Oxford University, 183

Paine College, 82
Paint Rock, Alabama, 28
Pan African Orthodox Christian Church, 192
Pang, Norman, 101
Paris (Texas), 217
Paschal Brothers, 134–36
Paschal, James, 134–40, 237
Paschal Mid Field Corporation, 136
Paschal, Robert, 134–40
Paschal's Concessions, Incorporated, 136
Paschal's Motor Hotel and Restaurant, 134–36
Patrice Lumumba University, 123
Patterson, James 56–57
Patterson, Louise Thompson, 15–20, 23–30, 35–37
Patterson, Mary Louise, 123–24
Patton, Sharon, 201
Payne Theological Seminary, 82
Pennsylvania Art Academy, 216
Pennsylvania State University, 64–65, 213–14
Pentecostal Assemblies of the World, 78
Pentecostal Church, 227
Peterson, John, Sr., 76, 96
Philadelphia, Pennsylvania, 110, 187
Pine Bluff, Arkansas, 22–23
Pioneers for Health Care Justice, 105
Pitts, James P., 11
Pittsburgh, Pennsylvania, 16, 29, 55
Plessy v. Ferguson, 15
Polite, Craig, 155
politics of class, ethnicity, age, gender, and sexual orientation, 238

"Politics of Hip Hop Culture, The," 153
Portsmouth City Charter, 176
Portsmouth, Virginia, 173
post-civil rights era, 49, 79, 155–56, 200, 228
postfigurative phase, 2, 235
"post-Me generation," 191
post-1960s, 235–36, 238
post-1960s clerics, 80
post-Reconstruction medicine, 104
post-World War II, 7, 30, 47, 65, 132, 137, 182
Potato Eater, (van Gogh), 229
Powell, General Colin, 183
PPOs, 128
Prayer at dedication ceremony, 34
pre-1960s, 235–36, 238
pre-1960s clerics, 80
pre-civil rights era, 155, 199–200
prefigurative phase, 228
Presidential Council on Minority Business Enterprise, 138
President's Medal of Georgetown University, 178
Prince, Arnold, 204
Prince Georges County, Maryland, 142
Prince, Steve, 206–8, 219–34
Prince, Valerie, 227
Princeton University, 178
Proctor, Samuel, 76, 96, 99
Project Hope, 176
Pullman Company, 135
Pullman Porter, 135, 159

racial divide, 189–90
racism, 8, 11–12, 43, 56, 59, 69, 71, 89, 90, 120, 137, 157, 163, 167, 170, 188, 201, 204, 206, 208, 211, 225–26, 228; changes in consciousness from, 11; coping and resisting in a racist society, 43; covert encounters with, 59; more blatant in World War I and World War II generations, 69; mutable forms of, 12; permanence of, 12; sophistication of, 71

Raleigh, North Carolina, 94
(Rattley), Florence, 165
Rattley, Jessie, 156, 158–73, 177, 181
Rattley, Robert, 165
(Rattley), Robin, 165
Reagan, Ronald, 34
Reaganomics, 182
Reconstruction, 15, 17, 104, 201
Reebok, 151
Regan, Tim, 240
"relevant black church," 90
Republican Finance Committee, 143
Republican National Committee, 144
Republican Party, 143, 183
Republican Presidential Trust, 143
Republicans, 28, 34, 87, 92, 140–41, 143, 172, 180
Rhode Island College, 204
Rhodes, Robert S., 114–18, 126
Rhodes Scholar, 183
Richmond v J. A. Croson and Company, 147
Robeson, Paul, 30–31, 62
Robinson, Benson (pseudonym), 138–44, 148
Robinson, Joy, 127
Rocafella Records, 153
Rock, John Sweat, 105
Roosevelt, Franklin D., 28–29
Roosevelt, Theodore, 32
Russo, Frank (pseudonym), 102, 118–23

Sacred Symphony: The Chanted Sermon of the Black Preacher (Turner), 80
St. Augustine College, 87
St. Cyprian's Parish, 85
St. Louis, Missouri, 78
St. Mary Seminary, 94
St. Thomas, Virgin Islands, 125
San Francisco, California, 18–19
Santayana, George, 73
Satcher, David, 105
Scott, John, 207, 223–24, 233–34
Scott, Robert C., 95–100
Scottsboro Boys, 28

Scottsboro Boys Action Committee, 29
Scottsboro case, 27–29
Seattle, Washington, 17
Second Baptist Church, 27
"Selfless Man, The," 115
Selma to Montgomery march, 1965, 177, 179
"servant of the people," 66, 68
Seven Minutes at the Mike in the Deep South (Borders), 31–32
sexism, 213–14, 222
Shapiro, Thomas, 146
Sharpton, Al, 77–78, 89, 94–95, 97–100
Shaw University, 174
Shiraz, Yasmin, 151–53
Shrine of the Black Madonna, 184, 187
Shuttlesworth, Fred, 83
Simmons, Charles F., 3–6, 36
Small Business Administration's set-aside program, 141
Smith, A. Wade, 132, 148
Smith, David, 207
Smith, James McCune, 105
Smith, Joshua I., 131–32, 138, 141–48
Smuts, General Jan, 23
SNCC (Student Nonviolent Coordinating Committee), 179
social gospel of liberation and reform, 97
Social Security system, 157–58
Sojourners for Truth and Justice, 30
Sorokin, Pitrim, 68
Soul of Black Worship, The (Walker), 75
Souls of Black Folk (DuBois), 20
South African Embassy, 84
South Carolina State College (now South Carolina State University), 115–16
Southern Christian Leadership Conference (SCLC), 81–83
Southern Illinois University, 204
Southern Normal School, 48–49
Southern Regional Council, 179
Soviet Union, 123
Spelman College, 50, 110–11, 178, 204

Spelman Seminary, 20
Spencer, Jon Michael, 30
Stanford University, 183
Steele, Shelby, 180
Steward, Susan Smith, 105
Stewart, James B., 64–67, 71
Stiff, Minnie A., 103, 113
Stillborn (Prince), 231
Stone Mountain, Georgia, 34
Study of the Negro Problem, The
    (Hope), 131
sugar story, the, 1, 9, 235; metaphor for
    changing black communities, 143;
    reactions to, 9; sugar bin half full at
    the turn of twentieth century in black
    community, 235
Suggs, Ernie, 54
Sullivan, Louis, 105
Supreme Court decision of 1954, 39, 51
Sutton, Deidra, 150
"Sweet Auburn Avenue," 106

"Talented Tenth," the (DuBois), 39
Talladega College, 49, 87
Task Force on Entrepreneurship, 143
Temple University, 226
Texas Southern University, 214, 216–17
Texas, University of, 178
Thee Generation, the, 240
Theisen, John, 216–17
Theisen, Olive Jensen, 216–17
"theology" of black liberation, 90
Third World countries, 84
Thirteenth and Fourteenth Amendments,
    15
Thomas, Clarence, 180
Thompson, Bart (pseudonym), 51–54
Thurman, Wallace, 26
Timberland Company, 178
Time magazine, 182
Title XVIII and Title XIX, 105
Topeka, Kansas, 62
"Top Ten Preachers of Black America,"
    Ebony magazine, 33
Towns, Gail H., 136

Toynbee, Arnold, 68
Tree House (Biggers), 215, 228
Triple "L" movement, 33
turbulent 1960s, the, 6, 15, 17;
    assassinations during, 6; changes in
    higher education during, 6; conflict,
    confrontation, and activism of, 17;
    protests, 4, 6
Turner, Henry, 76
Turner, William C., Jr., 80
Tuskegee Institute (now Tuskegee
    University), 40
Tyms, James D., 75–76, 81

Ujima spirit, 12
Uncle Tom, 24
UNESCO (United Nations Educational,
    Scientific and Cultural
    Organization), 217
Union College, 63
Union Theological Seminary, 21, 96
United Negro College Fund, 55
United States, 27, 29–31, 101, 123, 178,
    197, 204
United States Army Medical Corps,
    116
United States Senate, 17
Up From Slavery (Washington), 20
Urban League, 186
U.S. Air Force, 120
U.S. Army, 116
U.S. Conference of Mayors, 168, 190
U.S. Department of Defense, 142
U.S. Department of Education, 168
utilitarian individualism, 7; Euro-
    American culture, 7; values material
    acquisition, 7

Vanderbilt University, 116, 126
Van Gogh, 204, 229
Vietnam War, 89
Virginia Municipal League, 159
Virginia State University, 49, 125
visual artists, 199–200
Voter Education Project, 179

Voting Rights Act of 1965, 156–57, 177, 179, 181, 197
voucher system, 157

Walden, Jonathan (pseudonym), 89–92
Walker, D. Ormonde, 41
Walker-Taylor, Yvonne, 41–47, 54, 71
Walker, Wyatt Tee, 75, 96, 98–99
Walking With the Wind (Lewis), 178
Wallace, Governor George, 179
Walters, Cindy M., 150
Walton, Keith (pseudonym), 40, 68–72, 236
Warner, Clinton, 108, 113, 118, 237
Washington, Booker T., 16, 19–20, 22, 31, 35, 39–40, 108, 133
Washington, D.C., 84, 128, 227
Watergate scandal, 7
Watson, Glegg, 237
Watts, J. C., 183
The Way We Never Were (Coontz), 239
Wayne State University, 82
Weber, Max, 36, 76
"We" model, 236, 239
We Shall Overcome, 86
West, Cornel, 61
West Virginia State College (now West Virginia State University), 174
Wheat Street Baptist Church, 31, 33, 35
Wheat Street complex, 31
Where Do We Go From Here: Chaos or Community (King), 239
White House, the, 168
White, Josh, 214
"Who's Who among High School Students," 7
Widdiss, Claudia, 202–8, 234

Widdiss, Dorothy, 203
Wilberforce, Ohio, 143
Wilberforce University, 41–42, 44–46
William R. and Norma B. Harvey Library, 215
Williams, Hosea, 135, 179
Williams University, 178
Williams, Walter, 180
Wilmington, Delaware, 151
Wilson, Chaka, 153
Wilson, William J., 12
Wings Over Jordan, 108, 214
Winston-Salem College, 218
women's movement, 6
Woodruff Hale Show, 216
Woodson, Carter G., 104, 113
World War I era, 17, 20, 35–37, 46, 133, 235
World War I generation, 2–5, 15–16, 39–41, 44, 47, 49, 54, 62, 69, 71–72, 76, 96, 98–99, 105–6, 113, 124, 132, 236–38
World War II era, 83, 133, 173–74, 235
World War II generation, 2–3, 5–6, 8, 25–26, 36, 46, 54, 65, 69, 72–72, 75–76, 95–96, 98, 106, 113, 132, 236, 238

Xavier University, 207, 222–25

Yale Law School, 183
Yankelovich, Daniel, 7
YMCA (Young Men's Christian Association), 106
Young, Andrew, 135, 181
Young Black Republican Party, 91–92
Young, Coleman, 184, 190

About the Author

Lois Benjamin is Endowed University Professor of Sociology at Hampton University in Hampton, Virginia. She is the author of *The Black Elite: Still Facing the Color Line in the Twenty-First Century*, and *Dreaming No Small Dreams: William R. Harvey's Visionary Leadership* and editor of *Black Women in the Academy: Problems and Perils.*